LEADERS
Start to Finish

A Road Map for Developing Top Performers

ANNE BRUCE

STEPHANIE MONTANEZ

ASTD PRESS

ASTD Press is an internationally renowned source of insightful and practical information on workplace learning and performance topics, including training basics, evaluation and return on investment, instructional systems development, e-learning, leadership, and career development. Visit us at www.astd.org/astdpress.

Ordering information: Books published by ASTD Press can be purchased by visiting our website at store.astd.org or by calling 800.628.2783 or 703.683.8100.

Library of Congress Control Number: 2011944597
ISBN-10: 1-56286-813-6
ISBN-13: 978-1-56286-813-0

ASTD Press Editorial Staff:
Director: Anthony Allen
Senior Manager, Production & Editorial: Glenn Saltzman
Community of Practice Manager, Human Capital: Kristin Husak
Associate Editor: Ashley McDonald
Associate Editor: Heidi Smith
Associate Editor: Stephanie Castellano

Editorial, Design, and Production: Abella Publishing Services, LLC
Cover Design: Ana Foreman

Printed by Victor Graphics, Inc., Baltimore, MD, www.victorgraphics.com

Contents

Preface

A NEW AND IMPROVED LEADERSHIP GUIDE— GUARANTEED TO RAISE YOUR ORGANIZATION'S LEADERSHIP TO HIGHER LEVELS OF PERFORMANCE

Much has changed since ASTD's initial release of this book more than a decade ago. At the first printing of *Leaders Start to Finish*, no one had yet heard of the iPhone or Android—little, shiny rectangle devices that would revolutionize cell phone use by bringing us music, communication, web browsing, couponing, navigation, and even a flashlight—all literally at our fingertips, accessible by touch screen. These little devices are perfect symbols for how connected and accessible our world has become as people are now tapping into a virtual network of talent, knowledge, and opportunity.

New York Times foreign affairs columnist and bestselling author, Thomas L. Friedman, calls it worldwide "hyper-connectivity," and it's changing the way we will be expected to grow, brand, and develop top talent in decades to come. (Visit www.thomaslfriedman.com for up-to-date global leadership news and books that revolutionize the meaning of global leadership.)

Yes, what an extraordinary time this has been since the first edition of this book was written. And what an amazing time it is, right now more than ever, to be a leader in the making.

A NEW ERA OF OPPORTUNITY— KICKING PERFORMANCE AND PRODUCTIVITY UP

Almost a dozen years cannot slip by without challenges, of course. No one can forget September 11 or the economic stress that followed. While we could use such events and changes as an excuse to dwell in the land of discouragement, this new edition of *Leaders Start to Finish: A Road Map for Developing Top Performers* takes a positive and practical approach—delivering to you the inspiration and tools necessary to see this as

an era of opportunity. In fact, I believe that now more than ever is a prime time for managers, trainers, directors, business owners, HR leaders, and consultants to tap into the talent in the workforce and engage employees to become not only colleagues and co-workers, but star leaders!

You hold in your hand a new and improved leadership book and field guide. As I say in one of my leadership seminars and training workshops, "America's got talent in the workplace and it comes from all over the world and in many shapes and sizes, cultures, and age groups." Reflected in this leadership guide are the essential, back-to-basics tools and techniques that help make up the face of a new global leadership plan of action. It's time to embrace a new paradigm, and I'm asking you, as a developer of leaders, no matter what the level, that you begin making the shift today. If you do so, I'll make you a promise in return.

A LEADERSHIP PROMISE

The key to success is to use this book with great forethought and open mindedness for engaging new leadership ideas and approaches, while closely following the specific "how-to-dos" and "what-to-dos" between the covers of this book. If you do, you will not only start developing leaders at every level faster, you'll be raising your *existing* leadership to even higher levels of performance and productivity. And herein lies the **bonus** to just developing new and upcoming leaders. It's an opportunity to develop your existing leadership talent base at the same time.

I make this promise without hesitation, because in the past dozen years I have continued to test the formulas, lists, exercises, and worksheets in this book, and I've done this successfully all over the world—from Bozeman to Budapest, Denver to Dubai. The good news is that it works! The challenging news is that it will take you time, devotion to others, and an earnest commitment. In addition, you must have the desire to build a better, smarter, strength-based organization starting now, and to do so through people—one day, one person at a time. If you're reading this book, then I know you're up for the challenge!

STRENGTHENING YOUR PACK

Today, the term "leader" has more power and relevance than ever. Not only do today's leaders have greater responsibility to keep employees and free agents engaged as teams, they also must do more with less. Individuals are going out on their own to become consultants and contractors—using both economic downturns and upturns as opportunities to dig deep and pursue their true callings and gifts. Regardless of whether you are leading a team of thousands or venturing out to build your own business, adopting the skills and attitude of a leader will serve you well in your journey onward and upward. If you infuse your team members to become leaders, you are also creating valuable relationships and strengthening your pack as you travel ahead!

START WHERE YOU ARE

In this latest edition of *Leaders Start to Finish*, you will find more detail to the road map I laid out years ago. Like a GPS on your smartphone, I have tried to add not only a map, but also direction on how to get from here to there, as well as provide the information on what you might find along the way. I have updated directions with new roads—or routes to success—and highlighted potential dead ends. I've worked hard to make the journey accessible, and even fun—like a new app on your phone or iPad!

A NEW CO-AUTHOR TO HELP GUIDE YOU
ON YOUR LEADERSHIP JOURNEY

I'm thrilled to introduce my new co-author in this edition, Stephanie Montanez. Stephanie has been a great asset and friend, and she offers tremendous wisdom on the subject of leadership. Her contributions to the revisions in this book have taken the content you are about to read up a full notch. Thank you, Stephanie, for being a superstar leader.

In this exciting edition of *Leaders Start to Finish*, our goal is to infuse you to become a leader who not only is highly engaged, but who also spreads engagement to those you influence—whether it be your team members, clients, boss, or vendors. It's our goal to help you travel the road map as smoothly as possible and arrive at your destination with wisdom, enthusiasm, and measurable results.

GROW LEADERS UP

This book focuses on growing and developing leaders from the ground floor up. It addresses what must be done in order to create high-performing frontline, enthusiastic coaches; highly productive middle- and upper-level managers who put people first; and senior executives who walk the talk while renewing the organization's spirit. This book is a hands-on, how-to, no-nonsense reference and informative guide for developing and training leadership in cutting-edge environments, large and small. By focusing on the specifics of how we can develop leadership within our own organizations, this ASTD book answers the question: *What do leaders do?* Not, *how are they made?*

Fast and User-Friendly Tools We've Gathered for This Book—
A Gold Mine of Resources

The research compiled for this book consists of the interviews we have conducted over the years (in person and by phone) with hundreds of executives, team members, human resource professionals, instructional designers, and trainers around the world. Maybe you know of some of these people and their companies, or maybe you've read about them and admire their leadership style and capacity for bringing out the best in people.

Over the past 20 years, I have met, worked with, and interviewed countless CEOs and world leaders, from Herb Kelleher to Henry Kissinger, Ken Blanchard, and Tom Peters. I have had the privilege to work with inspirational gurus like Dr. Norman Vincent Peale and Zig Ziglar. I have also written about managers I've worked with who are not so well known, but who are just as powerful and effective in their approaches when it comes to developing leaders at all levels.

In addition, we have conducted extensive research over the years for numerous articles Stephanie and I have each authored, as well as hundreds of training programs we have written and delivered for companies large and small. There are organizations and people in this book that we have yet to meet in person or interview. Yet we have studied and researched them and their organizations for years, showcasing their impressive ways of doing business in our keynote speeches and leadership classes that we facilitate around the country and abroad.

This Book Is Written for You

If any of the following descriptions make you want to stand up and yell, "Hey, that's me!" then this book was written for you.

- An instructional design and development professional who is responsible for creating or enhancing an existing leadership training program.
- An experienced learning professional who wants to offer leadership development programs for one or more of the following groups: frontline supervisors, middle- or upper-level managers, senior- or executive-level managers.
- A training and learning professional whose organization does not presently offer a leadership program; someone who wants to start small, with just one or two leadership classes.
- A leadership developer who wants to build an entire leadership program from scratch, offering many subjects, at many levels of leadership, over an extended or specific period of time.
- A human resource professional who has training responsibilities and needs fast, easy-to-implement leadership skills and strategies!
- A tenured learning professional looking to glean new ideas and world-class practices on real-world leadership skills and techniques from the best of the best.
- A novice in the training field who's eager to learn how to quickly develop leadership programs.
- A human resources training and development professional whose organization's leadership curriculum could use some sprucing up.
- A leadership designer and developer who wants cutting-edge material that can be easily adapted to e-learning and distance learning programs and online e-letters.
- Virtual training organization designers who require fast and easy-to-use content for ongoing development and new training initiatives.

This book summarizes numerous business approaches to developing leaders in all of these areas and more. **It is based on the belief that leaders are developed, encouraged, and nurtured and that everyone has within them leadership qualities and competencies that can be tapped for the mutual benefit of developing human potential and creating high-performing organizations.**

We hope you will find this book not only thought provoking, but a practical and ongoing resource in the creation and enhancement of leadership development opportunities in your organization. It is our goal that you will glean the most appropriate and meaningful parts of this book and apply them as soon as possible, leaving your indelible imprint on the leaders of tomorrow.

Acknowledgments

This book could not have been written without the special contribution and creative collaboration of hundreds of people, beginning with the incredibly talented and hardworking people at ASTD Press, especially senior editor, Community of Practice Manager, and friend Kristin Husak; longtime ASTD colleague Justin Brusino; Nancy S. Olson, ASTD Director of Education Services; and brilliant book developer and close friend, Mark Morrow: you were the first to see this book as a worthwhile project from the start, and you've continued to support it to the end. A special thank you goes to the very patient and talented Ashley McDonald, our fearless copyeditor and ASTD associate editor; dear friend, publishing and marketing maven, Jocelyn Godfrey; to Elly Mixsell for your unwavering support year after year and for helping us promote this book with so much enthusiasm and creativity; to Phil Studdard, of Flip Design Studio, for spicing up our graphics and figures, chapter after chapter—you never failed us, Phil; to Betty Garrett of Garrett Speakers International for promoting and helping to sell the keynote speeches and training programs that accompany this book; to this book's amazing designers and layout team at Abella Publishing Services, LLC—great job; and to the entire ASTD production team for helping us meet our wild deadlines, a big thank you.

A note from Anne Bruce—A special thank you to all of the extremely kind and generous people who continue to follow my work and attend my seminars, leadership workshops, keynote events, and book signings—and still keep coming back year after year! Each and every one of you continues to enrich my life by allowing me to be a part of yours. To my co-author Stephanie Montanez, a big heartfelt thank you for all of those marathon late nights writing and bouncing ideas around, and for your unwavering "never-say-never" support and positive attitude! To all of my friends and family in sunshine and rain—I cannot list you all, but you know who you are. Your unconditional support and love make all that I do possible. And finally, with love and deepest appreciation for all you both do for me 365 days a year—my beacons of light and love—my husband David and my daughter Autumn. Because of you both, I get to shine in my career and in my life with you at home. You are my True North. I dedicate this book to you, Baby Barcelona. Oh what FUN we will have!

A note from Stephanie Montanez—Writing this book would have not been possible without the support, patience, love, and belief in me from my loving family and God. My husband Ramon inspired me by completing his bachelor's degree; he stayed up many long nights, and I figured if he could do it, so could I. My wonderful children have been so supportive and lifted me up daily by telling me that I can do it. Jaki, my intelligent and beautiful daughter, is so talented and has an unwavering spirit about her and brings sunshine to everyone she meets. My son Stephen is highly intelligent and has a free and happy spirit about him; his attention to detail is amazing, and he is always in the best mood and brings joy to all who meet him. Everything I do is for my family, and they inspire me to do great things; without them I would not be successful.

I cannot leave out my colleague, mentor, and friend, Anne Bruce. Without her, this dream could have never become a reality. She has so much energy and is always running at lightning speed. She is a wonderful writer, trainer, and mentor; she had faith in me and at times pushed me beyond my comfort zone, because she knew I could do it. There are times in your life when you know you have met a superstar, and Anne is that pinnacle in the sky called a "supernova"!

Finally, we both would like to extend many thanks and deep appreciation to the more than 100 organizations represented in these pages and to the helpful people in those organizations who so patiently responded to our nonstop emails, texts, and relentless phone calls.

Here's to your leadership journey. Make this road map yours!

Anne Bruce
Stephanie Montanez

Introduction

DEVELOPING LEADERS WHO CAN

"Whether you think that you can, or you can't, you are right." Henry Ford's words uttered during the Industrial Revolution are a powerful reminder, even to this day, that people will do only what they think they can do. The key in leadership development lies in inspiring employees to believe that they *can*.

Developing an "I can" leadership attitude among up-and-coming leaders is trickier than it seems. How do you promote undying hope and action amid change, uncertainty, and sometimes horrid economic news? In the aftermath of terrorist attacks, corporate scandals, and financial distress, the workplace isn't the same animal it was at the first printing of this book more than 10 years ago. Today, most companies must do more with less, or perish. Unemployment rates are pushing employees to work out of fear—often to the point of burnout (as our friend and leadership speaker Aric Bostick describes in his interview for this book on "Burnout to Breakthrough")—and managers are scrapping to meet their goals, let alone keep their staff engaged. In times of trauma or change, distractions like Facebook and smartphones zap productivity, as employees would often rather engage with friends and relatives than their stressed-out workplaces.

LEADERS WHO ENGAGE WORKERS

Did you know?

- Up to 70 percent of American employees say they are not engaged on the job.
- More than 90 percent of American employees say they leave their jobs because they have no emotional connection with their leadership.
- Less than 33 percent of workers view their leaders as strong individuals who walk the talk.
- Disengagement costs the United States economy $328 billion per year.
 (*Source: HumanResourcesSources.org website*)

SAVVY, REALISTIC, AND FLEXIBLE LEADERSHIP

One of our favorite leadership quotes is by Ralph Waldo Emerson, who once said, "Make the most of yourself. . . for that is all there is of you." Although some may use the economy as an excuse to hide under a rock and wait it out, we are also witnessing a birth of a new breed of leader. Today's leaders are savvy, realistic, and flexible as they map out their directions and work hard to push toward their goals regardless of the detours they encounter. Wise managers are taking this opportunity to refine their leadership skills and learn new and innovative procedures. (Our choice for most innovative leadership magazine to subscribe to? *Fast Company*. It's a must-have for leaders, chock-full of creative and innovative ideas and edgy solutions for real-world problems that every leader needs to read and then apply on the job. Grab a copy at the nearest newsstand and tell us what you think, or go online to fastcompany.com for a glimpse of the future.)

Even many who have been laid off are using their changes as opportunities to pursue consulting, developing new business, or obtaining a college degree. Leadership in today's business climate takes on new meaning; it is no longer reserved just for the elite, but rather is a quality that people at every level can embody. Like a glass of water, which replenishes people of all walks, leadership is a universal quality that infuses any sized workplace—from 1 to 100,000 and more—with energy.

In fact, leadership training and development in today's world has become a necessary quality for both managers and employees. People at all levels are often called to fill in for gaps left by vacating workers. Managers must take on more responsibility to train remaining employees—while keeping them engaged and maintaining a high-performing, high-producing, safe, and happy work environment. That's the future, that's the challenge, that's the expedition: developing and equipping leaders today who will weather the storms and carry your organization into tomorrow.

DEVELOP LEADERS WILLING TO *HEAR* THE LOWEST-TITLED PERSON IN THE ORGANIZATION

Many great ideas are born on a street corner, in the employee break room, or in an office building's revolving door. As a manager, how do you promote leadership as a quality in every employee, rather than just a position held by the elite? How do you internally motivate employees at all levels to see themselves as leaders who are crucial to your organization? Do you listen to the lowest-titled person in the organization as closely as you do the president of the company? Million-dollar ideas can bubble up from every level of leadership. People need to know you believe in them. That's the first step to developing top talent in any business.

Today's workplace needs formal leadership training and development as much as it did yesterday. In fact, we'll go a step further and say it needs more. It needs you, as the manager, HR director, chief of training and development, VP of people, or employee development coach, to emulate leadership practices that promote the development of greater potential in your employees. It needs you to act as not only "the boss,"

but as an ally and sometimes peer to your employees—one who is willing to hear that the lowest-titled person in your organization may have the million-dollar idea. Now there's something to ponder.

Get Zapped!

Zappos' leaders realized the value of their people when they created an annually updated book for new employees consisting of quotes from existing employees on what it is like to work for their organization. Their management chose not to edit out the negative comments prior to printing. Instead, they kept honesty as one of their core values and printed the book in entirety. Additionally, during economically difficult times, their leadership asked for ideas from all of their employees and utilized whatever worked. These are likely a couple of the reasons Zappos is known for having not only one of the most engaged workforces—employing people who often gather together well after work hours are done, and sometimes even share housing—but also why they are highly profitable—going from earning almost nothing in 1999 to more than $70 million in gross sales three years later. CEO Tony Hsieh realized that the value of his organization was not only in his ability to emulate strong leadership, but also in his willingness to treat each employee like a leader.

Employees think they can lead when they are given the training and freedom to be leaders of their domain. They are engaged to act when they see you—as a manager—acting like a strong leader.

In this book, we provide you, as a developer of top talent, with a road map as well as GPS-level instructions on where to go and how to get there. We position you with the skills you need so that you can be the voice of that GPS, eventually letting your employees know, "You have arrived at your destination."

LEADERSHIP IS EVERYONE'S BUSINESS— WHAT ARE YOU DOING ABOUT IT?

Once considered the elite domain of senior-level management, leadership is now everyone's business and responsibility. Employees are expected to lead by example and to take the initiative in preparing themselves to one day step into a leadership position. On the other hand, management is expected to provide such opportunities for each leader's personal and professional growth, while maintaining a high-performing, high-producing, safe, and happy work environment. That's the future, and that's the challenge: developing leaders today for tomorrow.

And that's where you come in. What are you doing to prepare tomorrow's leaders today? Are you committed to all that is required in realizing your organization's full potential and the potential of its employees? What areas of opportunity may be lacking when it comes to building leadership training programs that will create and bring greater success to your organization in the twenty-first century? Here's the good news. **Successful leadership is learnable—at all levels!**

This book focuses on growing and developing leaders from the ground up. It addresses what must be done in order to create a high-performing front line, enthusiastic coaches, highly productive middle- and upper-level managers who put people first, and senior executives who walk the talk while renewing the organization's spirit. This book is a hands-on, how-to, no-nonsense reference and informative guide for developing and training leadership in cutting-edge environments, large and small. By focusing on the specifics of how we can develop leadership in our own organizations, this book answers the question: **What do leaders do?** Not, **How are they made?**

PhDs NOT REQUIRED TO USE THIS BOOK AND DEVELOP LEADERS

You do not have to have a degree in organizational development, a formal coaching certificate, or years of training experience, design, or development to be charged with the responsibility of building a leadership program. Anyone and everyone is getting on board the leadership development train, often out of necessity. If you've got the background, education, and experience, then you are a step ahead of most, and you will find this book invaluable as a resource from which you will be able to easily adapt and apply the techniques described. However, today, mainly because of the multibillion-dollar training boom, many highly capable training enthusiasts with less experience have also taken on the crucial role of developing their organization's leaders. If you are seeking additional resources and guidance to help you get there, you will find it in this book. And the next time someone says, "What this place needs is a real leadership program," you'll be ready.

HOW TO USE THIS BOOK AND APPLY YOUR PERSONAL SPIN

In your individual approach to using this book, keep in mind that this is not intended to be a step-by-step leadership development training guide. There are no overhead transparencies to copy, PowerPoint slides to write, Prezi Presentations to create, classroom forms to duplicate, room diagrams to follow, or icebreakers to open a session. The American Society for Training and Development (ASTD) does, however, offer numerous top-quality training books and aids that are available through ASTD's website (www.astd.org), their catalogs, Amazon.com, and bookstores everywhere. Instead, this book offers you the critical building blocks that can be adapted easily and turned into high-impact leadership development, but not without your personal spin on things. If you adopt the leadership guidelines in this book, then you are agreeing to be an active participant in how this material will be delivered and utilized in your organization.

And here's the bonus for you: Although the book might not be your traditional training guide, there are plenty of takeaways, interactive exercises for fast learning, specific training tips, and practical trainer materials that you can pass on to your

leaders. The dual nature of this book is what sets it apart from the rest. Let this quick and easy format work for you. Let this book help you put an end to the busywork and start the work that matters when it comes to growing tomorrow's talent in your organization.

Select Your Approach to Using the Material Presented

How you go about creating a leadership program, or even part of a leadership program, is up to you. To get you started, here are the three situations and the appropriate guidance for how to use the book to build a thought-provoking curriculum for any level learner.

Situation 1: Help! I'm responsible for developing a brand new leadership curriculum. What do I do?

With this book, you can build an entire program from the ground up. You will find that the order in which the content is presented is conducive to the logical progression of a solid and comprehensive leadership program, beginning with the foundational components of leadership and gradually adding necessary skills, such as identifying leadership competencies, succession planning, coaching, and so on. Think of the chapters as separate learning blocks of skill development that naturally build on one another—one block at a time—one learning experience at a time.

Situation 2: Help! We need improvement with our existing programs—fast!

You also can use the information in this book to build on, or simply enhance, your existing leadership training. Let's say you have a program that offers basic leadership skill development on team building, or communications. Now, you'd like to expand your program to include performance management, knowledge management, or leadership planning. With this book, you can select the appropriate subjects from each chapter that meet your specific leadership training needs, while complying with your organization's culture and individuality, then insert that training component into your current learning curriculum.

Situation 3: Help! Our programs are outdated. We need to get with the times—now!

If you feel that some of the information and tools you offer now are inadequate for today's work environment or learning needs, you can supplement your current data with updated information and lessons available in this revised edition.

How to Apply the Information and Tailor Your Application

Keep it simple. Facilitate your leaders' success by keeping the learning easy to understand at every level. You probably know your organization's needs and the needs of its people best. Use the appropriate portions of this book that best match those needs. Adapt, modify, delete, expand, and work the material to meet your objectives, taking into consideration your learners' levels of competency when applying each lesson. Here are three suggestions for tailoring each lesson's application:

Consider your leaders' skill level: Ask yourself if your learners are novices, masters, or somewhere in between in their skill levels and abilities. Tailor all leadership

learning to the level of learner you are addressing. You wouldn't put a novice in a class with a master. This would not only squelch the confidence of the novice, but it would de-motivate the master.

Assess experience: Assess how much experience your learners have in the specific area in which you are offering development. Someone may have learned the skills, but may have never used them in the real world. Others who have lots of real-world experience will bring a different dynamic to the learning process—they've been there and done that.

Motivate and challenge: Employees who have lots of experience and have honed their skills are looking for a challenge. These folks need to be fired up! Always take advantage of a group that has lots of talent and great experiences to share with others. Keep them on their toes and challenge them often. If you don't, they will quickly become de-motivated and tune you out.

SPECIAL FEATURES OF THIS BOOK

In this revised 2nd edition of *Leaders Start to Finish*, you may notice that we are more to the point and definitely take a no-nonsense approach when it comes to delivering leadership tools to you and your aspiring leaders. We've done away with the icons for exercises, tools, case-in-point scenarios, and more. We've replaced these with faster, easier to reference key points, pull quotes, and a wealth of sidebars, including real-world case studies, plus a wrap up at the end of every chapter filled with thought-provoking discussion questions to help guide you and your team on the road to leadership development.

YOU'RE ON YOUR WAY!

There's a famous saying: If you don't know where you're going, any road will lead you there. By the same token, if you don't know where you're starting from, it can be a miserable trip getting to where you want to go! This book is about getting you, the reader, on a new and exciting path to doing even more great work as you develop top performers from start to finish. With this road map, we hope you will feel more empowered because we have helped lighten your load. It is our hope that this book has helped instill in you a new sense of drive, energy, and confidence. Road maps like this one help us to stop, think, and ask ourselves powerful questions, like: Can I take a better route? Could my destination be a place I've never considered visiting? Where am I now? Where do I really want to go, and where do I need to be? How did I get here to begin with?

HALLMARKS OF LEADERSHIP AWAIT YOU

Numerous chapters lie before you in this book. Each chapter covers one hallmark of leadership that is critical for success.

As on any road traveled, there are going to be places along the way where you feel compelled to stop and take in all that you can. And there may be points that you choose to bypass, because currently they hold little interest for you, or simply now is not the time. No matter what your stops along the way, or what your leadership development needs are, you can be sure this book will take you and your organization down an exciting and uncharted path to your next level of leadership development.

MAKE YOUR EFFORTS COUNT

Okay, here's the bottom line: Most of us spend more than half our life at work. So don't you want what you do and how you do it to make an impact? Sure, we all do. We all want to have a greater purpose in life, to be more than our paychecks and our titles. We want to make what we do count.

We're here to tell you that what you do—developing leaders at all levels—counts big time! We realize that you don't "need" us or this book, or a psychologist, a professional coach, a famous business guru, or an expensive weekend retreat to be successful. You've already got what it takes. What you most likely need is a bit of time to think through the process, get clear on your goals, and then infuse your own plan of action into it. We're just here to help facilitate and expedite the process.

It's time to get going. Thanks for taking us along.

Practicing Authentic Leadership and Ditching the Drama

There is a good reason that the first chapter of this book focuses on authentic leadership. Without authenticity, your leaders are sure to fail. Without an authentic presence, your leaders simply will go through the motions of the leadership principles discussed throughout the book. Without authenticity, those principles will be practiced without substance or backbone. Therefore, training in authentic leadership skills and behaviors is essential to developing your leaders at any level.

Authenticity in leadership is a proven, admired, and much sought-after characteristic among business leaders, and is now taught in recognized leadership programs worldwide. As the developer of a leadership program for your organization, you must explain the importance and introduce the criteria of authentic leadership—what it means and how it is practiced.

Here is where your leaders will learn about being authentic, why it is important, and how to develop this important characteristic in themselves. If you are developing leadership training from the ground up, this is your first step. If your training does not include this element, here is your chance to supplement your leadership development program to emphasize this vital quality.

What You Will Learn in This Chapter:

- ♦ Know who you really are. Leaders must
 - understand what "authentic" means
 - determine what sets them "authentically" apart from the rest
 - perform in a manner consistent with the way they see themselves.
- ♦ Apply self-knowledge and mastery on the job. Leaders must
 - acknowledge intuition and emotions
 - show their human side by talking freely about their mistakes and weaknesses
 - never ask someone to do anything they wouldn't do themselves.

WHAT IS AUTHENTICITY?

Authenticity gives us peace of mind and satisfaction. It tells the world that this is the real deal.

> **Authenticity:** *The condition or quality of being authentic, trustworthy, or genuine.*

It's human nature to want to know if something or someone is authentic. When a person buys a Picasso painting, he or she expects a certificate of authenticity to come with it. Authenticity can be measured by the clear "ping" that comes from tapping a piece of genuine Waterford crystal; in other instances, it's more subjective, such as the gut feeling you get when someone is—or is not—speaking the truth. Have you ever thought to yourself, "Hey, is this person for real?"

In organizations, employees follow leaders who behave authentically, and they support and respect them. These employees share their leaders' vision and trust that their leaders' decisions will be in the best interest of the employees.

LEADERS ARE TRUE TO THEMSELVES

An authentic leader is real and honest, and his or her authentic behavior is the prerequisite necessary to caring about and respecting employees. A leader's authentic behavior also reveals self-respect and self-esteem. A leader who is the "real deal" is always true to his or her principles.

It is your responsibility as the developer of your organization's leaders to help them understand that authentic leadership is not just something they do. Rather, it is something they *are*. Therefore, leaders cannot perform in a manner that is inconsistent with the way they see themselves. This is the crux of authentic leadership and the basic principle upon which authentic behavior thrives.

GET AUTHENTIC—STOP WORKPLACE DRAMA

Marlene Chism, speaker and author of *Stop Workplace Drama*, defines authentic leadership as "One who influences others because of who they are more than what their title is. Leaders walk their talk, and lead by example."

In the words of William Penn, "No man is fit to command another who cannot command himself." An authentic leader knows the distinction between power and force. Power comes from the inside and is purpose driven, while force involves manipulation and control.

Chism believes that committing oneself to authentic leadership also involves a life-long commitment to spiritual and personal growth. "You can only be as honest as your level of awareness," she states. She goes on to explain that **awareness is the ability to know that any drama around you is a mirror of the growth that is required of you—instead of the reflection of the flaws of others.**

"The outside circumstances only reflect what is on the inside of the leader," she states. "As the leader grows in personal power and authenticity, the outside

circumstances also start to change to mirror the growth." (The external is a reflection of the internal.)

Key Principle of Authentic Leadership: *Don't become the source of your own suffering.*

Five Traits of Authentic Leadership

Chism has identified five traits of authentic leadership, as outlined below.

1. **They do not participate in drama.** In Chism's book, she illustrates her interpretation of a transactional analysis tool known as The Karpman Drama Triangle (printed with permission by Marlene Chism), a concept originally developed by award-winning psychologist Stephen Karpman. The idea is that when relationships are dysfunctional, there are three prominent roles (each representing the three points on the triangle), the victim, the persecutor, and the rescuer.

 The leader does not act like a victim, complaining about the state of the economy or lousy employees. At the same time, the authentic leader does not encourage the victim role in employees by allowing them to blame other people and circumstances for their problems, hoping for the leader to come in as the rescuer. Nor does the leader persecute by using shame and guilt tactics to get results.

 Authentic leaders must simultaneously be involved in the situations and potential conflict among his or her employees, and also avoid getting pulled into the drama either by overcompensating, taking sides, using aggression, or applying other methods of game playing and manipulation to put people in their places. "They realize that it takes two to game play unless you are playing solitaire," states Chism. "They are not drawn in by listening to hearsay and gossip. In other words, if Sally comes into the office to represent Donna's point of view, the authentic leader asks Sally to invite Donna into the conversation. The expectation is that each person must represent himself or herself, and that eliminates the rescuing behavior on the triangle that creates misunderstandings."

2. **They take responsibility.** Authentic leaders take the *vow of responsibility*. They do not blame employees, the government, or outside circumstances for their lack of success or for the drama in the workplace. They understand the difference between job and responsibility. Like Harry Truman, the authentic leader says, "The buck stops here."

 Authentic leaders take responsibility for their communication. They speak about what they want, instead of what they don't want. They take responsibility for the energy they bring to a situation. Smart leaders also take responsibility to keep everyone informed about changes in the company and what is expected. Authentic leaders balance choice and responsibility. "The more one rises to the top, the more the responsibility must balance in proportion to the new choice, freedom or opportunity," states Chism.

3. **They promote empowerment.** The authentic leader expects and encourages responsible behavior in his employees. Chism explains that empowered leaders look for the four signs that indicate a lack of personal responsibility: blame, resentment, justification, and judgment; and they use coaching methods to teach responsible communication, instead of complaints, excuses, and regrets.

"They are not easily manipulated by drama stories because they realize that by your choices you reveal your commitments," states Chism. "They can identify an integrity gap—meaning that when words, actions, and results do not align, there is a lack of integrity in some area. Authentic leaders have radar for language that indicates a lack of responsibility and absence of personal choice. They listen with an open heart when an employee has a complaint, but instead of immediately fixing the problem, they ask for ideas so that the employee learns problem-solving skills instead of using the open door as a method to vent."

4. **They exhibit emotional mastery.** Authentic leaders are not afraid of their emotions, explains Chism. Human beings have five energy systems: physical, emotional, mental, spiritual, and environmental. Authentic leaders understand the complexity of their emotions, and they own their emotions instead of letting their emotions own them. They understand the need for physical rejuvenation, so they take regular times to rejuvenate and expect the same from their staff. When dealing with internal drama, instead of getting entangled into the emotion, authentic leaders know how to separate the facts from fiction. As Chism states, "They understand that while it's human nature to make up stories to understand the world we live in, knowing your feelings doesn't change the facts, but knowing the facts can change your feelings."

5. **They develop other leaders with attitude builders.** Authentic leaders understand the importance of training and development in all aspects, whether it's a short mentoring session in the office, an opportunity to shadow another job, or a formal training plan. The only way we grow is through the experiences we have, the places we travel, the people we meet, and the books we read.

One of the tools Chism has developed for leaders is "Attitude Builders," which is an easy way to offer staff development and enrichment with no prep, no plan, and no problems. Attitude Builders is an audio mp3 interview with an author, coach, business owner, or industry expert, complete with a learning guide and facilitation questions to guide a group discussion after listening to the audio.

This easy method of internal training and development allows employees to listen to audio interviews with all kinds of authors in various fields of personal development, health and wellness, and leadership. In addition, the discussion that is held after the interviews and facilitated either by the leader

or a team member, leads to critical thinking and camaraderie in the team. "The truth is, you don't need a ropes course to learn about teamwork, but you do need conversation, a new mindset, and connection to those with whom you work," states Chism. "Development tools like *Attitude Builders* offer an affordable way to generate conversation, build the team and offer personal development all at the same time."

A simple one-hour opportunity once a month can develop leaders to think differently and be exposed to a more well-rounded view of life in general. Check out www.AttitudeBuilders.com.

A Leader's Vow of Personal Responsibility

Chism has developed the following vow to help leaders achieve authenticity in their practice:

I vow to be responsible for my life experience.

I am responsible for how I use time.

I am responsible for how I use money.

I am responsible for the status of my relationships.

I am responsible for getting my needs met.

I am the creator of my experiences.

Even though I may not see my choices immediately in challenging circumstances or situations, I am willing to recognize the fact that choices are always available to me.

The more I recognize my choices, the more responsible I become. The less I complain, judge and blame others, the more empowered I become.

I am not a victim to my emotions or to the situation around me, or to other people's behaviors.

I agree to recognize that when I have an unwanted experience, and as a result fall into patterns of blame, resentment, justification or judgment, it is possibly because I failed to ask for what I want. Or perhaps I failed to set a boundary, failed to speak up, or I was unrealistic in my expectations, or in some other way unclear in my communication.

I accept that even in my disappointments there is an opportunity to grow, to learn how to communicate more effectively, to step into a new truth, and to see others differently.

I reap the rewards and the consequences of the choices I make, as well as the unconscious reactions I have.

Because I have choice, I am responsible, and because I am responsible, I am empowered.

I gladly accept the role of creator and take the vow of responsibility in all areas of my life personally and professionally.

Signed_____Date_____

7 Tips for Reducing Workplace Drama

Chism has created the following seven steps for reducing drama and leading authentically.

1. **Schedule regular staff meetings.** When done properly, regular meetings provide a forum for listening, problem solving, and honoring peak performance. Meeting mistakes include lecturing instead of engaging the team, inconsistent meeting times, no agenda, and no fun.

2. **Create clear guidelines.** Make relationships a priority and support the relationships with a standard operating procedure and employee manual. Review at least once a year and let the rules be the "bad guy" when it comes to discipline.

3. **Tweak the open door policy.** Change your open door policy from any time to specific hours and preferably by appointment. This prevents casual visits to vent or tattle.

4. **Promote problem solving.** When an employee comes to you with a complaint, acknowledge the complaint, and then schedule the employee to come back with all the facts, how the problem affects productivity, and an idea or potential solution.

5. **Stop office gossip.** If Sally comes to you and says, "Don't tell Donna I said this, but Donna is unhappy with. . . ," discourage hearsay with a calm question: "Why are you coming to me with Donna's problem?" Send the message that you do not tolerate "rescuing" behavior.

6. **Require rejuvenation.** No rest and recovery equals irritability, impatience, rude behavior, and more mistakes. Managing energy is crucial to peak performance and productivity. Make regular breaks mandatory at least every two hours.

7. **Lead by example.** Model the behavior you want them to have. Master your emotions, take regular breaks, be fair, listen, have integrity, show respect, and have fun. Remember the words of William Penn: "No man is fit to command another who cannot command himself."

WHAT SETS AUTHENTIC LEADERS APART FROM THE REST?

Authentic leaders put a great deal of time and effort into developing self-mastery, or what is also known as "self-knowledge." They gain self-knowledge by behaving in these three ways:

1. Acknowledging their intuition and emotions.
2. Showing their humanity by talking freely about their mistakes and weaknesses.
3. Never asking others to do anything they wouldn't do.

HOW TO HELP YOUR LEADERS DEVELOP SELF-MASTERY

Take your leaders through the following three steps to developing their self-mastery. Have them complete the exercises accompanying each step.

Step 1. Acknowledge Your Intuition and Emotions

Your leaders will do this by fine-tuning their internal compasses (their gut instincts) and responding to the emotional needs of their people. Authentic leaders care a great deal about how their employees are *feeling*, and their actions toward their workers aren't controlled or unemotional. Authentic leaders take the time to understand their employees' basic emotional needs and then support those needs by demonstrating their authentic concern. (See chapter 8 for more on this topic.)

Below is a list of the most common emotional needs of employees:

- recognition and praise
- achievement and advancement
- sense of belonging or being part of a team
- challenge and excitement
- pride and confidence
- love and support.

As an exercise, you can ask your leaders to describe in specific examples how he or she could demonstrate authentic leadership while supporting each of the emotional needs listed above. Suggest this example: If your leader knew that an employee had a strong need for challenge and excitement, the leader could address that need directly by matching that individual with many new and exciting projects and department challenges. By matching the person with a task that fills his or her strong emotional needs, your leaders can expect greater enthusiasm and greater productivity from their workers.

Another valuable suggestion is to have your leaders consider using the following phrases to demonstrate their authentic presence with their employees:

- "Help me understand how you're feeling. Tell me more."
- "Tell me your feelings and ideas about this."
- "What are you concerned about?"
- "What matters most to you about the outcome of this situation?"
- "How would you handle this?"

Step 2. Show Your Humanity by Revealing Your Mistakes and Weaknesses

Heck, celebrate them! Authentic leaders know that when they openly share their own mistakes and foibles, the likelihood is slim that their teams will be blindsided by the same errors. Teach your leaders that knowing and appreciating their own limitations as well as their glories will better equip them to build strong human relationships. Here are a few tips to share with your leaders on ways to celebrate their mistakes and weaknesses:

- Show your humanity. If you blow it, admit it. Employees want to know you're human just like them.
- Ask for help. If you don't know how to do something, tell people and get help. You'll be respected for your honesty.

- Celebrate a costly mistake by letting others know what happened so that they won't repeat the same error. They'll appreciate your taking the risk to be vulnerable.
- Always tell the truth. Don't try to cover up something or make things look different from what they really are.

Let your leaders know that it can be hard on the ego to expose and celebrate personal mistakes and weaknesses. It may be embarrassing. But in the end, they will gain the unconditional respect and admiration of their followers. If they still need some convincing, ask your leaders to describe a time when they made a mistake or needed help with something on the job, but kept it to themselves. Then have them share how celebrating the mistake or weakness might have been more beneficial and produced a learning experience for everyone involved. The objective here is to help your leaders understand the profound benefits associated with truthful leadership.

Step 3. Never Ask Others to Do Anything You Wouldn't Do

This is often referred to as "walking the talk." It is the ultimate expression of a leader's commitment to self-mastery. Help your leaders understand that they will learn the most from doing the things they expect of others. Leaders need to know that walking the talk develops a more powerful voice and makes a more profound contribution to the enterprise, thereby earning for a leader the respect and appreciation of everyone involved. Here are a few simple ways for leaders to show that they consider themselves as part of the group:

- Get out of your office and be with the people.
- Model the attitudes and behaviors you expect in others.
- Be a leader, not a boss.
- Show your dedication to community projects by participating in them.

In order to deepen your leaders' understanding of authentic leadership, have them write across the top of a piece of paper "The Most Authentic People I've Ever Known." Give them a few minutes to jot down the names of the men and women who come to mind. Next, ask them to reflect on what it was about those people that made them exceptionally authentic in their attitudes and actions. Point out that chances are good it wasn't their IQ or academic accomplishments that set them apart. Your leaders more than likely will discover that the authenticity they recall had more to do with their compassion and courage, their caring and empathy, their honesty, and their generous hearts.

AUTHENTIC BEHAVIOR CONNECTS YOUR LEADERS TO PEOPLE

Authentic behavior should be taught in any leadership program. It is the essence of who your leaders are, not just what your leaders do. It creates value through relationships. When your leaders learn to become truly authentic, they will be able to get in touch with their employees' feelings and concerns much more quickly, and they will understand and connect to their employees' fears, intentions, and aspirations.

By connecting at that deeper level, they will send the message that they care, and when that happens, employees will be eager to commit to their leaders' mission and to perform at their peak.

> *I am not always bound to win, but I am bound to be true. I am not always bound to succeed, but I am bound to live up to what light I have.* —Abraham Lincoln

LEADING AUTHENTICALLY

Use the following self-assessments to reach a thorough understanding of the key lessons in this chapter. First, do a quick review of the three ways to develop self-mastery:

1. Acknowledging your intuition and emotions.
2. Showing your humanity by freely revealing your mistakes and weaknesses.
3. Never asking others to do anything you wouldn't do.

Next, on a scale of one (lowest) to five (highest), do a quick self-assessment on your ability to implement the three authentic leadership behaviors.

Identifying Employees' Emotional Needs	1	2	3	4	5
1. Recognition and praise					
2. Achievement and advancement					
3. Sense of belonging or being part of a team					
4. Challenge and excitement					
5. Pride and confidence					
6. Love and support					
Celebrating Mistakes and Weaknesses	1	2	3	4	5
1. Show your humanity.					
2. Ask for help.					
3. Celebrate costly mistakes.					
4. Always tell the truth.					
Walking the Talk	1	2	3	4	5
1. Get out of your office and be with the people.					
2. Model the attitudes and behaviors you expect in others.					
3. Be a leader, not a boss.					
4. Show your dedication to community projects by participating in them.					

Every one of these behaviors increases your leaders' ability to be successful and authentic. Target for additional self-improvement those items on which your leaders rate themselves a three or less.

Questions for Discussion: Developing Authentic Leadership

1. Why do you think authenticity is an important part of leadership at all levels?
2. How will you set yourself apart as an authentic leader?
3. What is the strongest authentic leadership behavior you currently possess?
4. What challenges you the most about creating an authentic presence?

Wrapping It Up

It is unfortunate that many organizations separate the act of leadership from the leaders themselves. Don't make the same mistake. Help your leaders appreciate that authentic leadership is not something they *do*, but something they *are* deep inside. Authenticity surely is an important aspect of the human side of leadership—the topic of chapter 2. You can find more information on authentic leadership by visiting www.annebruce.com/humanpotential.html and clicking on *Human Potential Series*.

Civility and the Human Side of Leadership

It is vital that your leaders learn and understand from the start that business is about people and, therefore, their leadership techniques must embrace their humanness. This chapter addresses the timely importance of developing your leaders to the point where they can clearly recognize and appreciate the value of people not just as revenue producers, but as human beings. Here is where your leaders discover the meaning of embracing the human side of leadership. In other words, they learn how to nurture their nature. Understanding human behavior is a critical component to any leadership program. If your training does not include this element, here is your chance to supplement your leadership development program to emphasize this vital quality.

> *The deepest principle in human nature is the craving to be appreciated.* —William James, psychologist and philosopher

What You Will Learn in This Chapter:

- ◆ Determine whether you are abundant in or lacking in humanity. Leaders must
 - ● understand what civility is and how to activate it
 - ● understand what being "human oriented" is all about
 - ● learn how to relate as a leader to the whole person
 - ● grasp what the whole-person approach to leadership can do.
- ◆ Appreciate that people are worth taking stock in. Leaders must
 - ● take a close look at "whole-person" leadership in America's best companies
 - ● find and honor the soul of the organization and its people
 - ● commit to regarding people as the bottom line and to becoming more human oriented, caring, and soulful.

The Importance of Civility

The Importance of Civility

Leaders who are providing training to become more self-aware quickly understand the importance of building and maintaining professional relationships that represent their organizations in a positive light.

When treated rudely, 88 percent of employees say they plan to "get even" with their organizations and 94 percent say they "get even" with their offender.

Source: *The Cost of Incivility* by Christine Pearson and Christine Porath

> *How come when I ask for a pair of hands, I get a human being as well?* —Henry Ford

IS YOUR ORGANIZATION LACKING IN HUMANITY?

You're likely reading this book because you have an important position, like chief people officer, employee development coach, leader of talent management, VP (visionary person), people department manager, or designer of human resources and creative people development. If so, ask yourself this question: Is humanity lacking within my organization? That can be a difficult issue for some people to address. If there is a lack of humanity in your organization, you need to know that it probably profoundly affects the development of your leadership and their teams. Therefore, examine carefully the table of contents in this book and determine the areas of greatest need for training your organization's leaders in the human side of management.

You will find that people and humanity are the cornerstones upon which this book is written. From each chapter you will gain not only practical skills and lessons, but also a perspective on the human side of leadership and how that might look in your organization. You also will find numerous examples from world-class organizations that are emphasizing the human side of doing business by putting people first.

IS YOUR ORGANIZATION LACKING IN CIVILITY?

Do you ever have the feeling that civility is in hiding? There's no doubt we long for it in our organizations, but we just don't seem to have the tools to locate it. The search is crucial not only to the bottom line but to our society's very core. This section will help you find the necessary tools, use them, and get results.

Diana Damron's Three Cs

Civility and communications expert Diana Damron says the key is the three Cs: *communication, character,* and *civility*. In an interview, Damron explains, "We *communicate* our *character* by exercising our *civility*." In other words, we tell everyone *who* we are and *what* we are by how we treat other people and ourselves. We can get back on track, but it means getting back to basics.

> ## Incivility Is Expensive
>
> Did you know . . . ?
>
> - More than 80 percent of all workers believe it is important to work in a civil environment.
> - Incivility is often learned from leadership.
> - A worker who is treated rudely is often less productive, with lower performance levels.
> - 12 percent of employees leave their companies because of something to do with incivility (costing companies 1.5 to 3 times the employee's salary, with damage to company reputation and employee motivation).
>
> **Source:** The Civility Initiative at Johns Hopkins: *The Baltimore Workplace Civility Study* and Kenan-Flagler Business School University of North Carolina: *Workplace Incivility: The Target's Eye View.*

Damron talks about when she was a kid. "We'd be in big trouble with our moms if we didn't use the magic words, 'please,' 'thank you,' and 'you're welcome,'" she states. "We loved using them over at our friends' homes. Those moms always gave us extra brownies for being so polite. We learned early that courtesy counts and politeness pays!" Now, Damron says, if you're lucky, you hear, "please," "thank you," and "uh huh," or perhaps her personal favorite: "yup!"

The Price You Pay for Incivility

It's bad enough to get in hot water with your mom for not saying, "thank you" as a kid, but as an adult in the business world, those oversights and slights bear huge costs: millions of dollars!

Customers steer clear of businesses where they see employees treat each other poorly. Their impression of an organization that *permits* such treatment is poor, and they're not afraid to tell others that they too should avoid this business. Reputations can change quickly in the age of texts, tweets, and Facebook.

Even if you take customers out of the equation, the price is high for an organization that permits incivility. Even if organizational leaders are not aware of rudeness among teams, the impression for employees is that the business doesn't care—incivility is permitted. "It's hard for employees to think straight," Damron points out, "when they're the targets of either co-workers or leaders or both. When you're looking over your shoulder constantly, you can't function properly. That employee pays, the team pays, and the organization pays. It's robbery by rudeness!"

Leaders, put yourself in the shoes of someone who's treated rudely on a regular basis. Imagine trying to walk forward in a straight line while looking back over your shoulders. It's not easy, is it? But when you're waiting for the next verbal bomb to strike, or the next public humiliation, that's the result. Not much walking with confidence, just a lot of stumbling! Those stumbles can take down an entire organization.

The Vilification of Etiquette

"We banished manners, dumped etiquette, and now we're surprised that we can't seem to scrounge up much civility," says Damron. "We depicted etiquette as just a bunch of rigid and unnecessary rules for forks, knives, and spoons. Tragically, that image caught on, and we have paid a price."

Damron points to Peggy Post's statement in the 17th edition of *Emily Post's Etiquette:* "As fluid as manners are (and always have been), they rest on the same bedrock principles: respect, consideration, and honesty." Aren't those exactly the qualities we've been searching for? From politics to education, from courtrooms to living rooms, we all beg for a return to respect, consideration, and honesty. Once *accurately* defined, you realize that manners, etiquette, and civility are one in the same. Thoughtfulness is the Golden Rule: treating others the way you want to be treated. (Check out more on civility and business etiquette at www.emilypost.com.)

> *To make a pleasant and friendly impression is not only good manners but equally good business.* —Emily Post

Practice and Lead by Example

In her speaking, classes, and seminars (visit www.DianaDamron.com for more info on how to create a corporate culture of civility and how to engage confident leadership), Damron underscores the importance of practice. Practice becomes easier and more fruitful when we have an example. Leaders must be examples of thoughtfulness, civility, and kindness. What happens when they're not? Teams walk on eggshells, confidence wanes, and productivity starts to trickle away.

Finding a leader who is an example may be tougher than you'd think. Diana points us to *The Cost of Bad Behavior,* where the authors say that they're "always amazed how many managers, employees, and professionals tell us that they don't understand what it means to be civil." Okay, all together now: "Being civil means being thoughtful!"

So, leaders lead by example. However, what happens when a leader doesn't know *how* to be civil? This is when the problems arise. Employees leave, or at the very least, are disengaged. Loyalty to the organization sinks, and the bottom line suffers. It is estimated that employee disengagement costs American businesses $328 billion annually.

Between broken families, Hollywood's story lines, and some politicians' asinine antics, examples are hard to come by. Yet we desperately need them. In the book, *Wooden on Leadership*, UCLA Hall of Fame basketball coach John Wooden writes, "I believe there is no more powerful leadership tool than your own personal example."

For our workplaces to survive the current rising stress levels, it's vital that your leaders know they *must* lead by example. If they don't know how to be civil, help them. Civility coaches like Damron are passionate about transforming emotionally unsafe environments to places of respect and healthy teamwork.

Step Out of Your Shoes . . .

. . . and into theirs. Step into the shoes of your teams and your leaders. Look at yourself from their perspective. If *you* hate being reprimanded in public (and who doesn't), imagine how your team member feels when castigated in front a customer...or a fellow team member. If someone needs an attitude adjustment or a correction on policy, do it in private. Does your team or your leadership see you treating everyone with equal respect? Is there consistency? If not, you're not garnering support and loyalty.

In Case You're Wondering

Rude behavior, in the form of defensive behavior, can come from someone being poorly trained. Express your civility as a leader by ensuring that your teams are well trained. Are expectations clear? Are the methods and steps to achieve the goals reasonable and explicit? You can smile with great affection and speak with oozing warmth, but if you're not training your team, your concept of civility is misguided. Require that your leaders establish consideration and respect as a baseline for all professional behavior. Ask leaders if they want to be known as an organization where civility is a priority. The answer should obviously be yes, and then required standards of civility have to be set in place for everyone to follow.

Nike Up!

Nike definitely knows how to motivate. Their ads are clear and persuasive. Don't just talk; get up and do it! Leaders, it's time to Nike up. No sitting on the sidelines. Don't let your team get soft, inflexible, and tired. Imagine starting your team on a weight-lifting program. You're their personal coach. Help them to individually set goals and lay out a program to achieve those goals. Just like a personal trainer, your job is to *show* them how to get stronger. You're their example now.

Select specific skills. You might start with: 1) listen without interrupting; 2) use "please," "thank you," and "you're welcome" a lot more frequently; 3) put personal cell phones away during work hours; 4) re-read emails to ensure their clarity and civility before pressing "send"; 5) answer with words, not a grunt; and 6) smile! (Have you ever noticed that when you smile, even exercise or an unpleasant task seems easier...at least a little bit?)

Here's what you'll see: improvement! Your team will get stronger. That strength will allow for more flexibility and stability to handle whatever is thrown at them. With you as their coach, they'll get a better sense of teamwork and dedication to a goal. You will just do it! Thanks, Nike.

Time Is of the Essence—Tap the Power of Nice

Why are we making this so complicated? It's not nuclear physics. Civility is connecting with kindness—connecting by emotionally touching another human being. We're winning the race for speed. We email, text, and call within moments, but try to be nice...

Exercise: Civility and Your Team

Use this checklist and discussion stimulators for your next team meeting:

- ☐ Is civility in hiding in your workplace, or is it exercised regularly?
- ☐ Is civility exercised equally between coworkers and with customers?
- ☐ Is every customer greeted with a smile?
- ☐ Do you hear "you're welcome" regularly?
- ☐ Can you step into your team member's shoes?
- ☐ How do you look through your team's collective eyes?
- ☐ Are you a leader who inspires by example?
- ☐ Knowing you set the bar and are an example, have you made some changes to your routine?
- ☐ Is civility a priority for you? If yes, why? If no, why not?
- ☐ What does civility look like among your team members?
- ☐ Is civility a priority for your team? If yes, why? If no, why not?
- ☐ What motto can you write about being civil and treating others with respect? How will you use it as a leader?

well, that takes too much time. Seriously—folks are saying they just don't have time to be nice!

Actually, we don't have the time *not* to be nice. Our moods, our behavior—they're contagious. What do you want to spread in your organization? As a leader, that's your choice. Rushing is a risk that can have side effects you don't want. Taking the time to be nice and to exercise civility can have huge payoffs. In the book *The Power of Nice*, authors Linda Kaplan Thaler and Robin Koval speak glowingly of Frank, a much loved security guard in their Manhattan office building. He takes the time to greet each individual entering through the front door. The result has been the creation of a warm and welcoming environment that has actually led to big sales. Clients are human. They, too, appreciate kindness and that extra-special welcome. Their mood was primed for positive activity.

Don't let time dictate your behavior. Remember, you're an example. Your team is taking its cue from you. What mood will you be spreading today?

Step Away from the Device—Recapture the Human Touch

You know the feeling: You're in the middle of a serious conversation, you're just about to explain your idea of how to solve the problem, and someone picks up his phone and starts texting! Every bit of inspiration and excitement drain from you. You've been one-upped by a phone (or rectangular bully, as Damron calls it in her speeches) that really must be smart—you're playing second fiddle to it once again.

Civility requires that we get our priorities straight. Our communication techno-toys are tools, but people—our teams—are human! And before you think I'm stating the obvious, consider this: If it's that obvious, why aren't we treating our teams like they mean more to us? Really, take a moment. The next time you go to lunch, look around. Are the people sitting around you spending more time talking to their table companions or looking at a tiny screen?

So many problems in the workplace result from the fact that we know so much about technology, and so little about each other. We want to text and email to stay in touch, as long as we don't have to do it in person. Leaders have to get out of the office and in front of their teams. They must be the models of civility. One young woman wrote that her connection to her phone became an addiction. It was excruciatingly hard for her to stay focused in a meeting, at a meal, or with friends. What email was waiting to be read? What text impatiently waited for a response? What did Facebook know that she didn't?

You have this wonderful opportunity to change the face of your workplace by recapturing the human touch. The touch screen is convenient; the touch of civility is crucial.

Thick or Thin?

No, not the pizza crust, but the measure of your ability to roll with the punches. Are you thin-skinned? Do you take offense easily? You may be setting up your team for more drama than necessary. You have a sense of humor—use it more, take offense less. Just think what might happen if we *choose* to give the benefit of the doubt to the person who just said something inconsiderate. We've all done it—a thoughtless remark made without meaning anything offensive. How often would turmoil be terminated by a hearty laugh, a knowing smile, or a reassuring response?

Do You Dare?

You have the wonderful opportunity to change the complexion of your business by exercising civility. In the same way that your face glows after blood has been pumped to the skin through rigorous exercise, you and your leaders can pump life and vitality throughout your team by exercising—exercising civility.

You make the choice. Choose to be an example. Choose to be thoughtful. Choose to take that extra moment. Your choices are contagious.

Go and spread civility!

> *The philosophy of putting employees first is particularly important in our industry, because Marriott is in the people business, not just the service business. —J.W. Marriott*

WHAT IS A HUMAN-ORIENTED LEADER?

Peter Senge explains it best when he suggests that in the twenty-first century, it is not only going to be timely but also critical that we reflect on what we as humans beings have understood for a very long time: Work and working together hold a deep and gratifying source of meaning for people, and anything less than attaining that feeling of meaningful purpose is just a job.

It is essential that you teach your leaders to value and trust their workers, not only for their job functions but for who they are as people. And what about the leader in training who asks, "Who has time to spend on developing all of these relationships?" With that approach, those leaders will not be getting the most out of your organization's greatest asset—its people. (For more on that topic, see chapter 8.)

Successful Leaders and Organizations Relate to the Whole Person

No longer can organizations afford to compartmentalize their employees' lives. Drawing an invisible line that suggests a worker leave his or her personal life at the door when reporting for work ignores every aspect of humanness. That line from yesteryear's management rules now has become outdated and blurred. We know it is impossible for an employee to close off his or her personal life when coming to work because such behavior goes against human nature. One dimension of a person's life is affected by all others, and both the professional and personal lives of employees are closely connected. That is what is meant by the term *whole person*.

Encourage your leaders to take the whole-person approach when leading others. Tell them that when they do this, a variety of benefits will emerge from their people and throughout the organization—innovation, creativity, higher levels of performance and productivity, motivation, inspiration, caring, competencies, culture, tradition, values, feelings, expertise, intellectual capital, and integrity, among many others.

The Whole-Person Approach Requires Head, Hands, Feet, and Heart

Introduce your leaders to this whole-person approach by having them complete the following exercise. First, explain that this approach to leadership is a four-part process: part 1 is the leader's head, part 2 is the leader's hands, part 3 is the leader's feet, and part 4 is the leader's heart.

Ask your leaders to describe in specifics what makes up the whole person based on those human parts. For example, show them how the head may represent a person's unique expertise or knowledge in a certain area and how the hands may represent specific skills, hands-on coaching, and so forth. This effort will challenge your leaders to identify all of the human qualities and dimensions that go into making a worker as productive and high-performing as possible. Show your leaders Figure 2.1 and ask them to fill in the spaces associated with each of the four parts.

Debrief this exercise by having your leaders share aloud the various human dimensions and qualities they listed for each aspect. Ask them to discuss why they chose to list those qualities and talents where they did. Ask if some of these could be listed in more than one area. For example, customer service might be listed in both part 2 and part 4.

After you have completed this exercise with your leaders, show them Figure 2.2, which offers examples of suggested responses. Stress here that only when a leader sees and appreciates these human qualities can he or she effectively practice the

Figure 2.1 The Whole-Person Approach to Leadership

Whole-Person Approach to
LEADERSHIP

Part 1: **Leader's Head Represents**

Part 2: **Leader's Hands Represent**

Part 3: **Leader's Feet Represent**

Part 4: **Leader's Heart Represents**

Figure 2.2 Examples of the Whole-Person Approach

Part 1: **Leader's Head Represents**

Knowledge, education, unique expertise, intellectual property (i.e., patents, trade secrets, etc.), empowerment, competencies, attitude, motivation, character, integrity, and values

Part 2: **Leader's Hands Represent**

Skills, implementation, follow-through, hands-on coaching, customer service, production, and manufacturing

Part 3: **Leader's Feet Represent**

Foundation upon which the organization and its leaders are built, organization's culture, history, tradition, founders, organizational stability, and growth to move forward one step at a time

Part 4: **Leader's Heart Represents**

Caring, feelings, intuition, core values, emotional intelligence, pride, spirit, and hope

This represents the soul of the organization.

whole-person technique of leadership. Explain that the technique is requisite for effectively managing human capital, as described in chapter 8.

There is a difference between an organization with soul and one without it. To help your leaders understand that difference, point out the statement at the bottom of Figure 2.2: *This represents the soul of the organization.* Ask them to explain what that

means. Then suggest to them that there is a great difference between an organization that treats its employees as whole people and one that treats them as mechanical producers of a task for which they are compensated—in that difference lays the soul. Depending on your organization's comfort level in using the term *soul*, you also may refer to this concept as *spirit, meaningful purpose, inner passion, synergy,* or whatever word best suits your corporate culture.

What Whole-Person Leadership Looks Like in America's Leading Companies

Share with your leaders a few of the ways some of America's most successful companies demonstrate how they care about their people—seeing them not just as workers but as people with human needs and desires for more fulfilling lives. Isn't this the ultimate goal of any leadership program?

Starbucks Acknowledges Every Person's Desire for Health and Well-Being

Employees at Starbucks are considered family and are treated as such. Starbucks was the first private, and later public, company to offer full health benefits for all of its part-time workers. During a time when other companies were struggling to cut costs and eliminate benefits, especially for part-timers, Starbucks saw its people in a different way—not just as part-time staff with potentially high turnover but as people who were students and housewives—human beings juggling several activities to enrich their lives and make ends meet. Ask your leaders to identify which part or parts of the whole-person approach to leadership Starbucks uses in that example. (A possible answer is head and heart.)

Marriott Hotels Lead With a "Human Touch"

Marriott International, Inc., personalizes its treatment of employees by referring to them as "associates." With more than 80 languages spoken among Marriott's employees, this multibillion dollar enterprise also is multicultural in its makeup. Because of their cultural diversity, many employees must cope with complicated immigration procedures and social discrimination, in addition to such pressures as child care and housing problems.

The corporation makes a special effort to be in touch with the real-world personal challenges facing its employees by taking a whole-person approach to management. For one thing, the famous Marriott "Human Touch" is not reserved only for hotel customers. The corporation believes that what every troubled or worried associate needs is a bit of that touch.

In response to its people's needs, Marriott rolled out its 800 Associate Resource Line, or ARL. Any associate with a problem can call the ARL and immediately be connected with a trained professional social worker who listens and counsels and follows through until a solution is found. This humanistic program has produced drops in absenteeism, tardiness, and turnover.

Ask your leaders to identify which part or parts of the whole-person approach to leadership Marriott uses in that example. (A possible answer is head, hands, and heart.)

The Body Shop International—The Human Side of Doing Business

The Body Shop operates on a strong foundation of social activism, cultural values, and giving back to the community. The corporation prides itself on having employees whose ethics center around caring—people who aren't simply interested in a nine-to-five job but who want to find meaningful purpose through what they do at work.

Today, The Body Shop has 2,400 stores in 61 countries, and the late Dame Anita Roddick helped make this a reality by implementing her motto: "Bring your heart to work." According to Roddick, the workplace is less a factory for the production of goods and more an incubator for the human spirit. It is strongly believed at The Body Shop that by contributing to the greater good, employees build self-esteem and the ability to express themselves for common purpose and connection. As a result, all staff members are given one half-day of paid time off per month so they may take part in their choice of a community project. Not only does the program promote the organization's strong values-led belief system, but it also carries forward the tradition set by its founder. (The Body Shop International is now part of the L'Oreal corporate group and the second largest cosmetic franchise in the world.)

Ask your leaders to identify which part or parts of the whole-person approach to leadership The Body Shop uses in that example. (A possible answer is heart, hands, and feet.)

USAA Makes a Commitment to Human Skill Development

USAA knows how to enliven the spirit of its people, and it has gained a well-deserved reputation for employee dedication and a happy workplace. At this one-of-a-kind insurance company, there is great support not only for academic and professional development but also for personal growth and human skills development.

In an effort to help employees manage their personal development and prepare for the future, the company created a formal workforce development program. Employees get one-on-one consultation sessions with workforce development consultants. Sessions include skill assessment and action planning. Resource centers are located in USAA's major offices and are open 24 hours a day, seven days a week. Support services include self-reliance classes, interviewing tools, résumé preparation, networking skills, and much more. By doing this, USAA has taken the whole-person approach to successfully developing its people.

Ask your leaders to identify which part or parts of the whole-person approach to leadership USAA uses in that example. (A possible answer is head and hands.)

Use those real-world examples as points of discussion with your leaders. Ask them to think about other organizations they know of that use the whole-person approach to leadership. Ask what they have learned from those exemplary organizations and how they can apply the lessons to strengthen their own leadership styles.

People Are Worth the Investment

In the book *The Soul at Work,* authors Roger Lewin and Birute Regine write of the powerful ways that businesspeople are working in a new and global economy—where people are the bottom line and leaders and organizations have become more human oriented, caring, and soulful. Real-world examples of that leadership style have been provided for you in this chapter. Their successful outcomes in the business world, both in terms of performance and profitability, are testaments to the cutting-edge direction that organizations are taking, especially when it comes to women in global leadership roles. (Take a look at Regine's new book, *Iron Butterflies: Women Transforming Themselves and the World.* You can also check out her blog featured on the Huffington Post and visit her website at www.Ironbutterflies.com.)

Use this quick-reference tool when taking the whole-person approach to leadership.

Part 1: A Leader's Head Represents:	Part 3: A Leader's Feet Represent:
☐ Knowledge ☐ Education ☐ Unique expertise ☐ Intellectual property ☐ Empowerment ☐ Competencies ☐ Attitude ☐ Motivation ☐ Character ☐ Integrity ☐ Values	☐ Foundation upon which the organization and its leaders are built ☐ Organizational culture ☐ History ☐ Tradition ☐ Founders ☐ Organizational stability ☐ Growth to move forward
Part 2: A Leader's Hands Represent:	**Part 4: A Leader's Heart Represents:**
☐ Skills ☐ Implementation ☐ Follow-through ☐ Hands-on coaching ☐ Customer service ☐ Production ☐ Manufacturing	☐ Caring ☐ Feelings ☐ Intuition ☐ Core values ☐ Emotional intelligence ☐ Pride ☐ Spirit ☐ Hope

Questions for Discussion: Developing the Human Side of Leadership

1. Describe what role human nature and humanity play in effective leadership.
2. What do you think Henry Ford meant when he said, "How come when I ask for a pair of hands, I get a human being as well?"
3. What is a human-oriented leader?
4. The whole-person approach to leadership involves what four parts?
5. How are the HR role and the role of the learning professional profoundly affected by the whole-person approach to management?
6. In total, what do the head, hands, feet, and heart represent in an organization?

Wrapping It Up

For this chapter, your leaders have an important choice to make. They can view the leadership role as an exertion they are obligated to perform, or they can view the role as a vehicle that delivers a sense of meaningful purpose to both their employees and the organization. Taking a whole-person approach will enable your leaders to focus on the unique combination of talents and skills each worker offers first as a person, keeping in mind at all times that business is about people and their ability to strengthen relationships. Closing the gap and leading across the generational divide is the topic of the next chapter.

Minding the Gap on Generational Leadership

Generational gap leadership is one of the most complex dilemmas that face leaders to-day. Not everyone is like you or thinks like you! And it's a good thing. The world would be a boring place if we were all the same—not to mention that the world of in-novation would come to an abrupt halt. When leaders understand and appreciate the cultural diversity across multiple generations, they begin to unleash the success of their organizations. After all, an idea vetted by a diverse group of individuals will almost al-ways be stronger than an idea generated by a group of people sharing identical back-grounds.

If leaders could learn to bridge the gap between each generation in the workforce, their businesses would easily transform into high-performing, fully engaged organiza-tions. This chapter will help you to identify the specific traits, attitudes, and work styles of each generation—and show you how to communicate and coach these groups in order to build a high performance dream team.

What You Will Learn in This Chapter:

- ◆ The four generations currently in the workplace, including:
 - ● the background of the generations
 - ● preferred communication styles
 - ● ways to manage the generational divide.
- ◆ Important strategies to manage a multi-generational workplace, such as:
 - ● multiple communication strategies
 - ● flexible work environments
 - ● open communication techniques
 - ● goal setting for results.

MANAGE AND DEMONSTRATE LEADERSHIP BETWEEN GENERATIONAL GAPS

There are many differences found between the four generations in today's workplace. The distinction in thoughts, beliefs, actions, and tastes between these generations is referred to as the "generational gap."

Generational gaps have been common throughout all periods of history; however, the differences between the gaps have actually widened between the twentieth and twenty-first centuries. Today, generational gaps play a huge role in business, among other things. Companies are looking for ways to stabilize the workplace and balance the needs and views of individuals from differing age groups, who thus have differing work ethics and backgrounds.

Did you know that this is the first time in history that our global workforce is comprised of four distinct generations—all working side by side and under the same roofs in many companies around the world? The generations have many titles, but are typically called Traditionalists (or Pre-War), Baby Boomers, Generation Xs, and Generation Ys (also known as Generation Next or Millennials). Each generation brings different attributes, skills, and ethics to the workplace. It is these distinctions from which we all can benefit as they provide tremendously diverse skills, styles, and thought processes within a single workplace. The key for leaders is in learning new and effective ways to break through the communication barriers that can occur between generations.

In order to better understand the preferred work styles of these distinct generations, it helps to have insight into some of the life events that have shaped the values of each generation.

Traditionalists, or the Pre-War Generation

Traditionalists were born between 1922 and 1943. Employees of this generation value sacrificing for "the greater good," and they are known to crave the distinction of being considered the "most committed" generation.

Why? These individuals were born between two world wars. Many watched fathers leave to fight overseas while their mothers entered the workforce in order to pay the bills. Additionally, their values were shaped by the Great Depression. They never expected a handout. Rather, in this generation, everyone expected to work hard, save for rainy days, and take nothing for granted—not even "world peace." This generation is loyal to its company and to its employees, and expects job and financial security for this hard work and loyalty. It is not uncommon for Traditionalists to work at only one or two companies for their entire careers. This tends to be the most consistent generation and the one least likely to seek drastic or sudden change of the four groups.

Traditionalists

Traditionalists prefer:

- formal work environments in which they give and receive respect
- rolling up their sleeves and demonstrating self-reliance
- well-defined boundaries and clear expectations
- routine and methodical work assignments and processes
- to believe that "practice makes perfect."

Baby Boomers

Baby Boomers were born between 1944 and 1962. Boomers know how to "work to get ahead" or "live to work."

Why? Baby Boomers were created in the post-war economic boom—many growing up in new urban expansions called suburbs. While they witnessed the assassinations of reformers in the United States, such as the Kennedys, Martin Luther King Jr., and Malcolm X, they also came of age believing that man could indeed walk on the moon. They challenged society to tolerate rebellion when they championed free love and recreational drug use; however, as they matured, they turned their ideals toward improving society by championing causes ranging from civil rights to environmental issues. This generation thrives best in "high-warmth" environments where they feel cared for and included. Boomers value relationships, self-expression, and the spirit of youth.

Baby Boomers

Baby Boomers prefer:

- informal, casual communication styles
- harmonious teams and intimate work groups
- democracy—at home and at work
- building meaningful relationships
- recognition for a job well done.

Generation X

Generation Xs were born between 1963 and 1980. Gen Xs value "work-life balance." Unlike Boomers, who "live to work," Xs "work to live."

Why? They are a generation that started the computer age, so they expect both their computers and themselves to be gifted at "multi-tasking." And like those mavericks who pioneered the new age of technology, Generation Xs tend to act more like "free

agents" instead of committed loyalists to companies. Many of them were latchkey kids who witnessed their Baby Boomer parents work themselves to the bone to buy "things" for them, instead of spending time with them. Finally, Generation X started their corporate careers at the same time new words like "downsizing" and "outsourcing" entered our vocabulary. Believing that companies didn't give loyalty to its employees, Generation Xs tend to work for companies using a shorter term mindset than the previous generations. Many of them, in fact, pioneered their own businesses and value concepts such as those instilled in the popular 2009 book by Timothy Ferriss, *The 4-Hour Workweek*—wherein they are in charge of their own time and destiny.

Generation Xs

Generation Xs prefer:

- flexible schedules that allow them to balance their work commitments with their personal lives
- companies that value an entrepreneurial work style
- autonomy to make decisions and work independently
- individuality.

Generation Y (Gen Next or Millennials)

Generation Ys were born between 1981 and 2000. This generation strives to achieve "work-life integration" and they tend to practice a "live in the moment" philosophy. Generation Ys thrive on instant gratification.

Why? This generation came of age during times of economic growth. At school and on the field, they were less driven to compete for "first place;" instead, they were awarded trophies that said "good try" and "best effort." While older generations considered working together on school assignments "cheating," Generation Y does this as second nature; but instead of cheating, it's called "consensus building" and "collaboration." This generation came of age with information and social contact virtually on-demand—making these individuals less willing to wait to get what they want. Finally, as a result of the terrorist attacks on the World Trade Center, the Pentagon, and on the doomed flight that ended in Shanksville, PA, on September 11, 2001, Generation Ys in the United States are more comfortable giving up personal freedoms for collective safety—making Generation Ys more akin to Traditionalists than any other generation.

Generation Ys like to work in groups and are always asking for specific and measurable expectations. They are the most tech-savvy generation and can often multi-task circles around Generation Xs. This generation has a strong desire to please and wants to have development opportunities. They also do not want to just "put in their time" unless they are reinforced with results and praise. Generation Ys are likely to be visually oriented, and they learn and retain information well by using graphics, flowcharts, and diagrams.

> ## Generation Ys
>
> Generation Ys prefer:
> - training and development opportunities
> - team-based projects
> - to be told "why" when given work assignments
> - to work well in a structured environment
> - rewards and recognition today instead of waiting in line for older, more experienced colleagues or even their peers to first be recognized.

All four of the generations add powerful, unique work values when they are led with inspiration and proper direction. The best leaders understand the values of each generation, and they strive to harness their collective talents to elevate morale and performance across the workplace.

> ## The Benefits of a Multi-Generational Work Team
>
> - Diverse teams can recruit and retain additional top talent of all ages.
> - Multi-generational teams have greater flexibility and creativity.
> - Broad-based brainstorming tends to create superior decision making and stronger outcomes.
> - Diverse groups can speak to the needs of a more diverse population.

FOUR IMPORTANT STRATEGIES TO GIVE YOUR MULTI-GENERATIONAL WORKFORCE A BOOST

There are four strategies that can assist in managing a multi-generational workplace. These strategies are useful in any team but are particularly crucial in multi-generational groups. They boost communication, create a productive and safe environment, and help leaders to set and manage performance goals. Working in a multi-generational workplace is not a task for the weary or weak—but the strong and determined. The good news, though, is that these four strategies can be learned and mastered when practiced regularly.

Utilize Multiple Communication Channels

Every generation, just like every individual, approaches communication differently. The best leaders integrate the communication preferences of all generations and let the diversity of their group members serve as assets in addressing the issues at hand.

Here's an example: Baby Boomers often prefer face-to-face communication, while Generation Ys prefer electronic communication (for example, email, text messages, and instant messages). In order to meet the diverse needs of a multi-generational team, leaders may often need to share information via many formats:

● by email, which considers the audiences who prefer to read and re-read messages
● by short, impromptu, informational staff meetings—which take into consideration those who prefer more personable communication channels.

Does communicating via multiple channels sound like doing extra work? Maybe. But communication expert and leadership consultant Scott Carbonara (see chapter 14) reminds us that the old marketing adage called "The Rule of Sevens" applies here: "In general, listeners have to hear your message seven times before they are ready to act on that message. If you as a leader rely on one form of communication alone, you miss out on having your message readily heard, understood, and acted upon."

Imagine the power of your communication if all of your team members heard your message in *their own preferred language*. For communication to function, it takes appropriate repetition and the use of multiple channels on your part as a leader. Then it takes a nudge from you to ask your team to talk among themselves about what they heard. Finally, it takes follow-up on your part to ask your team, "So what did you hear me say?"

Foster a Flexible Environment Focused on Productivity

Every generation—again, like every individual—has preferences on what environmental factors influence them to produce outstanding work. Think of your own work preference. Do you like to listen to music? Do you require silence? Do you like to sit near a window? Or is it better if you sit facing a blank wall that has no movement or interesting objects? Obviously, what would create a high-performance environment for one person might create a tension headache for another.

The same holds true with flexible work schedules and performance. Some generations of employees crave the structure of the office environment to get things done. Others are more motivated by working outdoors—like sitting with a laptop on a bench by a lake. Therefore, it's important for leaders to realize that one size does not fit all. Instead of looking for a "one size fits all" solution, make sure that for all of the jobs your people perform, you have a means to systematically monitor and measure productivity. As a leader, you might not have it in your power to meet the various generational needs of each employee. But you can ask your employees what work environment they prefer. Remind them that you want to make them as happy and productive as possible. If you can't give them what they wish, explain to them what you can offer instead, and ask them how you can create more of the kind of workplace in which they perform best.

Encourage Open Communication

Demonstrate for leaders how to create a safe environment where everyone learns to accept the communication styles of multiple generations, while maintaining respect

and professionalism in the workplace. Encourage your employees to speak freely by creating an environment that doesn't "shoot the messenger" but rather encourages them to bring forward news even when the news is bad. Imagine a situation that can harm the organization, the reputation of the company, the morale of other team members, the customers, or the shareholders. Don't you want to have an environment that rewards open, honest communication?

Set Goals and Expectations

Turnkey companies address generational gaps by allowing flexibility in work environments, schedules, and job duties, and putting systematic programs in place to monitor productivity. But before an alternative work environment is implemented, make sure that you have taken the time to establish goals first. With established goals, all employees know what is expected of them and when each assignment is due. By creating a structured process that manages performance, employees have a tangible way of knowing when they are reaching the standards or when they are missing the mark, regardless of their personal work styles. Your structured processes become a way for you to reward your employees when they've earned it—but they also give you immediate feedback when someone requires performance coaching in order to reach the standards. This structure provides employees with the structure to "color within the lines," while still granting them freedom to choose whether to use a blue pen, or a red crayon, so to speak. In other words, they are told what to do, but given some choices in how to do it.

> **Key Point:** *The more you understand different generations, the more you appreciate and value all of the differences and contributions made.*

TRAIN YOUR LEADERS IN PROPER COMMUNICATION TECHNIQUES

The best way to help your leaders in a multi-generational environment is to teach and facilitate proper communication techniques. Each generation has a unique and specific way of seeing the world and interacting with leaders, peers, friends, family, acquaintances, and customers. The chart below more thoroughly explains this and can assist in bridging the communication gap.

The Way They See the World

	Traditionalists	Baby Boomers	Generation Xs	Generation Ys
General outlook	Realistic	Hopeful	Cynical	Optimistic
Work ethic	Devoted	Motivated	Impartial	Strong-minded
Authority	Courteous	Love or hate	Unenthusiastic	Polite
Leadership	Chain of command	Consensus	Proficient	Team up
Relationships	Personal sacrifice	Personal satisfaction	Reluctant to obligate	Inclusive
Turnoffs	Rudeness	Laziness	Cliché	Delayed gratification

Great leaders understand that the outlook for each generation is different. This assists them in having the ability to communicate properly and understand the "typical" viewpoints of each generation. In many organizations, leaders experience an "us versus them" mentality, which causes conflict between the generations. In this scenario, the more diversity you have between generations, the more conflict you will have. Such issues can bring employee engagement to a record low. Finding the solution to the generational gap conflict can "make or break" any organization.

To bridge the communication gap with Traditionalists, try these four techniques:
1. Provide them with written or face-to-face communication.
2. Do what you say you are going to do. Giving and keeping "your word" is of the utmost importance.
3. Since they tend to be productivity-driven, take care in not wasting their time.
4. Since they were brought up with the philosophy of "speak only if you are spoken to," they tend to internalize things rather than vocalize them. Do not expect a lot of feedback from them. However, since they value respect, they will open up if you ask them direct questions.

To bridge the communication gap with Baby Boomers, try these four techniques:
1. Use an open yet direct style.
2. Provide them with several choices so that they can make decisions on things that affect them.
3. Allow them flexibility to get the job done, but provide them with timelines and guidelines for a successful task or project; they are due-date driven.
4. Since this generation is perceptive, control your body language. They will know if your body language does not match the words that you say—which would eliminate your credibility with them.

To bridge the communication gap with Generation Xs, try these four techniques:
1. This data- and tech-savvy generation craves facts and statistics to explain the company's position. Be prepared for them to use a smartphone on the spot to check your facts!
2. Request their feedback and provide feedback on an ongoing basis.
3. Informal, casual communication works best with Generation X.
4. Keep them updated on the latest information that affects them or their overall performance.

In most cases, you can bridge the gap by understanding that the Generation Xs do not work effectively being micromanaged and rely heavily on data and statistics. When assigning work to a Generation Xer, give them specific timelines, targets, and expectations. It is not uncommon for them to bring back a finished product, on time, that meets all of the expectations. Typically, if they get in a bind and have additional questions, they are not afraid to ask for clarification.

To bridge the communication gap with Generation Ys, try these five techniques:

1. Explain the *why* behind things—from changes, to rules, to general instructions. Be sure to point out how things impact the team, organization, community, and them personally.
2. Provide them with job stimulation through challenges and encouragement to take risks.
3. Never talk down to them. They are young—but don't treat them as inexperienced or lacking sophistication. Be kind and considerate.
4. The preferred method of communication is instant messages and text messages. In a corporate environment, emails are acceptable but are not the preferred method of communication.
5. Create a fun, interactive, humorous work environment.

In most cases, you can bridge the gap with Generation Ys by giving them direction. They are quick to say "okay" and conform to changes that make sense to them. If the changes do not make sense to them, they will continue to ask questions. If they hear anything that sounds like, "Because I told you so," you will lose their attention immediately and their respect over time (if they continue to feel like you don't value them). They each want to be treated as smart and knowledgeable—not like the "new kid on the block." Generation Ys want to learn, be mentored, and be treated as valuable assets to their organizations. They also do not feel that they need to "put in their time" to get ahead; they instead feel that if they are doing the same job as another more experienced worker, they should receive the same rewards and pay.

The hardest communication is between Generation Ys and all other generations. Generation Ys like variety, need to know the purpose behind the rules (norms), and may appear to question "authority" even when, in fact, they are enthusiastic and want to please their leaders. They also thrive when they receive constant feedback and appraisal, if they have done the jobs or tasks well.

Test Your Knowledge

Test your knowledge of the generations by listing the generation group that corresponds to these phrases:

_____ The war made me even more loyal and patriotic.

_____ What do you mean I cannot collaborate on this with the president of the company?

_____ Trust in God; all others bring data!

_____ In this meeting, we should all come to a consensus.

HOW TO GIVE LEADERSHIP PURPOSE TO A MULTI-GENERATIONAL WORKPLACE

One dynamic and free way to boost to your employees' morale and performance is to instill them with a sense of purpose for what they do at work. Don't we all function best

in an environment where we are treated as individuals instead of just *numbers*? Some of these tips apply regardless of the generational gap in the workplace—but are especially necessary in cases where several generational groups exist. Here are some tips for engaging any workforce, but particularly a diverse one:

- Let your team members know the purpose behind their jobs, and the organizational goals.
- Make your team members feel that they are part of the "big" picture, and not just cogs in the wheel. Help them to use their diverse generational traits to serve a common purpose of helping the organization achieve success.
- Another way to add purpose and cohesiveness is to offer promotional opportunities to internal candidates before opening the positions to the public. Some employees may have been taking classes, completed a degree program, or have additional experience that the hiring manager was not aware of. Have ongoing conversations with your employees about their career goals, educational goals, and what it will take to get to the next level in the organization. These opportunities show that the leader cares about the success of the employee, and they help to bridge that gap between leadership and staff. All leaders started in a lower-level position at one point in their lives—and this technique also gives them an opportunity to give back what they have learned by mentoring an employee to success. When employees succeed with the assistance of a leader, that employee will be loyal to that leader for years to come. The leader can also step back and see the success story, and hopefully strive to find another success story.

Create a Purpose

At one time, Kodak's motto was, "We make memories." So employees in film processing plants were not film processors; they were "memory makers." Who would not want to put quality into making memories? In order to create this sort of purpose, you need to determine what your core product or service is, and then tie that into what your employees do so that you create their purpose.

Everything that leaders do, and inspire their employees to do, should be leading to the overall purpose of the organization. MedAmerica Billing Services Inc. (MBSI), based in Modesto, California, ties its purpose into its vision statement, which is: "MBSI's goal is to be recognized as the premier medical billing and practice management company by partnering with clients and employees to set the standard for our industry in service, quality, performance, and job satisfaction." What this means for employees across the generations is that they are setting the standard for quality, performance,

and job satisfaction for their clients. When their employees come to work, they know that they will do their very best for their clients, they know what the goals of the day are, and they will strive to meet or exceed these goals.

ACHIEVING GOALS IN A MULTI-GENERATIONAL WORKPLACE

In a multi-generational workplace, anytime you are about to initiate a change or act on a new goal, you can instill passion and purpose by using the four Ps. These techniques will help you to engage teams of diverse employees as they attend meetings, start a new project, form a new team, or have a brainstorming session.

The Four Ps Are Purpose, Processes, Payoffs, and Passion

Purpose: A savvy leader knows what the ultimate goal is, because all things hinge on this goal. They understand the time constraints, what actions are needed to be successful, and what it will take to accomplish the goal. Giving the team this information is imperative to its success and will build purpose by instilling trust and empowerment.

Processes: In order to function as a team to reach goals, proper processes need to be established. When everyone knows the proper steps to reach the goals, or is part of the team that creates the proper steps, purpose and pride are instilled in the team. They feel trusted to make proper decisions on the project, and it is an open and safe environment for them to brainstorm and share successes and improvements in the processes. Establishing processes also defines the decision-making process.

Payoffs: Smart leaders help their diverse teams to visualize what the payoffs will be when the projects are completed, so that the team has the drive and desire to reach the final goals of the projects. The payoff is when the ultimate goal is reached and the team can reflect on what went well and what could be improved upon for the future. This is a time when your team members can validate each person's input and respecting that individual for the value that he or she brought to the project. Perhaps you had a Traditionalist mentoring a Generation Y employee, or a Baby Boomer mentoring a Generation Xer. All generations enjoy reaching a goal and having the payoff instill pride and joy in them.

Passion: Leaders can instill passion in their workplace by allowing each team to function as a well-oiled machine—not by micromanaging them. When a leader trusts its employees and empowers them to be creative, it instills a passion that cannot be stopped. If employees are coming to work every day without passion, they will not produce the desired result and can be toxic to the rest of the team. Empower them, make them a part of the team, and let their individual attributes contribute to the organization's success.

What will you do today to add the four Ps to your meetings, tasks, projects, or day-to-day interactions with your employees? Refer to the sidebar for an exercise that tests how well you are using the four Ps.

Are You Using the Four Ps?

Mark each statement about your leadership methods as "true" or "false" to indicate if you are using the four Ps.

_____ Everyone understands the requirements, outcomes, and desired results.

_____ Each team member feels comfortable communicating openly in a safe environment.

_____ Each person is trusted and empowered to take justified risks to make the best decisions for the team.

_____ Each member of the team fully participates in the meeting, project, or task.

_____ Each team member is encouraged to bring their individual perspective without fear of reprisal.

_____ Each team member understands the proper decision-making process.

_____ Each team member is fully engaged and focusing on desired results.

_____ Each team member exhibits passion in their piece of the project or task.

If you have:

- 7-8 marked true, you have a fully engaged multi-generational team.
- 5-6 marked true, you have some engagement issues and need to refocus your team and provide them with additional tools or training and empower them to work toward the goals.
- 1-4 marked true, your team is in jeopardy of failure—and unless drastic steps are taken, the project may fail and the goals and objectives will not be met.

OTHER TIPS FOR MINDING GENERATIONAL GAPS

One major issue in managing generational gaps is leader-to-subordinate relationships. Leaders who are younger struggle when they try to manage their more seasoned employees. And older leaders struggle to manage their younger workers. One way to bridge this gap is to show that you care by respecting their time, asking for their opinions, treating them with respect, mentoring them, and trusting that they will do the work outlined to them.

To show them that you care, demonstrate a genuine interest in things that interest them, and learn about them as people—what their communication preferences are and what makes them tick. Acknowledge subordinates for their experience and the value that they bring to the organization. Every employee wants to feel valued, respected, and as though they have made a contribution to the organization. If you can help them to feel that way, they will work more cohesively together and, more importantly, be dedicated to you, their leader.

Build a Bridge and Get Over the Generational Divide

Below are 12 leadership techniques that bring multi-generational workplaces closer.

- Build a workplace culture of trust and sustainable talent.
- Appreciate the unique and valuable differences in others.
- Accept that a "one-size-fits-all" mentality no longer works.
- Find your own voice and your own unique ways to communicate with every generation.
- Demonstrate a genuine interest in others.
- Promote a cohesive workplace.
- Avoid making snap judgments about others whom you may not even know.
- Support each generation's values.
- Accommodate employee differences whenever you can.
- Be flexible in your leadership style.
- Respect and honor competence, experience, willingness to learn, and initiative.
- Be the bridge that you expect others to be and keep minding the gaps—big and small.

Here are 10 simple questions that leaders can ask their subordinates to bridge the gap and collaborate with all four generations:

1. How do you like to be communicated with (verbal, written, email, voicemail, text message)?
2. When you are recognized for a job well done, do you prefer private or public recognition?
3. What motivates you to be more productive?
4. Do you prefer a direct and straightforward approach or a collaborative approach?
5. What is your comfort level with technology?
6. What software are you familiar with, and what is your level of comfort?
7. What software do you want to learn, and how can the company assist you in learning it?
8. What goals do you have, and where do you want to be in one year, and in five years?
9. If you were running the company, what would you change?
10. Do you have any cost- or labor-saving ideas that can help do your job more efficiently?

Asking all of your subordinates these leading questions will assist you in understanding their communication styles, goals for future development, and how they want to be recognized.

Managers of low-performing work teams have poor leadership strategies. They expect everyone to be just like them, always focus on problems and mistakes, avoid risk and encourage others to avoid risks as well, and ignore positive contributions in the workplace. Managers of high-performing work teams encourage people to create new approaches to work, avoid judging ideas before they are fully explained, allow a variety of behaviors and attitudes unless they violate policies, emphasize and celebrate personal successes, and encourage risk-taking and learning from mistakes.

Benefits of a Multi-Generational Workforce

Some benefits of generational gaps include:

- Different viewpoints can generate more well-rounded ideas.
- Younger generations can assist in technology resources and question outdated processes.
- Older generations can assist with people skills; many organizations call these "soft skills."
- Everyone can collaborate and create a mentoring environment, which serves the needs of all generations.

Questions for Discussion: Bridging the Gap

1. Describe the different generations that are currently in the workplace.
2. List one communication preference from each generation.
3. What are the four steps you use that boost your workforce?
4. What are the 4 Ps, and how do they apply to your workplace?
5. Why is it important to understand the generations as applied to your workplace?
6. What are some of the benefits you have experienced in your own multi-generational workforce?

Wrapping It Up

By being aware of generational differences, we can assist leaders to modify their message for maximum effect—despite the task or relationship. Great business practices are based on understanding others' perspectives. Since many of us believe that the only right way is our way, we must now start to think that others can bring diversity and cultural competency to the table—looking outside the box for a well-rounded solution to complex problems. In order to work efficiently and effectively, and to increase quality and productivity, we need to embrace and understand generational uniqueness and learn how to use it effectively in dealing with each individual—while also keeping the common organizational purpose at the helm.

Brand and Expand Your Organization's Talent With Competencies

Some say the path to leadership success is through branding and expanding employee talent. Companies and leaders that invest in branding and in creating smart, self-reliant, always striving-to-improve, upgradable talent are the ones that will lead their organizations into the future. We happen to agree.

In fact, to make this process truly fly, we believe that managers and leaders should stop focusing so strongly on employee weaknesses, and instead start focusing on promoting their people's strengths and natural abilities. Books like Marcus Buckingham's *Now Discover Your Strengths*, as well as research published by leading positive psychology professor and author of *Authentic Happiness*, Martin Seligman, suggest that we experience more success by expanding upon others' strengths and the positive traits we find, rather than by trying to highlight or eliminate weaknesses. How, then, do you promote this type of leadership that expands upon competencies, while building them into the organizational brand?

In this chapter, and in the corresponding Appendix A, "Brand Leaders for Talent," your leaders will discover ways to incorporate the use of competency-building into their training. They will learn to promote and hire people with the competencies required for continued success and long-range achievement. If your leadership training does not currently include this element of recognizing, branding, and expanding your organization's talent, here is your chance to supplement your leadership development program to emphasize this vital quality.

What You Will Learn in This Chapter:

♦ Competencies are an important part of your leadership training and development. Leaders must
- focus on employees' individual strengths
- brand for talent among leaders
- understand the two basic categories from which competence is drawn: human ability and soft-skill intelligence; and technical skills and expertise, or cognitive ability
- create a list of appropriate core leadership competencies
- design a model for implementing core leadership competencies.

> ◆ Align competencies with organizational goals and strategies. Leaders must
> - practice using sample competencies as a model for creating their own core list
> - develop and build a framework from which to direct and implement a leadership style
> - better understand the overall value of establishing a leadership competency model that will build more cohesive teams and stretch people to their best abilities and talents.

BRAND AND EXPAND YOUR LEADERS USING STRENGTH-BASED TOOLS AND EMPLOYEE DEVELOPMENT PLANNING

An employee development plan is a written leadership strategy that provides a person with a step-by-step process to help achieve his or her career goals. Its purpose is to develop the strengths of a person to the greatest levels of talent and competency, achievement, and greater potential. It is also called a career development plan, individual development plan (IDP), or career-pathing strategy. In this chapter, we are giving you a template to follow that will help you to share this concept with the leaders you are developing.

Leaders Let Their Employees Shine and Set Everyone Up for Success

Employee development plans include the perspective of both a supervisor or manager and his or her employee. The goal is to make this plan reasonable and attainable—something that can be achieved with dedication, hard work, and focus. It's your job to set every employee up for success, not failure. We set people up for success when we let them shine at what they are good at, work at what they love doing, and continue to build a track record of success around those competencies. (See core leadership competencies later in this chapter and "Brand Leaders for Talent" in Appendix A.)

Leaders Focus on Employees' Talents and Strengths—Not Weaknesses

The most beneficial employee development plan focuses on an employee's talents and strengths. It does not focus solely on a person's weaknesses and how to improve them. Weak areas and challenges are certainly discussed and covered, but they should never be the primary focus for growing talent in an organization.

Weaknesses and special challenge areas of every employee should be discussed and then neutralized in an individual development plan, thereby making way for and allowing the employee's greatest talents to be fueled. Neutralizing weaknesses requires that you give people the help they need to do the job to the required competency level, but not necessarily to exceed that level. You don't want to spend an inordinate amount of time focusing on someone's weaknesses. And you certainly don't want to spend an inordinate amount of time pushing someone down a path that they hate, or developing a skill set that they despise doing—even if they are capable

of pulling it off. The results will be disastrous for not only the leader and his or her employee, but for the organization.

How to Develop Successful, Extraordinary Talent

By only focusing on the weaknesses of the person, we further make that person weaker and more insecure. When we neutralize weaknesses and redirect our energy toward a person's strongest gifts and talents, we create superstar performers, confident men and women, and extraordinary contributors to the organization's long-term goals.

Tell your leaders to identify and fuel their people's strengths, as it's their strengths that better equip them for growth and success, which in turn benefits the organization as well. First, you acknowledge that this is what your employee is hardwired for. Both leader and employee come together to create a career plan that brands and expands the organization, is in alignment with the organization's mission and vision, and meets the individual's desires and intrinsic motivation.

Leaders should be listening for their employees to say positive things about their jobs, their interests, and their future aspirations. For example:

- I love doing this job! It makes me really happy.
- I love writing strategic plans for our team.
- I love going to school and consider myself a lifelong learner.
- I enjoy pushing myself and stretching my abilities to new heights.
- I'm motivated by incentive plans and competition.
- I love learning the newest technology and then using it on the job.
- I enjoy experimenting and trying out new things.
- I'm introverted, so I love quiet time and being alone to think and plan ahead.
- Self-development helps me to reach my higher potential.
- When I am coaching others, I am learning the most.

An employee development plan lists both short- and long-term goals that an employee has pertaining to the current and future opportunities available in the organization.

Don't Just Teach What You Know

We teach what we know, and we often use the tools we feel comfortable with and have relied on time and again. And that's okay, to a point. It's human behavior to want to ensure the success of our efforts and the efforts of the people we are training and developing. Their ultimate success is a reflection on how well we've developed their potential and talent up to that point. But it's important to remember that your own career development is not the only reference point—or the only means to success.

How many times have you coached or trained an employee using some of the old-school methods you relied on back in the day? The approach may not be right or wrong, good or bad. It's just human nature that we sometimes instill in others what we know to be best for us, rather than what may be best for them at the time. One of the action learning points we teach in our seminars and workshops states, "We cannot coach people down a path that is inconsistent with the way they see themselves."

Every person grows beyond his or her developer and instructor at some point in all aspects of life, including the workplace. Our employees eventually grow beyond anything we could have imagined for them, and we may never know where our influence stops as leaders. Share this message with your leaders.

Teach Your Leaders How to Be Their Own Mentors

We may start off using our own methods and what worked best for us at the time when we started out as leaders, but eventually, to be able to develop people to their greater level of potential and performance, we have to relinquish our power and let them take the lead. (Anne writes about this extensively in her McGraw-Hill book, *Be Your Own Mentor*.) As leaders, it is our job to facilitate the success of others. It is the employee's responsibility to be his or her own mentor and make things happen in a unique way and with personal flair and style. We make the journey together, no matter where it starts.

Employee development plans have all got to be sturdy, substantive, reliable, strong, flexible, real-world, user friendly, easy to navigate and manipulate, and able to steer to the ultimate career.

Your ultimate objective as a leader is to provide each and every employee with the best tools and resources available to help ensure a successful journey and a safe landing. Once you've provided the map and compass, it's time for both you and your employee to take the ultimate leap of faith and implement the plan.

WHAT IS THE PURPOSE OF HAVING AN EMPLOYEE DEVELOPMENT PLAN?

The purpose of having an employee development plan (sometimes called an individual development plan, or IDP), is for leaders to grow talent and employee strengths within the organization. It has nothing to do with employee retention, or anyone paying you back, or appreciating what you've done for them by staying employed at the organization for 30 years! That's not the way it works. Like Zig Ziglar says in his *Little Book of Big Quotes*, "If you help enough other people get everything they want in life, you will get everything you want and more." This applies to employee development plans as well.

If your leaders help an employee plan a career strategy that is enormously successful and that person chooses to leave the organization, then so be it. Forget it and drive on! Regardless of where a leader's employee winds up—retiring from your organization, or accepting a fantastic job offer with another organization (perhaps one you could not match), a leader's intentions for their employees need to be pure and intended for each individual's growth and success. Whether you want to believe it or not, what goes around always comes around, and your leaders' intentions have to be authentic and not self-serving. Employee development planning is a long-lasting and powerful tool. How your leaders manage the responsibility for delivering the tool is up to them.

Few People Devote Their Careers to One Organization

Today's managers are well aware that if an employee (especially a younger employee) stays with an organization five or six years, that's a good run. Most Gen Xers and Gen Yers are not going to devote the next 30 years of their career lives to any one organization. Yes, it can happen, but it's unlikely. That's not the way our fluid, faster-than-ever, virtual workplace is built anymore.

If you get the best someone has to offer for five or six years, then that's about all you can expect. If you get more than that, consider it a bonus—take it and be grateful for the loyalty and dedication. But remember, plenty of people out there (maybe you are one of them) are extremely grateful for the mentors they have had and the development they've received. It may simply be time for them to move on for a wide variety of reasons. The key is in the relationships that we build along the way, not the people we hold hostage. Managers who continue to keep ongoing, strong, personal, and professional relationships with former employees find enormous benefit in the success that those they've mentored go on to achieve.

You're a manager and a leader, and you have evolved. Teach others to do the same. You'll be glad you did in the end.

AN EASY, SEVEN-STEP PROCESS FOR EMPLOYEE DEVELOPMENT PLANNING

The process for creating employee development and talent development plans can be whatever a leader wants it to be. Experience tells us that a collaborative effort in designing a plan is what makes it stronger and more fluid. As the manager, you can guide the process and facilitate the success of the plan by collaborating with your up-and-coming leaders on seven easy steps:

1. Competencies
2. Long-range goals
3. Short-range goals
4. Strategies
5. Action steps and timelines
6. Resources tool kit
7. Measurable outcomes

Getting Started

The process begins when you first sit down with an employee (and future leader) to identify big-picture goals, dreams, and objectives. Start by having a relaxed and casual conversation about the worker's unique interests and talents. Inquire about his or her current position and how things are going. Ask if there is any interest in special assignments, training courses, or ways to contribute to the department he or she works in. Write all of this down. It's a time to listen, not talk.

Would Your Leader Relocate for a Dream Job?

Inquire about your leader's different goals and obligations. Ask about family and community interests, because these are things that affect employee development planning big time. For example, a great position might be available at another location, so it may be timely to ask the person whether he or she might consider relocating to a different city or state. If the answer is yes, this could quickly become a goal in the plan. If the answer is no, then the plan will take a different direction and reflect those limitations. In addition, the person might share with you that right now would be a difficult time to move elsewhere; however, in two years, the timing would be good. Then you would add "relocating for a new position" to the long-range goal category of this person's plan.

Resources, Resources, Resources

Offer resources you know of that are available both inside and outside the organization. Leaders can consult an HR specialist for assistance in identifying additional resources or tools. As mentioned earlier, leaders often use their own career development as a reference point for guiding the development of others. We can all easily fall into this trap without even thinking. But what worked for you as a manager or supervisor back then might not be the best plan for the worker sitting across from you now. You should keep this in mind for yourself while advising your leader and, in addition, pass this message along so that your up-and-coming leaders remember this when they guide others.

As a leader, start the preparation of an employee development plan. Set up times to meet with the worker to assess progress and changes and help him or her revise the plan as you go along. Provide assessment resources so that the employee can establish a baseline of competency and score themselves in areas in which they can grow and flourish.

One important piece of advice: Do not wait a year before meeting again with the employee, or only use annual performance review time to go over this plan. This is a work in progress. It will require ongoing meetings to breathe life into the document.

Figure 4.1 is a template you can modify and adapt to your specific needs and the needs of your aspiring leaders. The phrases included here are to get you started; you and your leaders should add your own wording and flesh out these ideas in more detail to create a better, stronger personal and professional plan.

IF YOUR LEADERS DON'T KNOW WHERE THEY'RE GOING, ANY ROAD WILL TAKE THEM THERE

Give Your Leaders a Road Map and a Compass

The employee development plan you provide your leaders is the essential road map to helping them and their employees get to where they want to be. The **compass** is used to help them find their way—offering a personalized inner guidance system that propels them toward success. (For more on the process of discovering your True North, see Anne's book *Discover True North*, published by McGraw-Hill. *Discover True North* is

Figure 4.1 Employee Development Template

EMPLOYEE DEVELOPMENT TEMPLATE

Competencies

- [] Determine hard skills and soft skills.
- [] Stand up for your strengths and talents.
- [] I feel strong and amazing when: _____
- [] I feel depleted and exhausted when: _____
- [] Make assessments to identify talents and strengths.
- [] Match competencies and talents to career choices.
- [] Set up collaborative sessions, meetings, and discussions.
- [] Start draft of plan.
- [] Agree to neutralize challenge areas and weaknesses.
- [] What training will be required?
- [] How will research be approached?
- [] Define milestones.
- [] Determine what motivates you to your highest level of peak performance.

Long-Range Goals

- [] See the big picture.
- [] Determine future opportunities and parts you would like to play.
- [] Start acting the part now for what you hope to become later.
- [] What must be done long term?
- [] Consider degree certifications, new skill sets to learn, foreign languages to learn, and the possibility of relocation.
- [] How many coaches will you require?
- [] Who will you ask to mentor you?

Short-Range Goals

- [] What can you do today? Right now?
- [] What can you do this week?
- [] What can you do this month?
- [] What can you do by the end of one year?
- [] How will technology change your field and career in the next three years?
- [] What will you do to prepare for the future?
- [] How much money will it take?
- [] How long will training last?

EMPLOYEE DEVELOPMENT TEMPLATE

Strategies

- [] List specific strategies for both long-term goals and short-term goals.
- [] Who will be on your team?
- [] Who are the key players?
- [] What will you ask them to do?
- [] What will be your methods for moving things forward?
- [] How will your employee development plan become a strategic tool?
- [] How will you turn your strengths and talents into strategic weapons for winning and accomplishing your mission?
- [] Explain how you will handle change and make change work to your advantage.
- [] Adopt a can-do attitude, use attitude as a strategy to move you out of difficult moments to greater success.

Action Steps Timeline

- [] Determine specific actions to be taken.
- [] Determine contacts to be made.
- [] When will you make revisions to your plan? Review your plan with your manager.
- [] Revise again. Make a checklist of what's been completed.
- [] Schedule due dates for progress meetings.
- [] Rethink milestones and pace.
- [] Record and document all input you are getting.
- [] What works? How can you do more? What doesn't work? How can you eliminate it?

Resource Tool Kit

- [] Your resources include everything and anything that helps you to learn and grow, and understand at a higher level.
- [] Use and train for future technology.
- [] Use and train for human development skills.
- [] Seek out advanced mentors and coaches from inside and outside of the organization.
- [] Make a list of resources you need to move ahead, and share with your manager.

EMPLOYEE DEVELOPMENT TEMPLATE

Measurable Outcomes

- [] What did you love the most about getting here?
- [] Compare your initial assessments to your results now.
- [] Use self-scoring card for measuring improvement.
- [] What percentage of improvement would you assign to your growth and development?
- [] How has what you've done over time increased organizational productivity and performance? Be specific.
- [] What specific areas can you point to that you have changed and improved processes within for the better?
- [] Ask for feedback in all areas, measure its effectiveness.

filled with life-altering worksheets, interactive exercises, real-world stories, and inspi-rational quotations to help leaders make the most of themselves and their talents.) By utilizing tools and techniques for finding one's "True North" and applying it to the workplace, your process will go hand-in-glove with the employee development plan-ning you've set in motion by showing your leaders how to 1) rely on their inner com-passes for career direction; 2) make hard, critical choices that will move them forward; 3) focus on self-development without feeling as though they are abandoning others or teammates; and 4) help them to pinpoint their emotional and intellectual strengths for stronger decision making and creative thinking on the job.

A leader's employee development plan, along with a reliable compass, ensures that your leaders and others on the team will not lose their way. See Figure 4.2 for an out-line of the eight steps to employee development planning.

Figure 4.2 Eight Career Pathing Steps to Employee Development Planning

WHAT IS COMPETENCY?

Webster's Dictionary defines "competency" or "competence" as possessing a required skill, knowledge, qualification, or capacity or having suitable or sufficient skill, knowledge, or experience for some specified purpose.

In the work world, competency has many more meanings, sometimes relating to tasks and results, and at other times describing such characteristics of the people doing the job as values, humor, and skills. This is where the term "attribute bundle" comes from—a collection of all such competencies.

Competencies should link people with the organization's strategies, goals, and objectives. When people are in alignment with the strategic goals of their organization or department, they are much better prepared to meet the challenges their jobs present. This is the best way to prepare people to succeed before they even begin the job.

Make sure your leaders understand that no matter what issues or challenges people face in their careers, everyone shares one thing in common: They want to know where they fit in and what competencies are needed to succeed at the work they are asked to perform. That's the bottom line.

INCORPORATING COMPETENCIES INTO YOUR LEADERSHIP TRAINING

The competencies discussed here include two basic categories: human capability and soft-skills intelligence, and cognitive ability or technical skills and expertise. Observing what your leaders are faced with every day will help you determine which competencies your leaders ultimately will use as measurement gauges to develop and ensure the success of their people. (See chapter 19 for more about performance measurement.)

Leaders need to know that the technical skills required to do a job are often the easiest to clarify. For a scientist or technician, job-specific technical know-how and analytical thinking would be two competencies that might be listed in category two. Studies repeatedly show, however, that even among very technical people, the most important competencies to ensure someone's success often stem from the category of human capability and soft-skills intelligence. For scientists and technicians, those competencies might include the ability to influence, listen, and collaborate.

According to bestselling author Daniel Goleman (*Emotional Intelligence*, Bantam Books, and *Working with Emotional Intelligence*, Bantam Books), in studies conducted with more than 500 organizations, the necessary competencies that distinguish star performers and leaders in every field do not point to a person's IQ as the most important factor. Goleman says that, instead of advanced degrees and technical expertise, it is emotional intelligence that draws the unparalleled commonality among the world's greatest leaders. He emphasizes that influence, adaptability, self-confidence, self-awareness, and the ability to communicate are some of the premium competencies in today's global village.

10 Sample Core Leadership Competencies

Leadership competencies connect organizational strategies with people, and when people are in alignment with the strategic goals of the organization, they are better prepared to meet head-on the challenges that leadership requires in today's high-speed, global workplace.

In this chapter, we focus on 10 competency areas. They will serve as samples for competencies you may feel are appropriate for developing and training leaders at your organization.

Joan Smith is a competency expert who consults internationally with hundreds of learning organizations and training companies on how to design helpful competencies for training leaders at all levels. (See chapter 16 for more information on competency training.) The following sample leadership competencies were selected with her help to complement the specific leadership areas that are covered in this book. It will be your responsibility to adapt this list to your own organization's needs and to marry this information with the more technical skills and experience required by your organization's leadership opportunities. The goal here is to coach you along as you create and enlarge your own list of leadership competencies for specific management roles within your organization.

Here are the 10 core leadership competencies I have chosen for discussion:

1. Integrity
2. Trust and values
3. Team building
4. Listening
5. Influencing and persuading
6. Competitive spirit
7. Passion and intuition
8. Priority setting and decision making
9. Sense of humor
10. Vision and adaptability

For each competency there will be a brief description of its importance to the leader and an exercise or set of questions that will offer additional insights and ideas for your leaders when developing employees to reach each competency level. Additional behavioral characteristics are included.

As you introduce the importance of leadership competencies, explain to your leaders that many models for various leadership competencies are available. Tell them, however, that first focusing on and better understanding some of the more commonly recognized leadership competencies will help them begin to develop a framework from which to direct and implement their personal leadership styles. Over time, your leaders' personal mastery of each competency will help to define their own roles as leaders.

Applying the 10 Competencies

Below are some questions and exercises pertinent to the basic competencies of leadership. You can include them in your training program and watch them become powerful tools to be used in a leader's approach when linking people to the organization's required goals and objectives.

Competency 1: Integrity

Our integrity tells the world who we are and what we care about more than anything else. It says what our priorities are. There are two easy ways to evaluate a person's integrity and priorities: how that person spends his or her time, and how that person spends his or her money. Integrity can be viewed as a set of core values that each of us holds ourselves responsible for and demonstrates in our habits and behaviors.

Behavioral characteristics of integrity include sharing open and honest communication; providing helpful feedback, recognition, and rewards; behaving ethically; walking the talk; and doing what you say you're going to do.

Ask your leaders this question: If integrity were a crime and you were arrested for having it, would there be enough evidence to convict you? Have them list the undeniable evidence against them. Their lists should describe how they live and lead with integrity. Ask them to be as specific as possible in their responses.

Competency 2: Trust and Values

When we break our promises, we erode trust and lose credibility—and both are extremely difficult to regain once lost. The cornerstones of trust include:

- doing what you say you're going to do
- respecting others and appreciating their differences
- communicating openly
- acknowledging that trust is a mutual exchange.

> *Technique and technology are important, but building trust is the issue of the decade.* —Tom Peters, *The Circle of Innovation*

Ask your leaders the following questions regarding trust.

- Can you think of a time when trust was lost in your work environment?
- What was the situation?
- What were the consequences?
- Was trust easily regained? If not, why not?
- What do you think trust has to do with values and integrity?

Values are the guardians of an organization's integrity. They are important because they define the desired behaviors of leadership through a leader's personal conduct. As a basic leadership competency, values represent every organization's most competitive tool because they are woven into the fabric of its corporate culture.

It is critical that a leader's core values be in alignment with the core values of his or her organization. By completing this exercise, leaders will be able to examine more

clearly any possible discrepancies that exist between the two and to work toward closing the gaps.

From the following list, have your leaders circle the three values that are most important to them.

Friendships	Family relationships	Accountability
Advancement	Authority	Loyalty
Passion	Personal growth	Status
Self-respect	Excellence	Truth
Community	Wealth	Professional growth
Competence	Compensation	Competition
Home	Ethics	Achievement
Quality	Integrity	Trust
Honor	Respect	Courage

Key Point: *When you work in an environment where there is trust and you follow your passion and live by your values, the chances of greater balance in your personal and professional life increase dramatically.*

After leaders have made their choices, ask them to answer the following questions:

- Do you need to further develop these issues? If yes, how will you do this?
- Do you believe that values can be learned? If yes, how would you teach them to others?

Competency 3: Team Building

Teams are essential to a leader's success, and today's teams take on much more responsibility than they did previously. Leaders now are accustomed to encouraging their teams to act independently, make decisions, and even celebrate mistakes. A consistent leadership message you may hear is, "You figure out what needs to get done and then decide how you're going to do it."

There are three reasons why team building is an important leadership competency:

- Teams give employees a sense of belonging.
- Being a member of a team is energizing and motivating.
- Teams are more successful at solving problems.

Here are some questions pertinent to team building as a core competency. Suggest to your leaders that they use these questions to spark discussion among team members and build their core competencies.

- What should we do more often?
- Are there any activities that we should be rethinking or discontinuing?
- What do we do best?
- What do we need to operate more effectively as a team?
- How do you measure your performance effectiveness?
- Are we organized in the best way possible?

Ask your leaders if they have the following leadership characteristics required for team building:

- nourishing a cheerful team spirit and pride
- supportive and receptive way of listening
- ability to delegate authority
- an approach that encourages people to act on decisions
- interest in finding solutions
- willingness to allow team members to make financial decisions whenever possible.

Competency 4: Listening

Great leaders are great listeners. Listening is a skill and a character-building strength—a leader's most effective and influential tool. Competent listeners are other-centered. They don't just wait for their turn to talk; they make others feel important, worthy, and respected.

The following are some of the ways competent listeners behave. To demonstrate the effectiveness of listening behaviors, ask for two volunteers to partner in role playing. Have the partners demonstrate for others some specific examples of each of these actions:

Key Point: *The more you say, the less people will remember.*

- making eye contact
- assuming the listening position—sitting up straight, leaning forward, taking notes
- listening with enjoyment
- giving undivided attention
- asking questions.

Following the role playing, ask leaders to create a list of some of the ways leaders choose not to listen. Have them write down the behaviors that would typify a non-listener. Knowing what *not* to do when listening to someone can be just as valuable for leaders as knowing how to listen well.

Competency 5: Influencing and Persuading

The following are influential and persuasive behaviors common to all good leaders:

- using sound reasoning to persuade others
- writing clearly and with a convincing tone
- using body language and voice to influence others
- consistently gaining support for views and opinions
- effectively overcoming objections and concerns
- using tact at all times
- demonstrating persuasive selling skills
- knowing the facts.

Begin a discussion on why your leaders think these particular behaviors are important. Ask them to think of a time when they were influential in a situation that required their leadership. Ask what persuasive techniques they used in that situation.

Competency 6: Competitive Spirit

This competency describes the leader who is driven to be the best at whatever he or she does. Leaders with competitive spirit possess high energy and enthusiasm—whether it's for the job, a hobby, or a sporting event. Once people are involved and decisions to take action are made, a leader's competitive spirit becomes contagious!

No one keeps up his enthusiasm automatically. Enthusiasm must be nourished with new actions, new aspirations, new efforts, new vision. —From a collection of ancient Egyptian writings

Ask your leaders to describe their competitive spirit and energy. Ask them to recall a time when they put both heart and mind into an endeavor that resulted in personal or professional fulfillment.

Competency 7: Passion and Intuition

Passionate people do more than lead; they inspire. They strive against all odds to realize their dreams and hopes. Passion is a leadership competency once possessed by Walt Disney and John F. Kennedy Jr. It's a competency possessed by leaders today such as Gen. Colin Powell, whose passion is the future of America's children, and Amazon.com's Jeff Bezos, whose passion is changing the economics of the book industry by building—online—the world's largest bookstore.

Ask your leaders these two questions about their passions:
- For what are you a passionate advocate?
- In what areas are you passionate about growing your leadership talents?

Albert Einstein once said, "The really valuable thing is intuition." But Einstein was decades ahead of his time. Only in recent years has intuition become a credible leadership competency taught in leadership classes around the world. We've slowly learned that by trusting our gut feelings, we develop a keener perception and judgment on the job.

Characteristics of leaders who practice using their intuition and gut instincts include taking risks, having faith in the unknown, believing in oneself, trusting instinctively, taking a leap of faith for an important cause, possessing a vision of what is yet to be, and relying on that small voice from within.

Ask your leaders to consider this competency in their own work life and how important this "gut feeling" is to their job performance. Ask if they follow their hunches. Have them describe a time when they pursued a hunch. What was the outcome? Ask if there has been a time when they regret not relying more on their intuition.

Competency 8: Priority Setting and Decision Making

Establishing priorities involves instinct and decision making. Setting priorities in an organization is an art. Because people within the organization have their own priorities, the question is: Are those priorities in alignment with the organization's priorities?

Have your leaders list the three most important organizational priorities currently challenging them. Do those priorities and their personal priorities come together? Keep in mind that the way an organization's leader handles his or her employees' personal agendas often determines the success of the company.

Competency 9: Sense of Humor

Leaders with a sense of humor appear more human and approachable to their employees. When a leader uses humor at work, he or she automatically relieves pressures of the daily grind by releasing tension and instilling a feeling of camaraderie.

Humor involves doing something funny to make people laugh and relax. Some leaders tell jokes, and others have a dry wit that takes some getting used to. Others use puns, and some poke fun at themselves. Being just plain silly is another way to get people laughing. A CEO who wears a Donald Duck or Mickey Mouse tie to a quarterly employees' luncheon is sending out what kind of message to his people? Perhaps he wants his employees to take themselves less seriously, smile more, laugh out loud, or just relax upon meeting him. Remember, it's okay for leaders to take their jobs seriously and themselves lightly.

Use this exercise to get your leaders to share examples of the humorous things they do to put people at ease and to explain how humor works for them in a positive way on the job. Ask them to list three different ways their humor helps create a fun and positive workplace. What are the benefits? Examples might include reducing stress, building camaraderie, decreasing burnout, or eliminating tension.

Competency 10: Vision and Adaptability

Vision and adaptability go hand in hand. They are competencies that help leaders initiate and accept change. Without vision, or the ability to adapt to it, there is little or no sense of purpose in leadership. Visionary leaders see with their hearts and minds as well as their eyes. They articulate their vision so that everyone feels a part of it. And they can inspire others to buy into their vision because they are credible and trustworthy.

It is important that an organization's vision represent the collective aspirations, dreams, and desires of its people. That responsibility falls on the shoulders of its

leaders. Leaders must get their people to buy into the organization's vision because strategies alone will not sustain the organization through good and bad times. Employees must believe in their hearts that their leader's vision is also their vision. All of the previous nine competencies covered will provide your leaders with the foundation to actually create and communicate their vision as a leader.

Ask your leaders the questions below as they learn to adapt and build their capabilities to communicate a vision.

- A leader's vision can elude the individuals within an organization when it is far-reaching and nonspecific. How can you help your employees see the specifics and potential in your vision so they can visualize the big picture?
- Do you truly understand how the organization's vision specifically relates to you? Can you explain it?
- How will you effectively communicate your vision to your work team and across departments?

As a result of completing these exercises and ultimately better understanding the important role that establishing competencies will play in your organization's success, your leaders will now be able to

- build more cohesive and productive teams
- incorporate many of these competencies into the succession planning process
- create an environment in which trust and loyalty can be renewed
- prepare employees for greater success
- encourage employees to stretch by developing competencies they have not yet practiced
- hire the right people for the right opportunities.

MATCHING COMPETENCIES WITH ORGANIZATIONAL GOALS YIELDS BUSINESS RESULTS

The last step in this chapter is to help your leaders decide on specific organizational or leadership goals—for example, establishing a formal mentoring program or setting up a new community outreach project for their department. This step is critical because it provides business results for the organization.

Have your leaders identify and list specific business goals and then select the competencies needed to achieve them. Leaders should share this process with other leaders and team members. Based on what the leaders know about their organizations, they can determine which competencies will be required to ensure the success of their leadership efforts.

Leadership Competencies

Now that your leaders have a better understanding of what each core competency entails, ask each one to list their individual leadership goals to the right of each competency below.

Leadership Competencies	Corresponding Leadership Goals
1. Integrity	_____
2. Trust and values	_____
3. Team building	_____
4. Listening	_____
5. Influencing and persuading	_____
6. Competitive spirit	_____
7. Passion and intuition	_____
8. Priority setting and decision making	_____
9. Sense of humor	_____
10. Vision and adaptability	_____

Questions for Discussion: Developing Core Leadership Competencies

1. Why do you think it is important to match leadership goals to core competencies?

2. How might a core competency affect the end result of a leadership goal?

3. How can leaders use core competencies when matching an employee to a specific project?

4. All leaders need a road map and a compass that will show them how to get to where they want to be. What are some of the tools you will use from this chapter to begin developing individual development plans at various levels of leadership in your organization?

Wrapping It Up

In this chapter, you've learned that branding talent is an important job when developing leaders and that focusing on others' unique talents and strengths is more important than focusing on people's weaknesses. You've learned that competencies are powerful and effective tools that your leaders will sharpen with use over time. Employing competencies as a reliable gauge of potential success, your leaders will learn to hire, train, and promote workers in accordance with their own lists of desired competencies. By making such well-grounded choices, your leaders will be better prepared to create a successful leadership plan as well.

Coming up in chapter 5, you'll learn about the elements of leadership development and creating effective leadership plans.

Don't Lose Your Mojo— Create a Leadership Plan for Everyone Today

What's workplace mojo? It's your passion and excitement as a leader. It's your energy about your job and your self-confidence about the job you are doing. Leadership mojo has been written about by dozens of authors in books, prestigious business magazines, newspapers from the *Wall Street Journal* to the *Financial Times*, and blogs on Huffington Post, among other places. It's *that* important.

It's our leadership mojo that helps us to infuse the workplace with the best of what we have to offer. But sometimes it's easy to get off the track. As we get older and more set in our ways, we stop dreaming, and that's when it happens. We lose our mojo! So how do great leaders prevent such things from slowing them down? They help others to create a leadership plan that keeps aspiring leaders on their career paths—moving on and moving up. And here's the cool bonus you get from this chapter: A leadership plan is a map and a compass all in one.

Every leadership topic in this book on which you decide to train your leaders becomes an opportunity for each leader to attain his or her personal best—the kind of personal best that represents your organization's standards of excellence and high performance—and results from having a viable leadership plan to follow. That's the mojo we're talking about.

When your leaders actually *plan* how they will perform at their personal best while leading important and challenging projects for the organization, they become more capable of accomplishing extraordinary things in the process. By showing your leaders how to put together a leadership plan, you will be helping each of them to become a positive force in the organization.

Here is where your leaders will learn how to develop a solid and effective leadership plan. The purpose here is to guide your leaders—supervisors, team leaders, coaches, or senior managers—in initiating their own voyages of discovery and better understanding the crucial elements of leadership development. If your training does not include this element, here is your chance to supplement your leadership development program to emphasize this vital quality.

What You Will Learn in This Chapter:

♦ Create a leadership plan. Leaders must
 ● keep their mojo
 ● understand fully where they are right now
 ● focus on where they are going
 ● plan a course of action that will get them there.
♦ Voyage of self-discovery. Leaders must
 ● challenge the status quo
 ● stretch people and model the example
 ● take a specific course of action that gets results.

GOAL SETTING ISN'T ENOUGH

The concept of leadership planning has taken on a whole new significance from earlier days when simply setting goals was considered adequate. Quality-conscious, high-performing organizations today not only want their leaders to plan out their leadership projects and challenges, they also want them to do so while developing themselves to be the best leaders they can be.

As the developer of your organization's leadership program, you have two excellent opportunities: to help your leaders create extraordinary results for the organization by creating and implementing a plan of action for each and every one of their leadership challenges, and to help them further sharpen their leadership talents and capabilities.

Goal-Setting Exercise: Creating Your Leadership "Dream Map"

What would your organization look like if your team met its goals?

Speaker and success trainer Aric Bostick (see www.aricbostickcorporate.com for more on this leadership training rock star) recommends a system of developing a leadership "dream map" to visually reinforce the goals or direction an individual or team wishes to take. A dream map consists of an actual visual collage, representing life as if you had already "arrived" at your destination. Bostick likens this exercise to "tearing up the old script for what wasn't working, and starting anew."

Before creating the dream map, Bostick suggests having the senior leadership, management, and supervisors first develop their "dream lists." Bostick poses this key question to get leaders to think beyond the obvious, into what they would like to achieve: "What would you do if you knew you couldn't fail?"

The dream list should include a specific definition of success—and its components. For example, ask:

● How will your company be affecting and influencing the world at large?
● Where will it be positioned in its industry?
● What positive changes will have occurred in the workplace?

Then take the process a step further, and have your leaders define how the organizational success will positively affect their personal lives. For example, ask them:

- What will your dream life look, feel, and be like?
- What kind of work do you dream of doing?
- What will your physical health be like?
- How will you be positioned financially?
- How will your family relationships be defined?
- What kind of car will you drive?
- Where will you vacation?

Some of these questions may trigger additional personal goals that are beyond those of the organization. The idea is to get your leaders to think beyond the workplace so that their personal and professional goals are all moving them in the same direction— forward. As alignment occurs between their personal and professional goals, engagement in those goals is increased.

Get Visual

Then, to create the dream map, collect visual symbols of what it would mean to be successful, and paste these items on a sheet of paper. For example, a leader's dream map could include a picture of a large corner office (if one of the goals is professional advancement), a photo of a "greener" world (if one of your organization's goals is to improve the environment), or an image of a family relaxing on vacation (if one of the goals is to advance one's career and pay scale in order to afford more family activities, for example). On the dream map, also include phrases or quotes that inspire the organizational and personal goals to become reality—such as statements about perseverance, success, relationships, and goal setting.

Post It Where You Can See It!

Bostick suggests posting one's map on a bathroom mirror (if personal) or in a break room (if appropriate), or in a cubicle or leader's office, so it can be viewed every day. "Once you visualize success, it is easier to achieve it," states Bostick. "This map is geared to inspire you and keep you focused on taking action toward your ultimate vision of your life. Your mind doesn't know the difference between a real or imagined event. When you can see it on glossy paper, or in words in front of you every day, it enters your mind and it not only takes root—but it grows. I used this years ago when I started my career as a speaker—as I overcame the past and all the roadblocks I had, and instead built confidence in my capability to lead my own life and motivate others towards greater life satisfaction."

LEADERSHIP PLANNING—THE VOYAGE OF DISCOVERY

Your first step here is to identify for your leaders the four practices critical to exemplary leadership and explain why they are so crucial. The second step will be to help

themselves. In other words, leaders go first, and they wouldn't have it any other way. They model the way by personal example, not relying on their titles alone to gain them respect. Leaders who model the way know that it's their behavior that sets the momentum and inspires others to follow. They make certain that their actions are consistent with their words and ideas.

How do you measure up as a leader who models the example? Grade yourself here on a scale of 1 (lowest) to 10 (highest), circling the number that best reflects your present leadership ability in this area.

| 1 | 2 | 3 | 4 | 5 | 6 | 7 | 8 | 9 | 10 |

Much improvement needed Excellent

Have your leaders answer these questions to gauge their own personal best when it comes to how they will model the example:

- Can you provide an example of how you have modeled the way in the past and affected the behavior of those around you?
- What does it mean when we say a leader's actions are more important than his or her words or ideas?
- How does modeling the way strengthen employee commitment and trust?
- The daily acts of leadership model the way for others. How does that keep people moving forward and create progress within an organization?

Have your leaders make a list of the specific actions they will take to strengthen themselves in areas they've identified for improvement.

Practice 4: Taking Action

What it means: Do something. Do anything. Just do it. Leaders are action-oriented people. They don't sit on the sidelines watching the players; they're out on the field with the players! They implement ideas and action plans and encourage others to do the same. Leaders don't let themselves get bogged down in daily minutiae or perpetual committee meetings that cause the well-known analysis paralysis. Leaders should always take into account the ideas and feelings of others, but it's their responsibility to start things moving.

> *If Columbus had had an advisory committee, he would probably still be at the dock.*
> —Arthur Goldberg,
> former Secretary of Labor

The personal best in a leader is not seen in some grand and esoteric plan but more likely in the adventure stories leaders create, which are distinguished by taking on big challenges, steering projects toward meaningful purposes, and taking a stand whenever necessary.

Leaders not only set goals, they also implement them and then follow up to help their people achieve lots of small wins along the way. To do this, leaders break down

Then take the process a step further, and have your leaders define how the organizational success will positively affect their personal lives. For example, ask them:

- What will your dream life look, feel, and be like?
- What kind of work do you dream of doing?
- What will your physical health be like?
- How will you be positioned financially?
- How will your family relationships be defined?
- What kind of car will you drive?
- Where will you vacation?

Some of these questions may trigger additional personal goals that are beyond those of the organization. The idea is to get your leaders to think beyond the workplace so that their personal and professional goals are all moving them in the same direction—forward. As alignment occurs between their personal and professional goals, engagement in those goals is increased.

Get Visual

Then, to create the dream map, collect visual symbols of what it would mean to be successful, and paste these items on a sheet of paper. For example, a leader's dream map could include a picture of a large corner office (if one of the goals is professional advancement), a photo of a "greener" world (if one of your organization's goals is to improve the environment), or an image of a family relaxing on vacation (if one of the goals is to advance one's career and pay scale in order to afford more family activities, for example). On the dream map, also include phrases or quotes that inspire the organizational and personal goals to become reality—such as statements about perseverance, success, relationships, and goal setting.

Post It Where You Can See It!

Bostick suggests posting one's map on a bathroom mirror (if personal) or in a break room (if appropriate), or in a cubicle or leader's office, so it can be viewed every day. "Once you visualize success, it is easier to achieve it," states Bostick. "This map is geared to inspire you and keep you focused on taking action toward your ultimate vision of your life. Your mind doesn't know the difference between a real or imagined event. When you can see it on glossy paper, or in words in front of you every day, it enters your mind and it not only takes root—but it grows. I used this years ago when I started my career as a speaker—as I overcame the past and all the roadblocks I had, and instead built confidence in my capability to lead my own life and motivate others towards greater life satisfaction."

LEADERSHIP PLANNING—THE VOYAGE OF DISCOVERY

Your first step here is to identify for your leaders the four practices critical to exemplary leadership and explain why they are so crucial. The second step will be to help

your leaders put together their own leadership plan based on these practices and assist them in infusing the environment with eight important self-discovery steps, offered in this chapter by Hinshaw & Associates.

The four practices of successful leadership are

- challenging the status quo
- stretching people
- modeling the example
- taking action.

Be sure that you introduce and discuss these four practices with your leaders before you teach the leadership planning process. Although the two go hand in hand, the leadership planning portion of this chapter should be an extension built firmly on the foundation of these elements of leadership.

Use the following descriptions for each of the four leadership practices as a method of self-assessment and discovery for your leaders. Each definition provides instant feedback on how each practice should be conducted. Use the explanations to help your leaders target areas for their ongoing self-improvement and to uncover the action steps they'll need to take to reach their personal best.

Practice 1: Challenging the Status Quo

What it means: Leaders never stop challenging the process or pushing the envelope. They learn from their daring failures because they are pioneers who venture out into the unknown, sometimes without a map or a compass. They're not afraid to take the risks necessary to find a better way of doing things. They know that overcoming obstacles is just part of the leadership process and an opportunity from which to learn and grow or develop their personal best. They are gutsy when it's called for, and they bounce back from their failures.

How do you measure up as a leader who challenges the status quo? Grade yourself here on a scale of 1 (lowest) to 10 (highest), circling the number that best reflects your present leadership ability in this area.

1	2	3	4	5	6	7	8	9	10

Much improvement needed Excellent

> *Leaders learn by leading, and they learn best by leading in the face of obstacles. As weather shapes mountains, problems shape leaders.* —Warren Bennis, *The Leadership Challenge*

Have your leaders answer these questions to gauge their own personal best when it comes to practicing how they will challenge the status quo:

- What aspects of challenging the status quo are difficult for you to do? Why do you think you have that difficulty?
- What makes you a pioneer in leadership?
- When has taking a risk proved rewarding for you?

- How can you practice taking more risks?
- Just because "things have always been done this way" doesn't mean that's how you have to do them. What are some of the ways you might reinvent a project with a better process?

Have your leaders make a list of the specific actions they will take to strengthen themselves in areas they've identified as needing improvement.

Practice 2: Stretching People

What it means: Leaders continually must stretch their employees to improve. If a leader's employees aren't growing and stretching, they are probably complacent, not motivated, and not energized. As a result, performance and productivity suffer.

Stretching people requires that leaders give away their power. In order for employees to stretch beyond their obvious limitations, they must be given more responsibility, more decision-making power, and lots more information. When leaders stretch their people, the results can be extraordinary.

Employees want to stretch themselves even more when a leader encourages them to take ownership. The feeling that there is meaningful purpose behind the mission is what enables a leader's employees to push themselves beyond their own limitations. Raise the bar and watch your employees leap over it.

How do you measure up as a leader who stretches people? Grade yourself here on a scale of 1 (lowest) to 10 (highest), circling the number that best reflects your present leadership ability in this area.

| 1 | 2 | 3 | 4 | 5 | 6 | 7 | 8 | 9 | 10 |

Much improvement needed Excellent

Have your leaders answer these questions to evaluate their own personal best when it comes to practicing how they will stretch their people:

- What do you think are the positive results for an organization when people stretch themselves?
- When was a time you inspired someone to excel? How did you do that?
- Stretching people requires that they have confidence in their leaders. How will you instill that confidence?
- In a virtual organization, it can be more difficult to stretch people who are not working on site. What special challenges might that present, and how can you overcome them?

Have your leaders make a list of the specific actions they will take to strengthen themselves in areas they've identified as needing improvement.

Practice 3: Modeling the Example

What it means: In chapter 1, we made an important point about leaders developing their self-mastery: Leaders never ask their people to do anything they would not do

themselves. In other words, leaders go first, and they wouldn't have it any other way. They model the way by personal example, not relying on their titles alone to gain them respect. Leaders who model the way know that it's their behavior that sets the momentum and inspires others to follow. They make certain that their actions are consistent with their words and ideas.

How do you measure up as a leader who models the example? Grade yourself here on a scale of 1 (lowest) to 10 (highest), circling the number that best reflects your present leadership ability in this area.

1	2	3	4	5	6	7	8	9	10

Much improvement needed Excellent

Have your leaders answer these questions to gauge their own personal best when it comes to how they will model the example:

- Can you provide an example of how you have modeled the way in the past and affected the behavior of those around you?
- What does it mean when we say a leader's actions are more important than his or her words or ideas?
- How does modeling the way strengthen employee commitment and trust?
- The daily acts of leadership model the way for others. How does that keep people moving forward and create progress within an organization?

Have your leaders make a list of the specific actions they will take to strengthen themselves in areas they've identified for improvement.

Practice 4: Taking Action

What it means: Do something. Do anything. Just do it. Leaders are action-oriented people. They don't sit on the sidelines watching the players; they're out on the field with the players! They implement ideas and action plans and encourage others to do the same. Leaders don't let themselves get bogged down in daily minutiae or perpetual committee meetings that cause the well-known analysis paralysis. Leaders should always take into account the ideas and feelings of others, but it's their responsibility to start things moving.

> *If Columbus had had an advisory committee, he would probably still be at the dock.*
> —Arthur Goldberg, former Secretary of Labor

The personal best in a leader is not seen in some grand and esoteric plan but more likely in the adventure stories leaders create, which are distinguished by taking on big challenges, steering projects toward meaningful purposes, and taking a stand whenever necessary.

Leaders not only set goals, they also implement them and then follow up to help their people achieve lots of small wins along the way. To do this, leaders break down

Modeling the Example Through Leadership Planning at Junior Achievement

Junior Achievement (JA) is one of the world's largest and fastest-growing nonprofit economic education organizations. Its programs are taught by classroom volunteers from the business community in the United States and more than 100 countries worldwide. Leadership planning at JA is an important part of training leaders.

Community Leaders Inspiring Tomorrow's Leaders

At Junior Achievement, 382,637 volunteers teach 403,849 classes around the globe to more than 9,866,143 students a year. That's more than 27,000 students a day and more than 1,100 students an hour who become enlightened to learn about their own economic power and the future of business. JA is a remarkable partnership between business communities, educators, and volunteers, all working together to inspire global youth to dream big and reach for their highest potential.

According to one of team leader at JA, "Junior Achievement depends on its leaders within the organization to carry out its purpose, which is to educate and inspire young people to value free enterprise and entrepreneurship. We not only want youth to understand business and economics, but we want them to practice these things with integrity." JA calls this being workforce ready. JA students develop the skills necessary to experience the realities and opportunities of work and entrepreneurship in the twenty-first century global marketplace.

One manager said: "Because these are our leadership's expectations of others, it's essential that each leader within the organization model the behavior." JA trains its leaders to put together their own leadership and management plans and then trains them to implement those plans. "It would be incredibly difficult for any of us to meet our goals and follow our organization's vision and mission if we didn't have some sort of plan to follow that could make it a reality," the team leader adds.

Creating a Leadership Plan at JA

Some highlights from JA's leadership and management planning have included, but are not limited to, the following:

- long-, intermediate-, and short-range tactical goals
- a step-by-step plan for implementation that answers questions such as: Who needs to know? Who needs to tell them? How should the plan be communicated? and Who will be responsible for what?
- a plan for follow-up that describes what kind of follow-up is needed, from whom, how often, and in what form.

JA is a great place for your organization's leaders to share their ideas and help grow the young, up-and-coming leaders of tomorrow. Check out a JA office near you today and encourage the leaders you are growing now to get involved outside their own maps of the world. They'll learn just as much, if not more, about leadership, than their students. Visit www.JA.org for more information. Make JA a leadership project for growing your company's talent and building on their strengths.

8 Steps to Creating an Environment of Self-Discovery

According to Dolly Hinshaw of Hinshaw & Associates, we all need to give leaders "the edge" when it comes to creating high-functioning workplaces. "Influencing another person's journey to increase their own self-motivation, or greater mojo, is the greatest gift a leader can bestow on his or her workers," says Hinsahaw.

Hinshaw encourages her clients to create what she calls "workplaces of self-discovery" by using these eight steps:

1. **Live the standards you want your leaders to emulate:** Make a personal commitment to inspire creative and innovative thinking in your leaders and actually demonstrate what it is you want to see in others. Mentor expected behavior—every single day.

2. **Focus on leadership behaviors:** Pay attention and monitor your leaders' body language, verbal and written skills, cultural sensitivities, team building talents, technical expertise, and others' responses to their work ethic.

3. **Honor cultural skills that welcome feedback:** Create a continuous-learning environment where employee development and coaching are held in high regard. Demonstrate appropriate behaviors via role simulations, and expand the horizons of your leaders by creating new opportunities for growth. Tell them you welcome all feedback!

4. **Share creative pathways to your leaders' success:** Ignite passion, try new methods, build collaborative teams, embrace technology, and enhance communication tools. Provide physical environments conducive to idea generation whenever possible.

5. **Help leaders learn to diffuse stress:** Get to know what triggers stress, and have your leaders learn the signs, as well. Treat everyone with fairness and respect. Inspire taking initiative and using patience.

6. **Teach communication by design:** Everyone welcomes communication from their leaders. How much and how often needs to be customized based on preferences and performance levels.

7. **Challenge leaders beyond comfort zones:** Don't let your leaders get bored or stagnant. Extend your leaders beyond their comfort zones. Leaders like to stretch their abilities. Cheer them on!

8. **Celebrate success and increase leadership mojo:** Make everyone, at every level, feel special. All milestones on a leader's journey to higher levels of responsibility need acknowledgment. Give praise in progress. Leaders need to embrace the previous seven steps to collaboratively celebrate in their success.

Based in the Chicago area, Dolly Hinshaw is a highly regarded and successful businesswoman who combines out-of-the-ordinary-to-extraordinary thinking with an in-depth knowledge of changing markets to help clients celebrate their success with enthusiastic behavior and high levels of intrinsic motivation.

For more info on leadership whitepapers, productivity tools, motivational strategies, and more, visit: www.Hinshaw-Associates.com.

projects into small parts that are manageable and doable. This is also called "chunking down" pieces of a project.

How do you measure up as a leader who takes action? Grade yourself here on a scale of 1 (lowest) to 10 (highest), circling the number that best reflects your present leadership ability in this area.

1	2	3	4	5	6	7	8	9	10

Much improvement needed Excellent

Have your leaders answer these questions so that they may assess themselves and their own personal bests when it comes to practicing how they will take action:

- How would you go about chunking down a project into small parts so that it becomes more manageable?
- Why is it important for a leader to set milestones along the way to meeting the end result?
- Do you take action when you want to implement a plan, or do you procrastinate?
- Why do you think taking action is an important aspect of leadership?

Have your leaders make a list of the specific actions they will take to strengthen themselves in areas they've identified as needing improvement.

CREATE A LEADERSHIP PLAN THAT HELPS LEADERS KEEP THEIR MOJO

Now that you've seen how to guide your leaders in better understanding the critical elements of leadership by having them assess their own strengths and weaknesses in each of the four practices defined, it is time to teach your leaders how to create their own leadership plans for specific projects.

How to Use This Three-Part Planner

Use this planner as a prototype to help your leaders work through one particular leadership project they're dealing with currently or are likely to face. If your leaders don't have a particular work-related project they can use as an example, they may select a project that involves a club they belong to or a church or community organization project in which they're involved. Feel free to customize the plan to meet your specific industry-related needs or ask your leaders to come up with creative ways they can enhance portions of this sample plan. This planning effort will provide a step-by-step guide for developing the personal best inside each of your leaders.

Ask your leaders to photocopy and reduce their own leadership planners to fit in their daily calendars. With easy access to their leadership planners, they will be more likely to use the process for each project they undertake.

Sample Leadership Planner
Part I

Step 1: Describe the project you have selected to work through in this planner. Here are some examples: You're starting an online newsletter for your division; you're opening a new sales territory and introducing a new product line; you're going to be leading your team in implementing a new marketing project for your department and you're being met with some resistance to the change.

Step 2: Define specifically what the project goals are.

Step 3: Record the project's deadline.

Step 4: Outline your budget. Identify additional resources you will need.

Step 5: Identify your team for this project. List their names, titles, and the roles you expect each person to play. Describe each member's strengths and weaknesses and how you can maximize each one's talents relevant to the project's desired success.

Step 6: Think *virtual*. What other team members would you like to include in this project? Here are some examples of virtual teammates: your organization's customers, suppliers, and vendors; experts from other industry-related fields; even competitors. Don't make assumptions about who is willing to help and who isn't.

Step 7: Identify your stakeholders and what standards they will use to measure the success of the project.

Step 8: Make a list of words that describe how you feel about this project. For example, use words like *enthusiastic, excited, thrilled* or *terrified, hesitant,* and *apprehensive.*

Step 9: Anticipate any likely obstacles you may face. Identify the parts of the project you expect to be difficult or overwhelming. List those obstacles here and begin planning how you will overcome them.

Step 10: Answer these questions about the project you're planning: Why am I doing this? Why is this project important to the organization? To whom else is this project important?

Part II

This is where your leaders will have a chance to apply the lessons they learned earlier in this chapter on the four practices of successful leadership.

Practice 1: Challenge the status quo. By answering the following questions, you will be focusing on how to apply the leadership practice of challenging the status quo to this particular project.

- How do you plan to challenge the status quo regarding this project?
- How will you gather innovative ideas from the team?
- What experiments can you try?
- How will you motivate your team to think of this endeavor as an exciting adventure and not just another dull project to complete?
- How will you make it safe for team members to step outside the box?

Practice 2: Stretch people. Focus now on how to apply the leadership practice of stretching people to this particular project.

In part I of this planner, you listed words that described how you felt about this project. In doing that, you actually set up expectations or assumptions about how you or others on your team might treat this project, and thereby unknowingly set up barriers that may well hold you back from completing this project successfully.

Stretch yourself and your people by listing in one column how everyone feels about this project. In another column, list ways you and your team can turn any negative assumptions that might exist into opportunities to challenge the process. Then answer the questions below to help plan how you will stretch your people.

- How will you give your decision-making power to the team so that they will assume accountability and begin to stretch?
- To whom will you give more responsibility, and when?
- How will you enable your team to push itself beyond its own limits?
- What extraordinary results can you expect from stretching your people and raising the bar?

Practice 3: Model the example. What will be your leadership legacy? Imagine yourself a year from now. Your project has been completed successfully. What are people saying about you as a leader? How is your leadership on this project being described by employees?

- Write down how you hope people will describe your leadership legacy.
- Now it's the present and the question is this: What are you doing right here, right now, to help fulfill the legacy you just described?

Practice 4: Take action. Focus now on how to apply the leadership practice of taking action to a particular project. Answer the following questions, and then below you'll find some examples of actions to take to support your goals.

- By taking action, how do you deliberately set your people up for success?
- Once you've shared the goals of the project with your team, how will you set up a plan of action to accomplish those goals?
- How will you go about recognizing and celebrating the important small wins along the way to the end result for this project?

Here is an example of actions in support of goals:

Project Goals	Action Steps Needed to Get Us There
• Use customer feedback to improve processes and service. • Begin structuring the new customer service plan of action.	• Record all customer feedback data, whether good or bad. • Select feedback we plan to implement and assign a project leader.

Marking the milestones and celebrating their completion are important parts of every project. Here is an example of how to identify the small wins in pursuit of the

large victory: The ultimate goal of this project is to have a New Customer Care program rolled out in 15 regions by the end of summer.

Milestones That Will Mark Our Success	Date for Completion
• Hold initial team meeting to assign responsibilities and name team leaders.	January 10
• Outline customer care highlights and strategy for management approval.	January 25
• Obtain management approval.	February 5
• Disseminate information packets to regions.	March 3
• Celebrate project completion.	August 28

Part III

Plan to follow up. It's important that your leaders realize that the leadership planning process doesn't end with the completion of the plan itself. On its own, the plan is just a piece of paper. However, the plan to *follow up on the plan* is where successful leadership of a project lies.

Ask your leaders to determine for themselves the follow-up steps they'll need to take. Having them answer the following questions about their follow-up plan will provide them with a clearer direction. Tell them to take time to reflect on the overall project. Even the most exciting projects won't help them grow as leaders if they don't reflect on what they've learned and how they can continually improve the process. Use the following questions to guide you in your follow-up.

- What kind of follow-up steps will be necessary in order to measure this project's success?
- From whom will we gather our information?
- How often will it be necessary to follow up on this project?
- How will we document and report back our findings? What form of communication will we use?

Once your leaders have completed their plans to follow up, they'll be on their way to accomplishing greater achievements within the organization. They also will have answers to three important questions that all leaders want to know and that are mentioned in the beginning of this chapter: Where are they now? Where are they going? How will they get there?

PLANNING TO LEAD

Three things leaders want to know:

- where they are now
- where they are going
- how they intend to get there.

The four practices of leadership success:

- challenging the status quo
- stretching people
- modeling the example
- taking action.

Leadership Lessons From Steve Jobs

Steve Jobs was this century's Thomas Edison. Jobs changed the world. An extraordinary leader and innovator—that is how Steve Jobs will be remembered. This book was written on a Mac the first time around and once again in its new and improved format on Anne's MacBookPro, while researching content on an iPad.

What It Was Like to Be Alive When Steve Jobs Was the CEO and Chairman of Apple (NASDAQ: AAPL)

One day in the future, it is likely that your children, grandchildren, or great-grandchildren will be asking, "What was it like to be alive when Steve Jobs was the head of Apple?" Jobs was probably one of if not *the* greatest leaders of this century. Every golden nugget of wisdom he put posted on YouTube or TED Talks (check out his "How to Live Before You Die" speech), in his hundreds of famous speeches, or in his prolific writings will seem 100 times more significant as leadership lessons for us all now that he is gone.

A Few Lifelong Lessons That We as Authors Have Learned From Steve Jobs

- Connect the dots backward, not forward. From his famous 2005 Stanford speech, the concept here is that as much as we try to plan our lives in advance, there's always something that's unpredictable about life. We can only connect the dots looking back and trust that somehow they will connect down the road in your future. His message: Trust in something—your gut, karma, a higher being, spirit, or destiny.

- Listen to the voice in the back of your head. That voice will tell you if you are in the right place or not. Most leaders don't listen for that tiny voice. They simply decide to do something and do it. When we consciously decide we only want to make a lot of money, we snuff out the little voice of guidance and wisdom. Leaders are smart to listen to their inner voice, even if it tells you to leave your business partner, leave your company, move to China, or take the biggest risk of your life.

- Marry art and science. These are the greatest of all means of innovative creativity. This was one of the most profound leadership lessons that Apple taught its leaders. Many Apple leaders have backgrounds in anthropology, theology, and even poetry.

- Focus groups can't create your future. Jobs was the first to say that the customer does not always know what he or she wants, especially if it's something they've never touched before, like an iPad or the likes of an iPhone. Jobs trusted his intuition, like Picasso and other great artists. The iPad was a twittersphere joke for a day, until people held one. Then it became a must-have!

- Never fear failure. Jobs was fired by the successor he once chose. But he got right back up and went for his passion, his mojo. He was later diagnosed with pancreatic cancer

and told he only had weeks to live. As he says in his Stanford commencement speech: "There's nothing like your impending death to focus the mind."

- Surround yourself with the most talented people you can find. Apple is *not* Steve Jobs. In reality, Jobs surrounded himself with brilliance and talent. Jobs credited the team that no one ever sees.
- Expect a lot from your work, yourself, and others. Leaders have all heard the horror stories of Jobs yelling on the job or dressing down the staff. But, the staff says, "He gives a damn." He only wanted the best from himself and everyone who worked around him. There was an outpouring of emotion regarding Jobs' death because his people held him in such high esteem. Turns out that genuine talent and authentic leadership give a damn.
- Forget about being right; care about succeeding. Jobs said this after he was fired by Apple. Don't forget your current reality, he reminded everyone.
- Anything is possible with hard work, determination, and a sense of vision. Jobs could practically sum up all the chapters in this book with this statement. Even as a great leader, at the end of the day, Steve Jobs was a human being, a man, who took the whole-person approach to his leadership. We can all be just as special as he, if we follow the simple lessons he laid out in his leadership journey.
- Stay hungry and foolish. This is something Jobs wished for himself and said: "I wish that for you."

Steve Jobs died on October 5, 2011, at the age of 56, having battled pancreatic cancer for several years.

Questions for Discussion: Creating a Leadership Plan

1. Why is a leadership plan necessary? Why isn't goal setting enough?
2. Why is leadership planning considered a voyage of discovery?
3. What does developing a leader's personal best have to do with leadership planning success?
4. Why is it important to chunk down portions of a project?
5. Why do leaders include stakeholders' objectives in their plans?
6. Why do leaders use milestones along the way to measure ongoing success?

Wrapping It Up

This chapter teaches that when your leaders learn the various elements of leadership development, they will most likely implement a more creative project or process that management can get behind and equip them to accomplish. But first, it takes a plan.

Leadership planning is also the obvious precursor to developing a strategic plan and short- and long-term tactical plans that back it all up, as covered in the next chapter. We believe that this can all work in tandem and that when it does, it will enhance your leaders' long-term capabilities and success.

Leader's Guide to Developing Strategic and Tactical Plans

Recently, a well-known financial and insurance institution we worked with rolled out its strategic plan for its intact sales and marketing teams across the country. Although the rollout was well orchestrated (there was actually a road show of sorts set up to deliver the organization's mission and vision), reception for the document was lukewarm at best, and the plan's actual implementation was practically impossible. Follow-through on the action plan, commitment to the long-term strategy, and a passion to be a part of leadership's vision was met with shallow, ho-hum frontline effort. The plan, created by senior leadership, gathered little or no momentum, and the strategy failed to be implemented fully.

What went wrong? The leadership committee that wrote the strategic plan (that rarely is involved with the day-to-day processes of each job) did not ask for or include input from the field at any point during its development. Big mistake! Therefore, the most critical step in the entire process was overlooked. There was no feedback from the people who could actually breathe life into the plan's words—the workers performing the jobs. No wonder the financial institution's employees saw this as just another meaningless directive imposed from the top, and viewed these strategies as empty, created by people who have nothing to do with making them a reality. The greatest lesson we netted from this experience? Leadership committees should step aside when it comes to strategic planning.

It is in this chapter where your leaders will learn about the importance of constructing an effective approach for strategic and tactical planning—planning that adds real meaning to the organization and its people, and that is not just another hand-me-down directive from the top. Along with this strategic master plan, short-term tactical plans will be created along the way to ensure overall success. Your leaders will quickly learn here what it takes to write their own strategic and tactical plans with the help of everyone involved. They will also learn how to roll out the plan so that it meets with support and true enthusiasm for its message. If your training does not include the element of including both long-term strategic plans and short-term tactical plans, here is your chance to supplement your leadership development program to emphasize these vital components.

What You Will Learn in This Chapter:

- ◆ "Robust" strategic planning with short-term tactical planning to give real-world goals and meaningful purpose. Leaders must
 - ● share the responsibility for planning with all levels within the organization
 - ● create multilevel strategic and tactical planning teams
 - ● present every rollout as a work in progress.
- ◆ Step-by-step blueprint for creating an evolutionary strategic and tactical plan. Leaders must
 - ● build strategic partnerships within the organization
 - ● have a powerful vision statement
 - ● get people into alignment with the goals and objectives of the organization.

Analytical and stale processes in creating top-down strategic plans definitely have taken a brutal beating in the past few years. Business publications from the *Wall Street Journal* to *Fortune* magazine have helped spread the word about strategic planning's widespread disillusionment. Wide gaps between what gets created and what gets acted upon and measured for results (remember the old saying, "what gets measured is what gets done"?), as well as repeated failures to achieve strategic planning objectives, have been the main reason many organizations today have completely scrapped the idea of doing any strategic planning. In interviews with dozens of leaders on this topic, it was common to hear, "Strategic planning? Heck! We quit that wasted effort two years ago." Other leaders reported that at the very least, they were considering putting an abrupt halt to the process. This is why short-term tactical plans were created; if they are properly aligned with the strategic plan, the company should be able to see the strategic plan to success—taking the organization to the next level.

THE EVOLUTION OF STRATEGIC AND TACTICAL PLANNING

The first lesson in strategic planning for leaders at every level is this: Accept that the traditional approach to strategic planning is probably not adequate. The top-down approach and the linear procedures used by many organizations are on the way out. Strategic planning is no longer accomplished by a single group of elite executive managers gathering annually at a luxury resort to plot the future of the organization and its people. Instead, robust strategic planning—that is, planning with meaningful purpose, real-world goals and objectives, and action steps that make things happen on a daily basis—is now considered a continuous and evolving process that includes the entire organization.

Allow Short-Term Tactical Plans to Drive Long-Term Strategic Plans

Many companies meet more than once per year to create short-term tactical plans with quarterly or six-month goals to keep momentum strong. Short-term tactical plans are the engine within the long-term strategic planning process.

The important part of this process is to make sure that the tactical plans are in alignment with the strategic plans; otherwise they can move the company in a different

direction. These tactical plans allow the company to shift gears at a moment's notice due to business needs. They also shed light on critical areas that need to be modified in the strategic plan to help the company reach its organization's goals and objectives. (For example, technological advances may require modifications to the strategic plan. You may have experienced this in your own organization.)

The Difference Between Strategic and Tactical Planning

Strategic and tactical planning are two business objectives that are widely used in many organizations today. Businesses use strategic planning to set and focus on long-term goals that are between one to 10 years into the future. Typically, these long-term goals tie in with the vision statement of the organization and are determined by executive management.

THE STRATEGIC APPROACH—WHAT DO WE NEED TO BE DOING TO SURVIVE AND THRIVE?

Strategic planning answers broad questions such as, "Where should we be going and what should we be doing in order to remain in business?" These plans usually include several objectives that may affect many or all areas of the organization and are usually broad in spectrum, because they will morph continually depending on the times. Many companies use strategic planning to develop multiple strategic plans and alternatives. This way, the executive leaders can choose which strategic plan they feel would be best for the company after receiving input from all levels (potential future leaders) of the organization—including frontline and management employees.

THE TACTICAL APPROACH—HOW WILL OUR ORGANIZATION GET THERE AND WHEN?

Businesses use tactical planning to cover shorter periods of time weekly, monthly, quarterly, or every six months. In highly specialized fields, like commercial aviation, minute-by-minute and hourly real-time tactical planning goes into play during such events as winter ice and snow storms at airports like O'Hare International in Chicago. It doesn't get any more tactical than at a major airport during extreme weather conditions. Therefore, share with your leaders that short-term tactical planning is often relative.

Tactical plans address the guts of daily business operations and the "how-tos" of attaining the strategic objectives, and are typically very specific and goal oriented. Short-term tactical planning answers questions such as, "How will we get there? How much do we need to increase production in order to avoid hiring any new staff in the next quarter? What computer technology do we need to implement in the next six months to solve the current production problem?"

Middle Management and Supervisors Play a Key Role in Tactical Planning

Typically, middle management and the frontline supervisors assist in the development of the tactical plans. They are important in this process because they are the future

leadership of the organization, and their early involvement is critical to their long-term leadership development and success. Their role also creates buy-in from the staff that is directly working with the frontline employees and who have many of the most hands-on cost-saving ideas.

Make Tactical Planning Fun!

Cutting-edge organizations have taken their tactical plans to their employees in fun ways. Some companies have production competitions to set benchmarks on speed and accuracy, or have established monetary incentives for any employee who gives cost-saving ideas that the company later implements. Refer back to the introduction, where we underscore the importance of being willing to "hear" the lowest-titled person in the organization. The person doing the job is the most suitable for offering process improvements and ideas for saving money—and making it! This technique can become a leader's key strategy.

CUT TO THE CHASE: GET PEOPLE MOVING ON SHORT- AND LONG-TERM PLANS

Here is what to tell your leaders about strategic planning: Keep the process simple by providing employees with a straightforward, no-nonsense approach to developing their own winning strategies that get executed. Introduce leaders to these important components of a successful planning process:

- Put together multilevel planning teams, and get each level involved. Planning is not only a corporate function. Who's on your strategic planning team? If it consists of primarily top management folks, you've got a serious gap. Include team members from every level of the organization's structure. Let each level participate by providing ideas, and then, as a leader, utilize the best concepts from each level as you create a master strategic plan.
- Stop! Think about what you are doing. Don't just roll out a completed plan. The message you'll send is, "We did this ourselves, and we sure didn't need your input." Can you imagine anyone buying in to a plan that conveyed such a message? Always present a plan as a work in progress, and before finalizing it, get opinions on ways to improve it from employees at all levels. Soliciting broad input says you value the opinions and ideas of the people held responsible for doing the jobs.

Here is what you can tell your leaders about tactical planning: A simple process is necessary to ensure success, especially since tactical plans have a relatively short timeline. When creating the tactical plan, you should ask the question, "How does this align with our strategic plan?" If the answer is that it does not align with the strategic plan, then leadership should probably scrap the idea. Tactical plans usually align with the strategic plan so that you reach your ultimate planning goal.

Components of Successful Tactical Planning

Check out some of these important components of a successful tactical planning process and apply what works for you:

- Decide on which area of the business you want to focus on, and then comprise a team of subject matter experts (SMEs) from all levels of the organization for the team.
- Once the team is in place, the group then needs to create realistic goals, objectives, and timelines—and determine what resources are needed for the team.
- The team should review the strategic plan and carefully examine the goals and objectives of the tactical plans to make sure they are in alignment. If they are in alignment, then determine what the desired outcome of the tactical team will be.
- The tactical plans should be presented to executive management for final approval and allocation of resources (time, money, and human capital). If the plan is not approved, then the team should meet again to come up with a stronger initiative, until a green light is given. But first the team needs to find out why their first approach was rejected so that mistakes are not repeated.
- Once approved, the plan is put into place, and the timeline should be adhered to. Each part of the team should be held accountable to meet all deadlines. If the team falls behind schedule, they will need to determine if they require additional resources to complete the project, at or under budget.

Imperial Wallcoverings' Make-Ready Plan of Action

Imperial Wallcoverings is an east coast organization that had a strategic plan to become more efficient in making wallpaper. They set out to reduce the time it took to make their product by one-half, while simultaneously reducing waste. This was an aggressive goal, but the company was confident that they could reach it.

Next, they created tactical planning teams of employees, supervisors, and managers to see what processes could be improved so they could reach their goal and have less waste. The tactical planning teams worked hard to improve old processes, and managers started to listen to the employees and allow changes to be made. (In the past, only management made the decisions without consulting their employees.) The employees named the initiative the "Make-Ready Plan."

Results showed that the employees increased production, reduced waste, and met the company's strategic goals. All of the employees had a sense of pride and a feeling of accomplishment and belonging as they helped the company become more efficient.

An Upside With a Downside

The measurable downside of this successful tactical team is that the manufacturing plants became so efficient that the company needed fewer facilities from which to operate business and, therefore, closed some of its plants.

The bottom line is that Imperial would not have been successful without the buy-in and shared input from its employees. By getting them involved, the company reached its ultimate goals. And while some jobs were lost, the company overall kept its lights on—thus retaining many of its employees.

Planning Issues	Leadership Teams
Product development	Marketing mangers Technology supervisors
Service improvement	Frontline supervisors Team leaders Mid-level managers
Customer development and retention	Frontline supervisors Mid-level and upper-level managers
Functional processes for each department	Coaches Team leaders Frontline supervisors Managers at all levels
Competitive analysis	Department analysts Sales and marketing managers
Business growth	Upper-level managers Senior executives Financial analysts Legal analysts
Sales and marketing	Sales and marketing managers
Fix-it assignments	Anyone and everyone

Using the examples above, ask your leaders to add their own categories of leadership planning issues and specify the people who will be involved in writing and implementing their portions of the plan. Devise a series of questions and suggestions that each multilevel team can develop into its own strategic plan. Next, have everyone outline what will be the specific action steps necessary to make every issue in their plan a reality. Here's an example:

Strategic goal: Additional training programs on communications skills and customer service.

Actions steps necessary to make it a reality: Investigating off-the-shelf curricula, prices, and length of time to deliver; investigating the possibility of using in-house design and development people to prepare those programs; sending out a questionnaire asking for feedback on the specific communications skills and customer service tools employees need most.

Components of Successful Tactical Planning

Check out some of these important components of a successful tactical planning process and apply what works for you:

- Decide on which area of the business you want to focus on, and then comprise a team of subject matter experts (SMEs) from all levels of the organization for the team.

- Once the team is in place, the group then needs to create realistic goals, objectives, and timelines—and determine what resources are needed for the team.

- The team should review the strategic plan and carefully examine the goals and objectives of the tactical plans to make sure they are in alignment. If they are in alignment, then determine what the desired outcome of the tactical team will be.

- The tactical plans should be presented to executive management for final approval and allocation of resources (time, money, and human capital). If the plan is not approved, then the team should meet again to come up with a stronger initiative, until a green light is given. But first the team needs to find out why their first approach was rejected so that mistakes are not repeated.

- Once approved, the plan is put into place, and the timeline should be adhered to. Each part of the team should be held accountable to meet all deadlines. If the team falls behind schedule, they will need to determine if they require additional resources to complete the project, at or under budget.

Imperial Wallcoverings' Make-Ready Plan of Action

Imperial Wallcoverings is an east coast organization that had a strategic plan to become more efficient in making wallpaper. They set out to reduce the time it took to make their product by one-half, while simultaneously reducing waste. This was an aggressive goal, but the company was confident that they could reach it.

Next, they created tactical planning teams of employees, supervisors, and managers to see what processes could be improved so they could reach their goal and have less waste. The tactical planning teams worked hard to improve old processes, and managers started to listen to the employees and allow changes to be made. (In the past, only management made the decisions without consulting their employees.) The employees named the initiative the "Make-Ready Plan."

Results showed that the employees increased production, reduced waste, and met the company's strategic goals. All of the employees had a sense of pride and a feeling of accomplishment and belonging as they helped the company become more efficient.

An Upside With a Downside

The measurable downside of this successful tactical team is that the manufacturing plants became so efficient that the company needed fewer facilities from which to operate business and, therefore, closed some of its plants.

The bottom line is that Imperial would not have been successful without the buy-in and shared input from its employees. By getting them involved, the company reached its ultimate goals. And while some jobs were lost, the company overall kept its lights on—thus retaining many of its employees.

TACTICAL PLANS ARE ABOUT DOING, NOT PLANNING

It is important to point out to your leaders that tactical planning is more about doing than planning. And sometimes the actual doing comes *before* the planning. That approach can upset the traditional managerial mindset where the "plan then act" theory has been considered the logical way of doing things in the past. It may be logical, but certainly not creative, innovative, or motivating.

KEEP TACTICAL PLANS ALIGNED WITH THE STRATEGIC PLANS OF YOUR ORGANIZATION

As noted, strategic and tactical plans require constant recalibrating and alignment with each other. Once the strategic plan is created, the tactical plans need to be created and put into place as soon as possible to keep the momentum going. Remember, the tactical plans are what drive the success of the strategic plan. It's like a strategic, high-performing engine. Keeping this in mind helps the organization understand the importance of the tactical plans. Often, without some small built-in "wins" with tactical plans along the way to the ultimate goal of the strategic plan, the strategic plan will fizzle out and die. This is when organizations throw up their hands and employees get discouraged.

Let Employees "Feel and Experience" Ownership in the Process

An important point to keep in mind: Employees want to be a part of something bigger than themselves, and when they are involved in the planning, they take ownership of everything they do. When the employees take ownership, they become innovative—bringing forth cost-saving ideas, production improvements, and technological ideas. The act of empowering employees at all levels helps the organization to run like a well-oiled machine—one in which every department is intertwined with each other, all working toward the same vision and goals.

The keys to success in keeping the plans aligned are communication, planning, keeping momentum, and celebrating small successes along the way.

How you go about helping your leaders get from here to there in their tactical planning is an evolving process. There are many ways to help them reach their goals and objectives, but the effort can be simplified greatly for leaders new to this process if they first break it down into four parts.

A LEADER'S FOUR-PART BLUEPRINT FOR CREATING A STRATEGIC PLAN
Part 1: Create Tactical and Strategic Partnerships Using Mission and Vision Statements

It is critical that leaders at every level—supervisors, team leaders, coaches, managers, and so on—consider themselves strategic and tactical partners within the organization. That is most easily accomplished when all employees have a clear and thorough understanding of the organizational big picture—mission, vision, goals, and objectives.

A mission statement and a vision statement are not the same thing. A *mission statement* defines who you are. It doesn't stop short with a belief or philosophy. Instead, it goes on to describe succinctly how the mission will be accomplished. It states **this is who we are and this is what we stand for.**

Mission, Vision, Goals, and Objectives, Summed Up by the Best in the Business

Brilliant organizations who are laser focused on who they are and where they are going say it with simplicity and gusto.

Pixar: Pixar's objective and mission is to combine proprietary technological and world-class creative talent to develop computer-animated feature films with memorable characters and heartwarming stories that appeal to audiences of all ages.

3M Company: Solve unsolved problems innovatively. (Ever hear of Post-It Notes?)

Mary Kay Cosmetics: Give unlimited opportunity to women.

Merck: We preserve and improve human life.

Facebook: Facebook's mission is to give people the power to share and make the world more open and connected.

Pepsi: The choice of a new generation.

Ralph Lauren: Ralph Lauren's mission is to redefine American style, provide quality products, create worlds, and invite people to take part in our dreams.

eBay: eBay's mission is to provide a global trading platform where practically anyone can trade practically anything.

Disney: Make people happy!

Google: Google's mission is to organize the world's information and make it universally accessible and useful.

Microsoft: Microsoft's mission and values are to help people and businesses throughout the world realize their full potential.

Mission, Vision, Goals, and Objectives Set the Course for the Future

Looking back in time, you can see where a few world leaders used their vision and mission statements to take them into the twenty-first century.

Ford Motor Company (early 1900s): Ford will democratize the automobile.

Sony (early 1950s): We'll become the company most known for changing the worldwide poor-quality image of Japanese products.

Boeing (1950): Boeing will become the dominant player in commercial aircraft and bring the world into the jet age.

Is there any doubt that compelling statements such as these lead employees and their organizations into the future with a chance for greater success and leadership opportunities?

The Avnet Advantage

In the case of Avnet, Inc., they use branding, vision, and a motto. The company's success in building relationships among its employees and reaching its corporate goals and objectives speaks for itself.

Avnet may have once been a best-kept secret, but they are in the spotlight now. It is one of the world's largest transnational electronics distributors of electronic parts, enterprise computing, and storage products and embedded subsystems. This company provides a vital link in the technology supply chain (see www.Avnet.com).

Some of Avnet's recent accomplishments due to strategic and tactical goal setting include:

- Avnet was named number one in its industry on Fortune's "Most Admired Companies" for 2009, 2010, and 2011.
- It has been named in InfoWorld's top 100 five times in the last six years.
- The company was recognized in 2009 and 2010 by *Newsweek* magazine in its Green Rankings of the 500 largest U.S. companies.
- It has been ranked among the top 100 in the InformationWeek 500 for seven consecutive years.
- Avnet was the recipient of hundreds of global awards from leading manufacturers in the electronics industry.

Avnet has a company motto that encompasses its people, quality, and customer service: ***Avnet is a company whose leaders believe in developing their people, operational excellence, and profitable growth***. Avnet is an industry leader in the electronics arena and has been a world-class company for many years. They also value the alliances among their people in working toward their strategic plan and goals.

In a recent interview with Stephanie Montanez, Bernie Storm-Colvin, former operations manager of Avnet, states that at Avnet, the sky is the limit. Those who work hard and possess the skills necessary to do the job can start at an entry-level position in the company and work their way to the top. Storm-Colvin started as a general clerk and in a few short years was promoted to operations manager. She attributes her success to her previous manager, Ann Akagi, who practiced strategic, tactical planning and implemented succession planning in the organization. This process helped Avnet accomplish and encourage internal growth and movement. At Avnet, managers discuss areas that can be improved with employees, including each person's future goals and how leadership can help drive results and meet the aims of every worker. And perhaps most importantly, each of these questions ties back to and aligns with the organization's vision statement and strategic plan of action.

Vision Statements Are Not Wish Lists

Vision statements hold real purpose, and they say where you're going. The vision statement offers inspiration and hope for what the organization is capable of

becoming, but it's neither a wish list nor a description of the perfect organization. It's a realistic view of what the organization's success will look like when all of the strategies have been implemented. A vision statement should answer these four questions:

- What will we stand for in the future? (Select a specific future date for this question.)
- Where will we be in relation to our competition?
- What will we believe in and stand for? What will our philosophy be?
- What will our employees be saying and feeling about our organization?

By creating a vision statement that connects directly to the strategies of your plan, you paint an inspiring and unifying big picture for all of your employees. You also send a powerful message that says, "We can and will get there from here!" That gusto is expressed in the Sta-Rite Industries' Water Systems Group's vision statement. The group does a splendid job of detailing inspiration and hope for what it is capable of achieving (see the sidebar).

Sta-Rite Industries (Water Systems Group) Vision Statement

Profitably grow in the defined markets by increasing market share, introducing new products, and acquiring complementary product lines. It is our goal to be a global leader in our defined markets. We will be market-driven, focusing on the following areas: product performance, customer support, technical support/service. We will gain competitive advantage by building on existing strengths and developing new competencies. We will be the best-cost manufacturer.

Sta-Rite's strongest ingredient for success? Its people. Their motto is: "At Sta-Rite, Our People Make the Difference."

To help ensure your leaders' success, be certain that top brass within the organization is fully prepared to communicate the organization's overall goals and objectives in achieving its mission and accomplishing its vision. It would be extremely difficult for your leaders to move forward in either the tactical or the strategic planning processes unless upper-level management is clear about its goals and objectives.

Find out if your leaders really understand the organization's goals and objectives as they pertain to its mission and vision. If they don't, make that a part of the learning process before moving on to the second part of the planning blueprint.

Part 2: Get Departments and People in Alignment

Tell your leaders to observe what's happening in individual departments. Here's an important question for them to consider: Are individual departments and the employee

expectations within those departments supporting the overall mission, vision, goals, and expectations of the organization? If not, why not? Keep in mind that if the leaders' individual business units or departments and the people in them are not in sync, they will not be able to create a strategic plan that will successfully support the organization for the long haul.

To gauge the alignment of people and their departments, leaders should take the following actions:

- Ask employees to describe what success looks like in their departments, based on the specific goals and objectives set by leadership. Departmental priorities and expectations of people should always add up to and support the organization's overall goals.
- Decide if there are discrepancies between departmental and individual priorities. If so, work to close the gap for more unity and focus.
- Finally, ask how people believe that success should be measured in their departments. Measurements must be relative to the individuals who are charged with the responsibility for doing the work. Only the people who actually do the work should be determining what success looks like and how that success is best measured.

When leaders ask those questions and get people to think through this process, they almost instantly will be aligning people and departments with organizational direction. They'll also be creating strategic partners at all levels of the organization.

Getting Everyone in Sync—A Quick Assessment for Strategic Planning
Review with your leaders the top three priorities or goals and objectives of the organization, as established by top management. Here is an example of corporate priorities:

1. Customer service and retention
2. Stakeholder value
3. Competitive growth

Have your leaders match the organizational priorities and goals to those of your specific business units or departments, and then to the priorities of the men and women doing the work. Here is an example of departmental priorities and goals:

1. Customer service and retention
2. Bottom-line results
3. Higher performance for meeting competitive challenges

Here is an example of individual priorities and goals for one employee, "M. Jones":

1. Positive relationships with both internal and external customers
2. Helping reach all of our department's goals and objectives
3. Professional growth to remain competitive and marketable

It's evident in these examples that, like a ladder, each rung supports the others. Individual priorities and goals support specific business units and their goals, and both support the overall goals and primary objectives of the organization as set by top management.

The people and their departments throughout the organization must be in alignment with the organization's goals and objectives, mission, and vision before the strategic planning process can begin. If your leaders have identified gaps, use this opportunity to discuss and resolve whatever issue may present hurdles in your planning efforts. Point out that anticipating and preparing for likely obstacles makes the leaders better prepared to handle the bumps they may encounter along the way.

Part 3: Write the Plan

This is a good time to remind your leaders that everyone in the organization is going to have a hand in writing and developing the organization's strategic plan. The best way to go about this is to use the Einstein approach at all levels of leadership: Keep it simple, use common sense, and make it straightforward. Emphasize to your leaders that it is wise to ask the people who are in the ideal position to make recommendations—those doing the jobs on a daily basis—to offer their insights, ideas, and solutions.

Unfortunately, most companies rarely see their frontline people as strategists. What a mistake they are making! It's the leader's job to make employees at every level feel like they are an important part of the strategic planning process. Take a look at two of the primary roles frontline strategists may play in the organization.

- Frontline employees are the voices and mirrors of your customers—the ones who can most accurately bring customer opinions and feedback to the organization.
- Frontline employees are the organization's glue. Often working closely with other business units and departments, the front line observes firsthand what processes hold the organization together—what works, what doesn't, and why.

Organizing Multilevel Planning Teams

Depending on your industry, your leaders should be including other leaders at various levels to offer their input in designing your organization's strategic plan. Point out to your leaders that they should begin by organizing cross-functional teams to which they can assign a specific focal point of their plan. Be certain that the team is assigned to an issue or issues aligned with their expertise and experience. In that way, everyone who participates is set for success!

Multilevel teams comprise employees from various levels of leadership within the organization. Multilevel team membership may consist of frontline supervisors, coaches, and executive management, among others.

Here are a few examples of some of the planning issues various leadership teams might deal with and the level of leadership possibly assigned to each issue.

Planning Issues	Leadership Teams
Product development	Marketing mangers Technology supervisors
Service improvement	Frontline supervisors Team leaders Mid-level managers
Customer development and retention	Frontline supervisors Mid-level and upper-level managers
Functional processes for each department	Coaches Team leaders Frontline supervisors Managers at all levels
Competitive analysis	Department analysts Sales and marketing managers
Business growth	Upper-level managers Senior executives Financial analysts Legal analysts
Sales and marketing	Sales and marketing managers
Fix-it assignments	Anyone and everyone

Using the examples above, ask your leaders to add their own categories of leadership planning issues and specify the people who will be involved in writing and implementing their portions of the plan. Devise a series of questions and suggestions that each multilevel team can develop into its own strategic plan. Next, have everyone outline what will be the specific action steps necessary to make every issue in their plan a reality. Here's an example:

Strategic goal: Additional training programs on communications skills and customer service.

Actions steps necessary to make it a reality: Investigating off-the-shelf curricula, prices, and length of time to deliver; investigating the possibility of using in-house design and development people to prepare those programs; sending out a questionnaire asking for feedback on the specific communications skills and customer service tools employees need most.

Leaders now can assign a team or person to head up the discovery process and report back with specifics. This team or person also would be responsible for ongoing follow-up and evaluation of what's getting done.

Part 4: Take Action to Implement Your Plan

First you plan the strategy, and then you plan to carry it out—also known as implementing the strategy. That's the message you must convey to your leaders. Also, have them keep in mind the importance of getting people to buy in. If your leaders have included people from every level of the organization in the design and development of the process, they should not only have buy-in but also support and commitment from most of the organization. If this is the case, congratulate your leaders for getting over their biggest hurdle.

> *Good intentions mean squat without the action steps to back it up.* —Anne Bruce and Stephanie Montanez

Getting Leaders Engaged Through Action Steps

Initiate discussion among leaders on how they would go about implementing the following four action steps to their strategic plan. Start by having them discuss what a draft of their plan might look like and how they would seek input from the ranks and integrate that input into the plan. Then ask how they suggest lobbying for influential partners within the organization to help with the rollout of the program. Since upper-level management's buy-in is critical, ask how your leaders recommend tying together support from the top with the objectives that have already been set in place. How can this be done creatively? And, finally, what are some of the ways your leaders plan to motivate employees to act on the plan? How will they get others to drive home their strategies?

Action Step 1: Introduce a draft of the plan first. Remember, this is a work in progress. Don't roll out the actual finished product until people have seen the draft and have a chance to make additions, revisions, and further suggestions. You'll garner great respect for having been so considerate.

Action Step 2: Recruit influential strategic partners from various areas of the organization to roll out the plan. The executives can be present, but the job should be that of the people who represent the document.

Action Step 3: To get senior-level management's buy-in and support, be sure that you continually tie the strategies developed to the overall organization's mission, vision, goals, and established objectives.

Action Step 4: As the still-famous Nike ads once instructed, just do it! If you've done your job, your strategic plan will be a living, breathing document, and you will soon be seeing the results of your efforts on a daily basis.

Strategic Planning at The Ritz-Carlton

Strategic planning doesn't get any better than at The Ritz-Carlton Hotel Company. Not only is it simple and straightforward, it is also totally aligned with the organization's goals, mission, and values. And, more importantly, employees believe in it, support it, and act on it every day, bringing their strategic plan to life.

The Plan Is in the Gold Standards

When you want success, you study the successful. When you think of success, one of the first companies that may come to mind is The Ritz-Carlton. The Ritz-Carlton operates on a philosophy of Gold Standards, and that philosophy is the foundation of their hotel as well as their mission statement. Their Gold Standards represent the philosophies and values that they operate on every day. These standards support their business objectives and tie into their tactical plans, strategy, method, and finally the foundation on which the entire strategic plan rests: The Ritz-Carlton's Values and Philosophy, Gold Standards, Credo, Motto, Three Steps of Service, 12 Service Values, the Sixth Diamond, and the Employee Promise.

If you want to see a firsthand example of a strategic plan's daily effectiveness, this is where you'll find it. During every shift, in every department, in 76 hotels in 25 countries, from the Americas to Asia, from the Middle East to Europe, 38,000 employees start their day by having what they call a "lineup." These meetings bring everyone together to discuss one of the 12 Service Values, activities, VIPs that may be arriving, guest birthdays and anniversaries, and most importantly, a "wow" story wherein the leadership puts a spotlight on the great things that their "ladies and gentlemen" have done. They utilize this as a training tool to highlight excellence and their Gold Standards. This is a very important part of their strategic plan. On top of that, everyone around the world is discussing the exact same part of their Gold Standards on the exact same day (in different time zones, of course). When employees reach the 12th Service Value, they start all over again from the beginning. Can you imagine the synchronicity an organization gains when all of its people are following and believing in the same goals and objectives of their strategic plan, from San Francisco to London? Now that is amazing to have your entire organization focused on the same Gold Standards of excellence. Talk about synergy!

The Service and the Gold Standard

Ritz-Carlton strives to create the best experience possible for its customers, which is part of their Three Steps of Service. The second step of services relates to "anticipation and fulfillment of each guest's needs." Ritz entrusts each of their staff members to give the best Gold Standards to each and every customer, so that the employee can be empowered to do this without red tape or approval from the general manager. In fact, they allow each staff member to spend up to $2,000 on a guest. This shows that the management team really trusts and empowers their staff to make great decisions. Don't think that this money is only for problematic situations that may arise; the staff is really creative and uses the money to create the "Golden" experience for their guests. In an interview with *Forbes* magazine, Simon F. Cooper, president of The Ritz-Carlton Hotel, states the following on giving the Gold Standard to guests: "In Dubai, a waiter overheard a gentleman musing with his wife, who was in a wheelchair, that it was a shame

he couldn't get her down to the beach. The waiter told maintenance, who passed word, and the next afternoon there was a wooden walkway down to the beach to a tent that was set up for them to have dinner in." Cooper states, "A lot of the stuff that crosses my desk is not that they overcame a problem but that they used their $2,000 to create an outstanding experience" for their guests.

The Ritz-Carlton Gold Standards are known worldwide as a standard of excellence that is hard to match. Each of their standards is listed below:

The Credo

- The Ritz-Carlton is a place where the genuine care and comfort of our guests is our highest mission.
- We pledge to provide the finest personal service and facilities for our guests, who will always enjoy a warm, relaxed, yet refined ambience.
- The Ritz-Carlton experience enlivens the senses, instills well-being, and fulfills even the unexpressed wishes and needs of our guests.

Motto

At The Ritz-Carlton Hotel Company, LLC, "We are Ladies and Gentlemen serving Ladies and Gentlemen." This motto exemplifies the anticipatory service provided by all staff members.

Three Steps of Service

- A warm and sincere greeting. Use the guest's name.
- Anticipation and fulfillment of each guest's needs.
- Fond farewell. Give a warm good-bye, and use the guest's name.

The Employee Promise

- At The Ritz-Carlton, our ladies and gentlemen are the most important resource in our service commitment to our guests.
- By applying the principles of trust, honesty, respect, integrity, and commitment, we nurture and maximize talent to the benefit of each individual and the company.
- The Ritz-Carlton fosters a work environment where diversity is valued, quality of life is enhanced, individual aspirations are fulfilled, and The Ritz-Carlton Mystique is strengthened.

12 Service Values: I Am Proud to Be Ritz-Carlton

- I build strong relationships and create Ritz-Carlton guests for life.
- I am always responsive to the expressed and unexpressed wishes and needs of our guests.
- I am empowered to create unique, memorable, and personal experiences for our guests.
- I understand my role in achieving the Key Success Factors, embracing Community Footprints, and creating The Ritz-Carlton Mystique.
- I continuously seek opportunities to innovate and improve The Ritz-Carlton experience.

- I own and immediately resolve guest problems.
- I create a work environment of teamwork and lateral service so that the needs of our guests and each other are met.
- I have the opportunity to continuously learn and grow.
- I am involved in the planning of the work that affects me.
- I am proud of my professional appearance, language, and behavior.
- I protect the privacy and security of our guests, my fellow employees, and the company's confidential information and assets.
- I am responsible for uncompromising levels of cleanliness and creating a safe and accident-free environment.

The Ritz Carlton's strategic planning efforts have paid off handsomely, as the company has won not once, but twice, the prestigious Malcolm Baldridge National Quality Award—the first and only hotel company ever to receive such an honor. If ever there was an organization from which strategic planning techniques can be gleaned, it's The Ritz Carlton.

In addition, The Ritz-Carlton Leadership Center has welcomed thousands of senior executives, managers, and line staff from a variety of industries. The Leadership Center has flourished as a resource hub for guiding organizations interested in benchmarking many of these business practices.

INCLUDE EVERYONE WHEN IMPLEMENTING A STRATEGIC PLAN

Every successful tactical or strategic rollout that your leaders will be a part of will require a call to action. In other words, someone has got to implement the strategy or campaign by taking action and demonstrating the potential of its success. Your leaders will need to inspire buy-in from everyone on the team and from leadership above—bottom to top. When leaders inspire buy-in from the entire team, they will automatically build high morale, instill positive attitudes, and create enthusiasm for carrying out the strategies desired at all levels within the organization. No one should be left out—a serious mistake that leaders often make when they want to take control of a new concept or announcement.

In San Jose, California, Samaritan Medical Care Center and Gateway Family Medical Center, partners of CEP America (California Emergency Physicians, based in the Northern California Bay Area of Emeryville), doctors, office managers, and supervisors rolled out a strategic customer service program and culture-coaching event for both clinics and their teams.

The campaign strategy, called We C.A.R.E., was based on the four core values established by the practices' two medical directors, Dr. Samuel Cipoletti and Dr. Melanie Martin, along with Dr. Diana Fink and Dr. Elham Louis.

First, the two practices joined together for an overall team building seminar, which included dinner and an interactive personal and professional development session, facilitated by Anne and our colleague, Anmarie Miller. Everyone on staff attended, including all the doctors, who set the tone for teamwork and a culture change that was about to be unveiled. This meeting set the stage for changes to come and created an environment of high energy, trust, excitement, and a feeling of "family." The changes to take place would prove beneficial to all and create a new and improved environment of professional healthcare and customer service loyalty.

The first team gathering gave everyone a chance to improve relationships between intact work groups and learn how to better appreciate and utilize the unique differences everyone had to offer both practices.

Approximately eight weeks later, Anne and Anmarie returned and worked with both medical practices to roll out a 2012 campaign that would introduce a significant culture shift and improve customer care relations between staff, leadership, patients, and the local community.

We C.A.R.E.

First, a medical practice development model was established. The model was values-based, because values drive behaviors, and without behavioral changes, strategic plans can easily get off track.

The message was sent, loud and clear, that the values of the practice drive behaviors; behaviors drive customer/patient services; and customer service drives financial results, productivity, and higher performance. And who wouldn't want to be a part of that?

The four core values selected to drive the campaign spelled the word C.A.R.E.

Communication

Attitude

Respect

Empathy

Another evening presentation was held, and everyone attended. This time, the campaign was received with even more excitement and enthusiasm. Everyone got to participate and offer their input. Both teams were engaged throughout and were given specific boundaries and expectations when implementing the customer service tools, patient feedback surveys, and personal "vows" regarding the "My Commitment to C.A.R.E." sheet, signed and dated by all staff, which highlighted expected behaviors of the entire staff.

The campaign rollout was a success, and the "We C.A.R.E." promotional materials paved the way for ongoing team building events and strategic implementation of various collateral materials. In other words, by this time, everyone was a stakeholder in the successful outcome of the plan, and everyone had an important role to play—all while having fun in the process!

FIGURE 6.1 We C.A.R.E. Campaign Kit

A LEADER'S SIX-PART BLUEPRINT FOR CREATING A TACTICAL PLAN

Once you have created a strategic plan, it is time to create tactical plans to support it. Here is a process to make sure that your tactical plans align and are effective.

Part One: Setting the objectives of the tactical plans is the first and foremost step. The objectives should be achievable, measurable, and crystal clear for the team members. Each team member should have a clear understanding of the requirements and how the tactical plan will support the strategic plan. All results must be measureable and able to be tracked, so that the team will know how to evaluate the success and what success means for the organization. Finally, the objectives should be achievable; if the team is unsure if the goals and objectives are achievable, it will negatively affect the team's passion as the plan is executed. Keep in mind that a well-organized tactical planning team should have clearly defined goals and timelines that keep them from casting blame on others if the project is not successful.

Part Two: One of the prime steps that should happen prior to developing a tactical plan is to **evaluate potential threats to the project's completion,** or roadblocks that may come into place. Recognizing obstacles that may deter the objective, identifying them, and setting up plans to help control them, are necessities. Many businesses fail to do this step, and their tactical plans have a high propensity of failure.

Part Three: The next task in the tactical planning process is to **determine what resources are necessary** and evaluate what will be required to lead the team to success. If additional resources are needed, then upper management will need to be consulted for approval. Some of the resources that may be necessary are allocation of monies, intellectual power, or additional equipment—this is the step that is necessary to identify the need.

Part Four: There is a benefit to **learning from projects and team members who have accomplished similar tactical plans**. Having a culture of sharing in successes and failures and evaluating the results (often called a "postmortem") can assist in higher success rates for future tactical plans. Focusing on these learned lessons helps to create a culture of learning and knowledge. This can assist in creating the models, determining necessary tools, and allocating the resources that businesses use to provide to workers who are working on the achievable objectives. Communication is an important part of this step in the tactical planning process; it assists in the success and encourages both failure and success in the final analysis. Keeping in mind all of the identified obstacles and resources evaluated, you should verify frequently if the results are still clear, measureable, and achievable. And most importantly, you should remember to ask: Do these results support the strategic plan? If the tactical plans are not supporting the strategic plan, stop the project immediately, re-evaluate with leadership, and make an appropriate decision that aligns with the strategic plan.

Part Five: Have open communication sessions to gather great ideas from the team and make sure you express complete appreciation for the ideas they bring forth. This step helps team members bring their best ideas to the table. When the project members are allowed to bring in their own ideas, it adds individual accountability to the team members. It stresses that each team member is in charge of their assigned tasks and must meet the team deadlines for completion. Accountability becomes an important part of the tactical planning process and will lead to project success—it helps everyone to strive to reach goals, while pushing forward to obtain success and personal improvement.

Part Six: For the final step, you need to **build a contingency plan that can consider what could go wrong.** An important question you should ask is, "What would your team do if the project failed?" Smart leaders always have a contingency plan in case something goes awry. Without a back-up plan, the team is unsure where to go next. If and when the project fails to stay on schedule, determine with the team what changes need to be made so that it can get back on course. (If necessary, set new deadlines.)

Finishing the tactical planning projects can be challenging, especially when integrating them into the final project and finalizing a successful strategic plan. One thing that was not mentioned above was the frequency of the tactical planning meetings. This should be determined by the project leaders; the team should initially meet every week, then longer timelines between meetings can be set as long as everything is on schedule. Toward the end of the project, the team will most likely need to meet weekly again to keep all of the parts moving. Many of the meetings will be short and to the

point. These meetings move the project along quickly and keep every team member accountable to their piece of the project. Team members who are falling behind are quickly identified and can be corrected or replaced on the project team. There is also peer pressure among the team since no one wants to show up at a meeting unprepared and let the rest of the team down. Reaching the end of the tactical planning sessions and seeing the ultimate goal of a successful strategic plan can bring great celebration to an organization. Reaching this goal is easy by implementing the six steps!

Questions for Discussion: Developing Strategic and Tactical Plans

1. What is the purpose of strategic planning?
2. What is the purpose of tactical planning?
3. How can leaders best share the responsibilities of strategic and tactical planning with lower levels of management?
4. How should the rollout of a strategic plan take place?
5. How should the rollouts of the tactical plans take place?
6. How can an organization's leaders measure whether people, departments, and organizational goals are in appropriate alignment?
7. Why are mission and vision statements important to the development of a strategic and tactical plan?

Wrapping It Up

This chapter has taught that a well-crafted, big-picture strategic plan driven by smaller tactical plans is a living document of action—action that will be carried out with zeal and commitment to the greater benefit of all members of the organization. Once your leaders have a good feel for writing and rolling out their strategic and tactical plans, they will be ready to embark on another critical planning process, one that develops tomorrow's leaders today. That process is succession planning, and it is the topic of the next chapter.

Bonus for your leaders: For more information on strategic and tactical planning, write to Stephanie Montanez at Steff@HumanResourcesSources.org, or by visiting www.HumanResourcesSources.org for more information and guidelines.

Chapter 7

Succession Planning Takes Talent Management

Succession planning is no longer just a concern for company presidents, CEOs, or other top management; it affects leaders at all levels within the organization. In exhilarating times of rapid change, there's little time for leaders to stop what they're doing and suddenly start grooming leaders. Instead, leaders today must be growing and developing potential leaders at all levels and simultaneously doing their own jobs.

Succession planning (also referred to as continuity planning by some) is key to the future success of every organization, but working on a plan to replace themselves is probably not at the top of most leaders' priority lists. The irony is that the only real way a leader can advance is by having someone ready to fill his or her shoes when the opportunity arises. This thinking may require a paradigm shift on the part of some of your leaders.

Here is where your leaders will learn about the art of succession planning and the steps necessary to put one into place. Every leader must prepare to pass the baton willingly and without hesitation. If your program does not include this element, here is your chance to supplement your leadership development program to emphasize this vital element.

What You Will Learn in This Chapter:

- Real-world succession planning. Leaders must
 - implement successful talent management while enhancing a commitment to developing leaders from within
 - initiate succession planning rather than simply hiring replacements
 - appreciate the organization's culture as a competitive and useful tool
 - study the best-of-the-best world-class organizations and their methods.
- Critical components of succession planning. Leaders must
 - attract talented workers
 - grow leaders from within the organization
 - offer ongoing career development opportunities.

A CALIFORNIA LEADER IN SUCCESSION PLANNING: SUTTER HEALTH PAVES THE WAY

After interviewing Erika Duffy, Managing Consultant of Executive Development Programs and Program Leader for Sutter Health's Leadership Academy in Sacramento, California, we knew right away that her organization's take on a world-class succession planning strategy deserved a mini-case study on the organization's brilliant road map to ensure ongoing success. We will begin our discussion on succession planning by examining this organization's ability to blend talent management with the inevitability of passing the baton.

Sutter Health is a world leader in succession planning and talent development. Serving patients and their families in more than 100 northern California cities and towns, Sutter Health doctors, not-for-profit hospitals, and other healthcare service providers share resources and expertise to advance healthcare quality and access. The Sutter Medical Network includes many of California's top-performing, highest-quality physician organizations as measured annually by the Integrated Healthcare Association. Sutter-affiliated hospitals are regional leaders in cardiac care, women's and children's services, cancer care, orthopedics, and advanced patient safety technology.

Identifying Future Leaders Is a Critical Part of Leadership Transformation

Erika Duffy told us that several years ago, Sutter Health began taking bold steps to transform healthcare. As part of its strategic plan, the organization embraced a vision to deliver high-value services by providing expert, personalized care that is both high quality and affordable.

"In the years ahead," says Duffy, "delivering high-quality care as efficiently as possible will become even more important. Under federal healthcare reform, the government will provide health coverage to 32 million uninsured Americans. Over the next decade, Medicare will reduce reimbursement to Sutter Health by nearly $2 billion. At the same time, the state of California faces a massive debt—and it is very possible that Medi-Cal will also reduce its payments to doctors and hospitals."

Sutter Health senior leaders recognized that every employee plays a vital role in improving healthcare and growing the system into a highly coordinated, integrated network of care. Sutter Health also recognized that many key employees and leaders were nearing retirement age. Identifying and developing future leaders remains a critical part of Sutter Health's transformation.

Dashboard Metrics and High Leadership Standards

An early step in Sutter Health's transformation included aligning the network's business objectives around a common set of dashboard metrics and leadership behaviors. The Sutter Health Dashboard measures **"what"** leaders must accomplish in the areas of finance, quality, growth, service, community, and people. The Sutter Health Leadership Standards define **"how"** leaders should perform their duties by identifying

The Dashboard Metrics Approach

Leaders are often exposed to a mind-boggling array of metric systems (finite measures of performance). Whether they use spreadsheets, graphs, models, charts, or financials, leaders must keep their fingers on the pulse of what is happening. We recommend a dashboard metrics approach because it refers to a limited set of important and relevant numbers that leaders need to comprehend the status of things in the moment.

When you are driving your car, you glance at your dashboard to quickly gather a few "localized" numbers that tell you how smoothly things are running—speedometer, gas gauge, oil levels, and so on. These are all measurements that you, the driver, have complete control over. If you run the car to empty, or push your speed to 100 mph, there are consequences. Leadership teams who use the same dashboard metrics system know exactly how they are doing, when they are doing it.

essential leadership behaviors. The Dashboard and Leadership Standards together define success for leaders.

Cultivating Future Generation Leaders

"To successfully meet strategic business goals, every organization must have the right people, with the right skills and behaviors, in the right positions at the right time—the ultimate goal of succession planning," emphasizes Duffy.

As Baby Boomers near retirement, Sutter Health—like numerous other organizations—will face the loss of many strong and vital employees. To cultivate strong current and future generation leaders, Sutter Health has built key people-oriented processes and programs systemwide. At the heart of these people processes/programs stands a renewed philosophy to develop leaders from within. These three integral and interrelated processes and programs support Sutter Health's success in transforming its culture and developing its next generation of leaders:

- integrated talent management system
- talent review and succession planning process
- Leadership Academy program.

An Integrated Talent Management System

It's clear that common systems and processes are vital components of Sutter Health's strategic goals. After establishing a common set of Dashboard Metrics and essential leadership behaviors, Sutter Health installed an integrated, web-based talent management system. Internally branded as Performance Success and Development Process (PSDP), the system supports networkwide goal alignment, performance management, and succession planning around Sutter's core metrics and behaviors.

Using PSDP, Sutter Health leaders easily cascade organizational objectives to help ensure alignment of employee performance objectives with the organization's business

goals. The talent management system also improves employee efficiency, creates a "paperless" performance review process, and enables and integrates succession planning with performance reviews and development planning.

Talent Review and Succession Planning

The Sutter Health talent review and succession planning process is completed annually as part of the overall talent management process. In quarter one, performance reviews are conducted for the previous year. This is followed by talent review and succession planning in quarter two. In the third quarter, the focus is on development planning; and in the final quarter, employees work on goal setting for the upcoming year.

Through a series of facilitated talent review meetings, leadership teams assess and discuss leadership talent (an employee's performance and potential) using a nine-box grid. The meetings also provide a forum for open discussion of potential successors to key roles and development opportunities and needs for an identified successor.

The team enters decisions and data from the meetings into PSDP, where reports and additional analysis help identify leadership bench strengths and gaps, readiness of identified successors, high potentials, and development plans. "These talent inventory reports support Sutter Health's Human Resource leaders as they seek internal candidates for critical roles across our system," adds Duffy.

What Gets Measured Is What Gets Done— Driving Results at Sutter Health

Although Sutter Health's talent review and succession planning process continues to evolve, early outcomes show promising results. The network enjoys systemwide unity in identifying, assessing, developing, sourcing, and deploying talent. In 2005, only the top 300 senior leaders were assessed, potential successors were discussed only at the most senior levels, and data was housed in a home-grown spreadsheet. Today, more than 2,100 leaders are assessed annually, ranging from frontline managers to senior-level leaders. In 2003, Sutter Health filled 28 percent of senior-level positions with inside talent—by 2011, the average was 65 percent.

A Top-Notch Leadership Academy to Support Succession Planning

Identifying and developing leaders from within the organization is another important component to achieving Sutter Health's goals. The system's Leadership Academy offers an opportunity for Sutter Health's next generation of leaders to develop their skills through an intense, year-long executive readiness program. Comparable in time, effort, and development to an executive MBA program, Sutter Health's Leadership Academy is a key stepping-stone to gaining senior-level positions in the organization. Participants are selected through Sutter's annual talent review and succession planning process.

Launched in 2004, the Leadership Academy was redesigned in 2007 to enhance and advance the program. Key components of its current design include:

- group learning
- action learning challenges with real Sutter Health opportunities and challenges sponsored by members of the System Management Team
- executive coaching with 360-degree feedback
- learning from scholars and executive leaders, internal and external to Sutter Health
- case studies
- books and articles on current and classic thinking about leaders and leadership development.

The measures of success for the Leadership Academy include:

- promotion rates into senior-level positions
- assignments to key system initiatives
- individual leader effectiveness.

According to Duffy, as of September 2011, more than one-third of Leadership Academy graduates (2008 classes and beyond) have been promoted into senior-level roles. The Leadership Academy alumni network is more than 120 strong with six graduating classes as of July 2011.

Sutter Health attributes the success of its Leadership Academy to two key factors.

- Strong support and participation of Sutter Health's CEO and System Management team: As guest presenters, sponsors of action learning challenges, and leaders committed to providing honest and direct feedback to students, their engagement lends credibility and confidence to the process.
- High-caliber participants: Sutter Health's discerning selection and screening process ensures that only the highest-potential candidates participate in the program.

It Doesn't End Here

Duffy concludes that several years ago, Sutter Health set out on a journey to deliver the highest-quality patient care in an affordable way. "People play a key role in achieving these goals. By aligning strategic objectives, implementing a successful talent-management process, and enhancing its commitment to developing leaders from within, Sutter Health has started on a path to leading care delivery transformations," Duffy adds.

For more information and ways to track this industry leader, or for more on the not-for-profit Sutter Health network, please visit: www.SutterHealth.org, www.Facebook.com/SutterHealth, www.YouTube.com/SutterHealth, or www.Twitter.com/SutterHealth.

SUCCESSION PLANNING VERSUS REPLACEMENT HIRING

It's important that your leaders do not confuse succession planning with replacement hiring, which commonly happens in organizations. Replacement hiring is just that: "We've got to replace her right away, so let's fill this position now!" Notice the angst in that decision? This is exactly what you want your leaders to avoid.

Succession planning requires continually striving to identify and develop talent that will carry the organization's strategic planning into the next generation of leadership. Succession planning ensures continuity for all leadership positions by developing a plan that builds star talent from within.

Here's an example that clearly compares the difference between the two. It will help your leaders stay focused on planning the transition of employees to leadership positions, rather than just quickly replacing an employee or filling a vacancy.

Replacement Hiring Is...	Succession Planning Is...
• reacting to fill a position fast	• being proactive and planning in advance who will step in to fill a vacancy
• a narrow and temporary approach to filling a position	• in sync with the organization's overall strategic plan and goals
• a substitution	• a renewed commitment
• trying to head off a crisis and to cope	• long-term talent building
• inflexible	• flexible
• hiring the best of the worst	• hiring the best

Continuity

Continuity and well-thought-out planning are going to be critical to the future of your leaders. However, those easily can be dropped when people are busy and their organizations are changing and moving at breakneck speeds. One way to ensure that the job gets done is to help your leaders chunk it all down into parts. That requires separating the five most important components of the succession planning process:

- attracting and retaining the best talent
- building leaders from within the organization
- developing the careers of potential successors
- implementing a strong, long-term talent development and management process
- encouraging employee development plans and leadership coaching.

ATTRACTING AND RETAINING THE BEST TALENT

Don't let your leaders be fooled. Succession planning starts first and foremost with attracting, hiring, and retaining the best talent available. Leaders should adopt the attitude that they always will be looking for star talent—not just when there's an opening to fill. Scouting for talent should be taken very seriously. Leaders who do this consistently seldom lack quality candidates. Review the Sutter Health mini-case study early in this chapter. Their words of wisdom may save you years of time and baptism by fire.

Selling Culture as a Hiring Tool

This is where your leaders can learn to combine the organization's culture with their individual scouting efforts. Promoting the most attractive aspects of the culture is an effective tool in gathering talent. It can draw applicants to an organization no matter how short the supply of labor. (You'll find more about how this works in chapter 9, "Leading With Integrity, Values, Intuition, and Stronger Ethics.")

But leaders can't hire people who don't apply, and direct financial incentives are not the only things that attract good people. More organizations today attract and retain star talent with cultural values that honor their employees and help them to balance both home and work lives, and by offering supportive perks such as on-site day care programs and stock options.

Ask your leaders to discuss what some of their organization's cultural selling points are. Have them come up with a list of ways they can effectively sell the organization's culture to attract qualified job candidates in various departments.

Hiring Smart Means Hiring Close to Home

When companies hire smart, they start their recruiting efforts close to home, among their own workers. Such employee referral techniques have gained great popularity as effective employee recruiting tools, in organizations big and small. More than 40 percent of all new hires at Microsoft come from employee referrals. The philosophy is that an organization's employees want to spend time, both personally and professionally, with people like themselves.

It would be worthwhile to initiate discussion with your leaders regarding the pros and cons of hiring friends of employees, and how they might turn such an idea into effective employee recruiting.

Finding star talent doesn't stop with hiring employee referrals in some companies—it goes a step further. Organizations with advanced hiring practices encourage family members of employees to join the team. The theory is that blood is thicker than water, and who better to hire than the relatives of your organization's superstar talent! Successful companies that encourage leaders to use the gene pool as a talent pool believe that families who work together often stay together, and that keeping families together can sometimes work as an effective retention advantage.

Regardless of your organization's rules for hiring relatives, this method of recruitment has definitely become a growing trend and merits discussion among your leaders. Discuss in depth your leaders' opinions on the matter. Ask what their concerns might be if they were to hire their employees' relatives and what good experiences they may have had with nepotism in the workplace.

If your leaders agree that it's wise to tap their employees' gene pool when expanding their staff, here is a word of caution: Have them set a rule early on that one family member cannot supervise another. Doing so can eliminate possible uncomfortable situations or favorable treatment of relatives.

Model for Smarter Hiring

This is a good time to ask your leaders to reflect on their years of hiring. Have them analyze what separates their star talent from their minimum producers. In other words, what separates the great hires from the not-so-great hires? In every industry, whether finance, healthcare, computers, transportation, or hospitality, the answer to what separates star hires from mediocre hires can be summed up in one word: attitude!

Have your leaders study the steps in the following hiring model and use these best practices to create a successful hiring model of their own.

Step 1: Hire for attitude and train for skill. It all boils down to this: What people know is far less important than who they are. Cutting-edge organizations like Cantor Fitzgerald, Zappos, Pixar, Nordstrom, Southwest Airlines, Rosenbluth International, Nucor Steel, and Whole Foods Market believe that successful hiring is a matter of finding people with the right mindset or attitude, not simply experience. The basic belief is that people with the right attitude can always be trained in the matters they need to learn. A bad attitude is something you can't easily un-train.

So how do companies gauge attitude? Interviewers say they give people a chance to show a sense of humor and to declare passion for what's meaningful in their lives. Some organizations begin identifying a candidate's attitude from the minute he or she walks in the door the receptionist may ask questions of an interviewee and later report both responses and attitude to the interviewer.

Step 2: Believe in the Popeye Principle. The Popeye Principle relays that the cartoon character Popeye the sailor probably was right when he said, "I yam what I yam." The most common mistake that leaders make when interviewing someone else is to be taken in by the candidate with a glowing résumé—all of the right skills and experience but none of the right attitude or mindset. Never hire someone on the belief that they can be changed. They can't. Almost any time a leader thinks that he or she can change a potential employee, it's a serious mistake. Basic personal traits tend not to change. Maybe you've heard the phrase: "That zebra won't lose its stripes anytime soon."

Step 3: Use behavior to predict behavior. For decades, researchers have tracked the behaviors of people by studying various personality types, observing actions, and interviewing friends and families. The conclusions? The best predictor of future behavior is past behavior. That is not to say that people do not change for the better and grow in a positive direction, but a leader may use a person's past behavior to get a hint of how he or she will act in future situations.

Rule #1 when interviewing: Do not ask theoretical questions. For example, a query like "What would you do if...?" only invites a person's hopes and dreams. A good rule of thumb when interviewing is to "stay out of the *woulds*." Take the time to craft productive interview questions that narrowly define what a candidate has done or achieved under specific circumstances. You will be probing for desirable behaviors and competencies that help identify star talent. For example, ask, "When have you worked under extreme pressure to meet a deadline and then missed it? Tell me the specific circumstances and what you learned from the experience."

Hire for Attitude Sample Interview Questions

1. How would others describe your attitude? What adjectives would they use? (Look for creative answers with energy and real enthusiasm.)

2. When have you used your attitude on the job to reverse a negative environment or situation?

3. What would your toughest critics tell me about your attitude and its specific impact on others? Describe your impact and its effect on people around you.

4. What do you do to get in the right frame of mind and keep that frame of mind, even on tough days? Describe your techniques and be specific.

5. What have you read or seen that exemplifies an amazing attitude you'd like to emulate? Who do you know who sets that example constantly? What have you learned from them about the importance of a positive attitude on the job?

6. How do you rate the importance of a great attitude on a scale of 1-10? (Look for someone who says 10.)

7. Tell me about a time when your attitude completely changed everything for the better. Provide specifics.

8. When have you learned from bad attitudes and their negative impact on people? Does a bad attitude, in your opinion, cost the company money, time, and productivity? How so? How would you turn the tables fast and effectively?

Targeted selection is a popular hiring tool based on this step. It rests on the principle that the best way to select people who will succeed in an organization is to identify the competencies and behavioral characteristics of the organization's star performers and then go after people with those same qualities. (How to understand and identify core competencies is discussed in detail in chapter 4.)

Step 4: Implement peer hiring. Whole Foods Market, a publicly held company whose profit margins are approximately 50 percent higher than those of the average grocery chain, not only boasts more than a billion dollars in annual sales, but boasts about its hiring process, too. People are not just hired at the nation's biggest natural foods supermarket chain; they have to be voted in by a team of their peers or fellow employees.

With the heightened worry about organizational fit, interviewees frequently are being quizzed by the people with whom they'll actually work. This is taking place at every level within the organization. For example, pilots and flight attendants at New York–based JetBlue Airways interview candidate pilots. Input from a candidate's potential colleagues is considered valuable information to most organizations seeking long-term relationships with their employees.

Step 5: Try simulating the job. Simulation or task performance has become another popular tool used in the model for hiring star performers. In South Carolina, BMW built a simulated assembly line. Over a period of 90 minutes, job candidates get

an opportunity to perform several job-related tasks, and those who don't meet the requirements necessary in BMW's rigorous workplace are not hired. Other manufacturers, such as Subaru, Toyota, and Cessna, have initiated the same process.

Remind your leaders that this model for smarter hiring is a thumbnail sketch of the hiring process. Each leader should devise a model for smarter hiring based on the organization's existing hiring program and on the specific competencies required in the jobs for which he or she will be hiring. (Refer your leaders to chapter 4.)

BUILDING LEADERS FROM WITHIN THE ORGANIZATION

Now that you've thoroughly covered one of the most critical components of effective succession planning—finding and hiring great people—it's time to address the second critical component: building leaders from within the organization. The goal here is to maximize and identify current and future talent who already work in your organization, and then select your dream team from among them.

For discussion purposes, ask your leaders how they would go about replacing a key position in their department if suddenly it were to become vacant. Then ask how they would fill that same position if they knew it was going to open a year later. Look for gaps in their preparedness when it comes to planning for succession.

As President John F. Kennedy once said, "The time to repair the roof is when the sun is shining." That sound advice applies when preparing your leaders to establish a systematic means for replacing key leaders with qualified incumbents before the need arises. Doing so requires identifying:

- key positions
- critical competencies
- potential successors
- the ideal team.

Identifying Key Positions and Critical Competencies

For years, organizations have focused primarily on management positions in their succession planning, with the CEO position taking top priority. Today we know that succession planning must be carried out for leadership positions at all levels.

To introduce this concept, use the following chart to help your leaders identify specific positions that they now should be preparing for succession. Have them start the process by listing their own positions first. Remember, the only way a leader can advance is to have someone ready to fill his or her shoes when the opportunity presents itself. Next, have leaders identify the specific competencies necessary to perform the jobs they've listed. Help your leaders in doing this by directing them to the "performance builder" tool in chapter 19. This tool was designed to uncover employees' competencies and strengths as well as their areas of needed improvement.

Point out that an employee's strengths will help determine his or her potential for succession, and that areas needing improvement will call attention to what must be addressed in the career development portion of the succession plan. Also have your leaders list the names of potential successors on this chart.

Call to Action: Leaders—Train a Replacement Your First Day On the Job!

When it was announced that Myra deGersdorff, then general manager of the Kansas City Ritz-Carlton Hotel, would be leaving her post to take over the hotel operations at another Ritz-Carlton property, the transition was accepted among the ranks without the slightest twinge of employee anxiety, and it was handled with great ease.

When asked how she would quickly prepare her successor to run the highly successful and profitable property that she'd helped shape over a period of three years, deGersdorff responded, "That's easy. I've been training my successor since the day I took this position." **The Ritz-Carlton requires that every leader hire and train his or her own replacement the moment he or she takes on a leadership position anywhere in the company.** "That way, when any one of us is promoted or transferred, or even leaves the company, hotel operations continue running smoothly and our customers never pay the price for a change we have going on in management," says deGersdorff.

Identifying Potential Successors

When identifying potential successors for a position, point out that sometimes a leader has to look beyond the obvious to find the highest potential within the organization. For example, some employees simply stand out as superstars from the start, and so it is often these folks who get the greatest opportunities for advancement. However, there almost always are supporting players who quickly can be developed into superstar talent with a little work on their performance quality. The potential is there but your leaders will have to look a little harder for it. Remind leaders that the best successor's talent might not necessarily lay right at the surface. Leaders have to think of themselves as continuous excavators of people potential.

Identifying Your Dream Team

Before career development plans can be prepared for potential successors, key positions and priority of successors must be established. Have your leaders make a "dream team chart" to name specific key positions and the top three possible successors for each position. Rank those successors in the following order:

#1. _____ is ready to step in immediately.

#2. _____ will be ready in one to two years.

#3. _____ should be ready in three to five years.

Your leaders should complete this exercise for all "key positions" on their team. When your leaders have completed their lists, the next step will be to determine the professional development needed for these contenders.

Targeting Key Positions for Succession

Key Positions	Competencies Required to Do the Job	Potential Successor	Career Development
My Position Here:			
CEO			
President			
Sr. Vice Presidents			
•			
•			
Vice Presidents			
•			
•			
Directors			
•			
•			
Staff Management			
•			
•			
Supervisors			
•			
•			
Team Leaders			
•			
•			
Coaches			
•			
•			
Sales Team			
•			
•			
Technicians			
•			
•			
Customer Service Representatives			
•			
•			
Administrative Support			
•			
•			

DEVELOPING THE CAREERS OF POTENTIAL SUCCESSORS

A career development program for a potential successor is the third critical component to succession planning. Your leaders' ability to meet the organization's internal promotion needs will depend on how well prepared the organization is to meet each potential successor's individual needs for advancement.

A well-conceived career plan can bridge the gap between a potential successor's present talent and his or her future ability. Your leaders should be prepared to commit to a detailed employee learning and development program. Career development should focus not on job title but on specific competencies required to do the work. The following career development form can be used by your leaders in preparing their employees for ongoing development and readiness.

Career Development Tool

Name of successor: _____

Present position: _____

Length of time in this position: _____

Key position successor is preparing for: _____

Successor's career goals: _____

Career development objectives mutually agreed on by successor and leader: _____

Targeted methods of successor's career development, specific steps to be taken, and targeted dates of completion: _____

Measurement method to be used for this position: _____

The goal during the career development process is to have your leaders' potential successors eventually reach a level of readiness that enables them to step into the position and manage all of its responsibilities.

There are many methods of professional development and growth. Have your leaders review the following list of suggested career development options and add to the list their own ideas and suggestions. Career development options include:

- professional employee development and coaching programs
- in-house and off-site training programs
- public seminars
- job rotation
- mentoring and coaching programs
- shadowing

- computer-based training programs
- one-on-one customized coaching
- team training
- degree-granting programs
- self-directed learning
- continuing education
- study groups
- distance learning.

Check out Anne Bruce's bestselling book on creating employee development plans, *Perfect Phrases for Employee Development Plans* (McGraw-Hill), and you'll find lots of real-world templates and tools for setting up both personal and professional plans on the spot.

Career Development at the Bank of Montreal

A leader in encouraging essential career development within the organization, the HR department at the Bank of Montreal offers employees access to its Possibilities Center. That name alone sums up the organization's approach to growing and developing people to reach their full potential. The center is used as a key resource in preparing employees for succession opportunities. What will you name your center?

THE ULTIMATE TEST: PASS THE BATON AND GET OUT OF THE WAY

The ultimate test of your leaders' true commitment to the organization's future and to developing an effective succession program will come when it's time to pass the baton and get out of the way. Some leaders spend a lifetime preparing their followers to take over, but when the time comes to let someone else take the lead, they can't do it. Teach people that being a winning leader means having confidence in what they've taught others, and then trusting that the job will get done.

Quick Quiz on Succession Planning

Circle True or False.

1. Succession planning starts when an employee leaves or retires.

 True False

2. Succession planning is also referred to as continuity planning.

 True False

3. Succession planning creates an ongoing talent pool from which to draw.

 True False

4. One of the many benefits of a succession plan is that it helps to ensure the success of the organization and its people.

 True False

5. When implemented correctly, a succession plan eliminates replacement hiring.

 True False

6. Life's events always take precedence over a person's job.

 True False

7. An organization's culture has nothing to do with attracting and keeping talented workers.

 True False

8. There is a trend toward employee referrals in hiring.

 True False

9. Nepotism will surely kill a succession plan.

 True False

10. A good question to ask a job candidate is, "What would you do if you were hired for this position tomorrow?"

 True False

11. Job simulation has become a popular way to audition potential employees in real-world scenarios.

 True False

12. Peer hiring is a bad idea that easily can backfire.

 True False

13. Hiring to competencies is part of a solid succession plan.

 True False

14. Job rotation and mentoring are two effective career development methods.

 True False

15. The ultimate test of a leader's success is being able to pass the baton.

 True False

Quick Quiz Answer Key:

1. False	4. True	7. False	10. False	13. True
2. True	5. True	8. True	11. True	14. True
3. True	6. True	9. False	12. False	15. True

Questions for Discussion: The Art of Succession Planning

1. Describe the difference between succession planning and replacement hiring.
2. What are the dangers to an organization that doesn't have a succession plan in place?
3. What are the three critical components of a succession plan?
4. What are some of the ways a leader can identify a potential successor?
5. Why is succession planning important at every leadership level?
6. Why is employee development and career planning important to succession?

Wrapping It Up

With increasing regularity, many organizations are citing succession planning as one of their top leadership priorities because it accomplishes three objectives that we've discussed in this chapter: 1) it sets the tone for identifying potential star talent internally, 2) it encourages employee growth and development, and 3) it creates a continuously stocked talent pool from which new leaders can be drawn.

So now that your leaders are attracting and hiring the best candidates, how do they plan to manage all of that valuable human capital? In the following chapter, we will cover some essential ways for your leaders to manage by leveraging your organization's culture.

Leadership and Corporate Culture: Strategies for Developing Human Capital

THE WHOLE-Y GRAIL OF CORPORATE CULTURE

Whole Foods values its corporate culture and human capital big time!

According to leadership, most companies do not want "average" as part of their culture or human capital. Whole Foods believes that every single hire has the potential to impact the company brand or the bottom line, in both large and small, and good and bad ways. This is why they hire the best of the best, never the best of the worst. It's all about hiring for attitude and training for skill. If you settle for less than your culture's standards, you will wind up with a systemic and toxic problem internally. That is an option at this market.

Companies like Whole Foods look to *complement* and *enhance* their corporate culture. They call this the "it" factor. The "it" factor is the result of developing top-notch human capital. If you shop here, like we do, you immediately have a "cultural experience" the moment you walk through Whole Foods' doors. Their leadership trains everyone to be positive and engaging. And it's immediately evident that Whole Foods values both its internal and external human capital.

Leaders need to be made aware that company culture has taken on a brand new meaning in the past decade. Today, it's becoming the norm for companies to embody proactive traits like fun in the workplace, casual dress (five days a week, not just on "casual Fridays"), corporate core values, and the freedom and encouragement for its people to achieve ongoing professional training, as well as personal growth. It's an organic process, never forced.

You cannot force culture. But you can infuse change in your work environment and influence a creative new approach. Culture is the culmination of your organization's core values, rites and rituals, rules, languages, processes, personality, and all of its leadership combined. Your organization's leadership—good or bad—is the most instrumental in creating corporate culture and influencing it to improve and get better. Leaders create the right conditions in which culture is encouraged to flourish. They do not create the culture itself.

A Culture Built on Doing the Right Thing, Because It's the Right Thing to Do!

Once upon a time, organic food could only be found in small specialty shops or at outdoor food stands run by semi-capitalistic hippies. But along came Texas-based Whole Foods Market and changed the landscape of grocery shopping by bringing in local organic farmers and their offerings, gourmet delights, and affordability.

Whole Foods exemplifies a strong corporate culture and a strong leadership that values its human capital. The organization has more than 51,000 employees, called "Team Members," and nearly 90 percent of those folks are full-time workers. Whole Foods has stores in almost 300 countries and in more than 38 states.

And here's the kicker. Whole Foods Market ranks on *Fortune*'s "100 Best Companies to Work For." And if you're wondering why, the average salaried employee rakes in more than $70,000 annually. Not bad for a grocery store. But it takes a lot more than salary to make that prestigious list. This culturally competent business values diversity and has more than 40 percent of its employees, women and minorities, telecommuting. Of course, if you're a checker, that might be tough. But there are other benefits, like the fact that Whole Foods pays for 100 percent of healthcare premiums and offers subsidies if you join a gym and get moving.

Managing Human Capital at Lands' End

Another great organization named by *Fortune* magazine as one of the top 100 companies to work for in America, Lands' End considers human capital management to be one of its most important leadership initiatives, and a defining part of its culture. Here is how the leaders at Lands' End manage human capital:

- "Down the Road" presentations are given at which employees learn what's going on with the company and share their ideas and suggestions for making the organization better.

- Previous and current leaders meet with creative staff off-site over several days to discuss what the company is all about.

- Quarterly meetings are conducted to inform employees about how the company is doing and what lies ahead.

- Monthly communications meetings are held with either the CEO, CFO, or COO. At those meetings employees are told what's going on with the organization and are asked to share their thoughts.

FIVE LEADERSHIP STRATEGIES FOR LEADING HUMAN CAPITAL AND CULTURE

In planning ahead, your leaders should understand the guiding role they will play within the organization and that the role is likely to become more complex and challenging as technology and global business requirements continue to evolve. If your leaders are to make the organization more efficient and successful, they will have to master the following five basic leadership strategies for managing human capital within the organization's culture. Using these tactics will help them galvanize their own leadership personalities to the organization's personality—its awesome culture.

Review the strategies below, and at the conclusion of this chapter, you'll find a job aid that leaders can use as a reminder to help them implement these crucial strategies.

Strategy 1: Take advantage of the organization's environment, location, and decor to design the perfect workplace around the people and talent you want to attract and keep. The organization's environment can be its greatest influence. It describes the organization's culture and how things are done there. The *environment*—meaning what's hanging on the walls; how core values, mission statements, and vision statements are displayed; the decor; and how special artifacts are showcased—is a powerful tool. Leaders can customize and design it to attract and retain superstar workers by creating a feeling of family, warmth, friendliness, safety, or whatever cultural message the organization's leadership wishes to convey. The environment can prompt people to say, "That's a place I'd love to work!" or "This is a place I am proud to be a part of and where I want to stay."

Strategy 2: Put it out there! Prominently display the organization's core values and principles for all the world to see. Values and principles are the soul and spirit of any organization's culture. Core values and principles are not some afterthought to enhance culture or manage human capital, but rather they are the foundation upon which the organization operates and leads, clearly defining its own unique corporate character. They need to be shouted with pride to both internal and external customers.

Strategy 3: Promote and encourage heroism and develop situational heroes who personify the culture, its values, and principles. America's companies need heroes because heroes don't just manage—they create cultures with great vitality and optimism for tomorrow. Situational heroes rise to an occasion to embrace change and leap into uncharted territory, blazing new trails and enthusiastically demonstrating for others what lies ahead. This may be for just a moment, or such a hero may go on performing acts of heroism for years, if the environment encourages it.

Developing situational heroes doesn't involve managing people; it involves managing intellectual capital and infiltrating the culture with handpicked people who model optimum workplace behavior. Situational heroes not only influence others; they also inspire and bring out the best in people with their simple and humble actions, or their undeniably brave

> **Key Point:** *A situational hero is someone who rises to the occasion and enhances the organization's culture with his or her behavior.*

Southwest Airlines Encourages and Celebrates Heroes

Southwest Airlines certainly is known for its colorful and vibrant culture. Almost a decade ago, the airline devised a way to identify and honor some of its unsung situational heroes who perform positive and influential acts of goodness behind the scenes. Southwest created a recognition program that fit beautifully with their culture: "Heroes of the Heart." Each year, a behind-the-scenes work group at the airline, such as technical services or customer service coordinators, is presented with the Heroes of the Heart award. It's Southwest's way of saying "This is what's important around here" to the employees who rarely are seen by the general public and who don't hold a high profile within the organization.

and vigorous feats of courage and servant leadership. It's critical for organizations to identify and encourage heroes so that they may shape and fine-tune the organization's culture on a people-to-people basis, from the heart.

Key Point: *Looking through the lens of the media, some leaders have come to believe that heroes are the people with charisma. To the contrary, however, organizational heroes come in many shapes and sizes— from shy and quiet to bold and hard-nosed. Situational heroes represent a wide variety of people and personalities, and charisma is not a requisite of the job.*

Strategy 4: Appreciate and share with others the rites and rituals of the organization. The rites and rituals of an organization are demonstrations of its culture in action. They also provide an effective vehicle of ongoing communications among workers. The rites and rituals honor employees and inspire innovative thinking over conventional wisdom. Rites and rituals are absolutely necessary in an organization. Without expressive events and celebrations, an organization will die. Ceremonies and traditions are to the organization's culture what music is to dance, or the lead character is to a novel: The two go hand in hand. Without traditions and rituals, an organization's values and principles will have little or no impact.

Examples of what rites and rituals might look like in an organization may include a variety of events and ceremonies, such as the following:

- Halloween costume parties
- awards banquets
- walk-the-talk awards
- community involvement and charitable causes
- annual conferences
- CEOs who give presentations to the field every year
- sales contests

- softball teams
- well-known anecdotes and company stories
- new-hire orientation
- company picnics
- annual retreats
- strategic planning sessions
- verbal rituals
- day-to-day rituals.

Whether it's a cultural extravaganza or a simple "Way to go!" for passing a particular milestone, performing the rites and rituals of the organization will help build a

stronger culture and encourage people to produce greater results through higher performance.

Strategy 5: Create a culture council or culture committee. Build a culture network that keeps the organization's spirit alive and cherished.

We've worked with dozens of organizations who keep their culture alive and well through culture councils and culture committees. And it works! The selected group makes sure that the company's history, special celebrations, and rituals are carried out and passed on to new hires. Other terms you can use include cross-functional culture team, and cultural competency committee. The purpose is to make it easier for your leaders to support the culture, boost morale, develop human capital, and simply have a great time at work!

> *When it comes to culture, you are on the outside what you are on the inside—no debate!*
> —Herb Kelleher, Founder, Southwest Airlines

Did you know that keeping the corporate culture alive has become a full-time job at many organizations? Some titles we've heard include manager of culture development, minister of culture, director of cultural competency and diversity, affinity council leader, and employee cultural resource manager.

Leadership Is Tested When Cultures Merge

In these days of frequent mergers, acquisitions, and joint ventures, it is not unusual for cultures to be combined overnight. When this happens, there are typically three possible directions that cultural shifting will take. It's important that your leaders be aware of them.

1. **When east meets west and no one yields.** This happens when a merger or acquisition occurs and the two cultures decide to remain separate and keep their individual identities. Perhaps both cultures are so polarized that keeping them separate works in the best interest of its stakeholders. Such might be the case with America Online and *The Huffington Post*, a buy-out and merger that brings together two distinctly different cultures—one young, tattooed, and sporting tank tops and shorts, and the other embodying the more traditionally staid, button-down-collar mentality of the publishing and broadcasting worlds.

2. **Survival of the fittest prevails.** This takes place when there is one dominant culture that takes over after a merger. When Hewlett Packard bought Apollo, for instance, it trained Apollo's people quickly to adopt the "HP way." And that was that. The same scenario occurred when Intel bought one of DEC's semiconductor plants. Intel's management announced that the plant would now operate by Intel methods and culture from that point forward. These clearly were the dominant cultures.

3. **Integrated cultures blend.** Yes, two cultures can successfully blend with one another if they take the best of both cultures for the most desirable outcome following an acquisition or merger. One way of doing this is by benchmarking various systems and processes against each other to try to produce new and improved procedures. An example of doing this might be taking the best HRD (Human Resource Development) system from one organization and the information systems from the other.

THE POWER OF CULTURE AND HUMAN CAPITAL

If your leaders truly are going to understand the important role that the organization's culture will play in their leadership journey, they must see the culture and its human capital as a collective and powerful force made up of behaviors, values, personalities, environments, storytelling, and much more. Knowing that workers do not respond well to unpredictability, chaos, and change, your leaders can take full advantage of the organization's culture by using it as a dependable and stabilizing force whenever the ship starts to rock.

If your leaders learn to use the organization's culture effectively and depend on it as the most stable part of the organizational structure, they will stand a much better chance of surviving major changes with greater confidence and success.

Quick Culture Evaluation Exercise

For a quick evaluation of their organization's culture, have your leaders use this on-the-spot questionnaire:

1. What do you see, hear, and feel as you walk the corridors of the organization?

2. Describe the environment—e.g., architecture, artwork, decor, furniture.

3. What are the people wearing?

4. How are the people working together?

5. What are the organization's tales and stories, rites, and rituals?

Five Leadership Strategies for Managing Human Capital and Culture

Here is a job aid leaders can use as a reminder of how to implement crucial leadership strategies.

Strategy 1: Take advantage of the organization's environment to design the perfect workplace around the people and talent you want to attract and keep.

Strategy 2: Put it out there! Prominently display the organization's core values and principles for all the world to see.

Strategy 3: Promote and encourage heroism and develop situational heroes who personify the culture, its values, and its principles.

Strategy 4: Appreciate and share with others the rites and rituals of the organization.

Strategy 5: Create a culture council or culture committee. Build a culture network that keeps the organization's spirit alive and cherished.

Questions for Discussion: Managing Culture and Human Capital

1. What do an organization's culture and managing its human capital have to do with one another?
2. What does an organization's environment reveal about its culture?
3. What do an organization's rites and rituals, celebrations, and traditions have to do with sustaining its culture?
4. Can an organization's culture be changed easily? If not, why not?
5. What are some of the strategies that leaders use to influence and sustain culture?
6. What are the three directions an organization takes when cultures merge?

Wrapping It Up

This chapter has taught that in order to harness their followers' brainpower, your leaders will have to know where to find it and how to use it effectively within the specific cultural walls of the organization. In the next chapter, we'll consider some critical leadership attributes that should be active parts of an organization's culture: integrity, values, intuition, and stronger ethics.

INTEGRITY: THE HIGHEST FORM OF HUMAN INTELLIGENCE

Integrity has become a required characteristic behavior of leaders in today's society. In fact, integrity has been described by some organizational development professionals as the highest form of human intelligence. Integrity is not only an expansion of human honesty and trustworthiness, it is what remains when we strip away all of our credentials and reputation—our moral fiber and conscience, our principle beliefs and values. Elizabeth Dole, former president and CEO of the American Red Cross, underscored the meaning of integrity in saying, "Integrity is the one thing every person has 100 percent control over."

In some of America's top business schools, the pendulum may have swung when it comes to what's considered the academic ideal. Leadership courses and classes on entrepreneurship have become accepted curricula for teachers at America's most popular graduate schools. As a result, students are learning more than finance and marketing; they're now learning the important lessons of integrity, values, vision, ethics, and how to lead by example.

Northwestern University's Kellogg Graduate School of Management has successfully broken the stereotype of theory-based business school learning and plans on continuing the effort. Where students were once best known for their top grade point averages and business acumen, some are known for having flocked to take the highly publicized "Dynamics of Leadership" course taught by adjunct professors Oprah Winfrey and Stedman Graham, held a decade ago. Topics of the condensed 10-week leadership course they taught included learning what it means to be a leader, understanding personal visioning and applying it to reality, identifying your beliefs as a leader, and knowing your whole self. Business, marketing, and economics course may have changed over time, but the "emotional intelligence" curricula taught by Oprah and Stedman remain relevant as ever to this day. In fact, we'd go as far as to say that this was the pivotal Ivy League Business School "real-world" leadership program that shifted paradigms on B-school leadership curricula worldwide.

PEOPLE WILL DO WHAT THEY SEE THEIR LEADERS DO

The bottom line is this: People will do what they see their leaders do. This is the essential meaning of "leading by example." It is your responsibility to convey that important message to the leaders you are developing today, as well as to the leaders you'll be developing in the future. Let them know that their lives and jobs as leaders carry enormous responsibility and that the key criterion for their future success is integrity. By that, we mean doing the right thing by not succumbing to fair-weather morality or, as it's so eloquently stated in Pfizer Pharmaceutical's mission statement, "We must do more than simply do things right—we must also do the right things."

> *We will honor all commitments to our customers, employees, and shareholders. We will conduct our business with unwavering high standards of honesty, trust, professionalism, and ethical behavior. We will communicate what we know, when we know it.*
> —Avis, speaking on integrity

ROI = RETURN-ON-INTEGRITY

According to one small, privately held, global holding company that provides investment banking services, financing, and insurance to its niche clients, its most important asset is its great "tradition of trust," or its long-standing reputation for integrity in the marketplace. In accordance with that reputation, the corporation emphasizes that it will not tolerate lapses in ethics or integrity and that no one's personal bottom line is more important than the reputation and integrity of the firm.

The small Kansas City–based firm interprets the term *ROI* as "return-on-integrity." While this type of ROI may not appear on the organization's financial statements, the company believes strongly that return-on-integrity is worth protecting at any cost because it is the bedrock of the organization's prosperity and pride.

Is this ROI the bedrock of your organization's prosperity and pride? It should be. Ask your leaders to answer the following questions about integrity. Have them form teams for sharing ideas and brainstorming, and use their responses to prompt further discussion on the importance of integrity.

- A leader's integrity can be built or destroyed by many patterns of behavior. Why do you think it is important for a leader's behavior to be consistent?
- It is said that successful leaders are transparent, meaning that they do what they say, they walk the talk, or practice one hard and fast rule: Do what you say you're going to do. Why is this important to building a leader's integrity?
- What do you consider to be some of the essential characteristics of integrity, and why? (Examples include: personal conviction, truthfulness, courage.)
- In the words of the Peter Drucker Foundation, "Out of the marriage of humility and courage is born the child of integrity." Explain what this means to you as a leader.
- Leaders who possess integrity are not caught up in manipulative game playing or a constant state of comparison with others. Their security comes from within and gives certainty about which direction to take or which path to choose. How do you think a leader with integrity distinguishes between right and wrong, wisdom and foolishness?
- If you are a leader in a nonprofit organization, you probably are aware that society already expects greater integrity from you than from your counterparts in the general business community. The public's trust of tax exemption and contributions from people at all income levels require that leaders in nonprofit organizations adhere to the highest levels of integrity and ethics. How can you as a leader live up to this promise?
- There is a saying that trust within an organization can never be achieved without integrity. Explain what that means.
- As a leader, how do you plan to demonstrate ROI, or "return-on-integrity," to your organization? Be specific in your response.

After your leaders have completed this exercise and you have initiated an open discussion on the importance of integrity, instruct your leaders that you would now like

them to make a commitment to providing ROI to the organization. Have someone read aloud the following ROI pledge. Ask everyone in agreement with the pledge to sign and date it.

My Personal Commitment to Providing ROI (Return-on-Integrity)

I make my commitment to (name of your organization here), that as a leader in this organization, I will provide a return-on-integrity for the trust that has been placed in me, and to include, but not be limited to, the following behaviors and their positive outcomes: truthfulness, walking the talk, doing what I say I am going to do, honesty, accountability, reliability, ethical behavior, and doing unto others as I would have them do unto me. In addition, I will be clear in my personal convictions, values, and principles, and model these behaviors daily with purpose, while distinguishing right from wrong.

Signed: _____ Date: _____

Recognizing Behaviors That Lack Integrity

Ask your leaders to spend the next few weeks monitoring their character habits using the following checklist to note each time they act in contradiction to their pledge in one of the following ways:

- ☐ Neglecting to tell the whole truth
- ☐ Not fulfilling a promise
- ☐ Dropping the ball on completing an assignment or project
- ☐ Betraying a trust
- ☐ Treating someone in a manner in which you would not like to be treated.

Let this checklist remind your leaders of their human frailties—everyone falls off course now and then. Ask them to pay close attention to how their actions may not support their personal integrity and value systems.

As a developer of leaders in your organization, you must establish the highest ethical standards of behavior and conduct for your leaders. Be aware that the behavior and habits of the leaders you turn out will continue to be a direct reflection on your organization's quality of character.

Key Point: *You tell the world who you are by the integrity that lives within your organization's leaders.*

STAND FOR SOMETHING OR FALL FOR ANYTHING: THE VALUES-LED APPROACH

If values-led leadership has taught us anything, it is that organizations don't have to sacrifice social consciousness on the altar of maximized profits, and that values do translate into a healthy bottom line. It used to be that consumers bought products and services

despite how they felt about the companies that sold them. Today, however, know that a values-led organization appeals to consumers on more bases than just a well-advertised product or service that uses sporty cars and sex appeal to gain market share.

Convey to your leaders that a values-conscious organization transcends every purchase made by connecting with people and making them actually feel good about doing business with the organization and its people because of the values they hold.

Share these values-led examples with your leaders. The late Paul Newman's company donates to charity every penny of profit from his incredibly successful Newman's Own food line. One of Hershey's marketing campaigns included putting Treats for Treatment coupons in Sunday newspapers, then giving money to children's hospitals in exchange for each coupon redeemed. One car dealership donated a fleet of fuel-efficient cars to Tree People, a tree-planting organization in Los Angeles, and then planted a tree for each new car sold. Target gives away millions of dollars in profits each week to the communities in which they operate their stores.

Shared values tell everyone what the organization stands for and that its leaders subscribe to a clear and explicit philosophy of how to conduct themselves in business. Because your organization's values can influence greatly what employees actually do on the job, it is important to emphasize to your leaders their individual responsibility in shaping and enhancing the organization's value system.

Remind your leaders that polls continue to show that the most successful companies and their leaders place enormous emphasis on company values. Included in that group are the Fire Department of New York (FDNY); Saks Fifth Avenue OFF Fifth; Volvo; Target; Ben & Jerry's; McDonald's; Kellogg's; the Charleston, SC, Police Department; The Body Shop; Patagonia; Whole Foods Market; Odwalla; Newman's Own; Reebok; Johnson & Johnson; JetBlue; Intel; Starbucks; Amazon.com; Zappos; Disney; Virgin Group, Ltd.; and even the Chicago Bears. Some of these organizations go as far as to conduct social audits and publish statements of social responsibility.

Values at American Express

At American Express, all activities and decisions are based on and guided by what are called the American Express Blue Box Values:

- Placing the interests of clients and customers first.
- A continuous quest for quality in everything we do.
- Treating people with respect and dignity.
- Conduct that reflects the highest standards of integrity.
- Teamwork—from the smallest unit to the enterprise as a whole.
- Being good citizens in the communities in which we live and work.

Ben & Jerry's Social Mission Statement

To operate the company in a way that actively recognizes the central role that business plays in the structure of society by initiating innovative ways to improve the quality of life of a broad community: local, national, and international.

Underlying the mission of Ben & Jerry's is the determination to seek new and creative ways of addressing all three parts, while holding a deep respect for individuals inside and outside the company and for the communities of which they are a part.

Innovation Is Not Enough Without Values

We are reminded of what happens when corporate core values are lost when we consider some of the largest corporate scandals of our era, in contrast to some of the most vital successes.

First consider Enron: Once employing more than 22,000 people and serving as one of the foremost natural gas, electricity, communications, and paper companies in the world, revenue in the year 2000 was at nearly $101 billion, and *Fortune* magazine recognized the company as "America's Most Innovative Company" for six consecutive years. Fast forward to 2001, when the company was forced to declare bankruptcy after gross accounting fraud—a case that rocked worldwide trust in the way big businesses operated. What lay at the heart of this scandalous fall? We could boil the failure down to a lack of integrity among a core group of leaders, who apparently placed more value on personal gain than on more universally advantageous values such as empowering its employees to live better lives, leading by example, and modeling success through honest efforts and practices.

Innovation, Intuition, and Passion

In contrast, consider Apple, a company known for its unprecedented innovation. In a rare speech about corporate values delivered in 1997 at the launch of Apple's "Think Different" ad campaign, then-interim CEO Steve Jobs stated:

> To me, marketing is about values. This is a very complicated world. It's a very noisy world. And we're not going to get a chance to get people to remember much about us. No company is. And so we have to be really clear about what we want them to know about us.
>
> The way to do that is not to talk about speeds and fees. It's not to talk about bits and megahertz. . . . Our customers want to know "Who is Apple and what is it that we stand for?" Where do we fit in this world? And what we're about isn't making boxes for people to get their jobs done, although we do that well. . . . Apple is about something more than that. Apple at the core—its core value—is that **we believe**

that people with passion can change the world for the better. . . . And we have had the opportunity to work with people like that. We've had the opportunity to work with people like you, with software developers, with customers, who have done it. In some big and some small ways. And we believe that, in this world, people can change it for the better. And that those people who are crazy enough to think that they can change the world are the ones that actually do."

This campaign helped Apple turn around a reputation that had at times been struggling, and placed them on the Forbes "Most Admired Companies" list year after year. Apple is led from a place of values first—a value of passionately seeking to improve people's lives. Apple went so far as to reward its workers who contributed to this value, through the Apple Fellows program, awarded to employees who contributed exemplary leadership in their contributions to the world of personal computing.

The strength of Apple's brand has become less about the widgets they sell, and more about the way in which their brand proactively strives to push the envelope on what can be done for the people they serve. One of the driving forces in this value of "passion" is in Apple's intuitive way of developing products. The *Telegraph* reported in a January 20, 2011, article by Steve Lohr that Steve Jobs was asked what consumer and market research Apple had done to guide the development of the new product. "None," Jobs replied. "It isn't the consumers' job to know what they want." In other words, Jobs knew that he needed to use intuition to anticipate what customers would need or want and develop it for them.

In 2007, Jobs announced a name change from Apple Computer, Inc., to Apple, Inc., as they revealed that they would focus less on personal computers and more on the mobile phone industry. They have since been the pioneers in mainstreaming technology such as the touch screen, which is now integrated not only in their iPhones and iPads but in virtually every competitor phone carrier's equipment. Apple has revolutionized the way we use our technology and has made what was previously "techy" seem fun, alluring, and indispensable.

Forging a Value System

Alert your leaders that they now are going to forge a leader's value system, and that it will be of critical importance because they cannot perform in a manner that is inconsistent with what they believe in, how they see themselves, or what they hold as core values. To underscore that truth, start by explaining the following four facts of values-led leadership:

Fact 1: Our values reflect how we see ourselves.

Fact 2: To reach people and touch them, our values must have heart and soul.

Fact 3: Our values determine how we make our decisions.

Fact 4: Our values determine how we behave and how we spend our time and money (just take a look in your day planner and checkbook).

Identify the Organization's Core Values

Have your leaders list here the core values of the organization. If none have been formulated, have your leadership class form a list of its own. After each value has been listed, ask your leaders this question: If values-led leadership were a crime, would there be enough evidence to convict you?

Because your leaders have just learned the importance of reflecting their values by their behaviors, form two-person teams to describe on-the-job behavior that correlates with each of the core values they listed. The purpose here is to take each core value and make it a real-world experience to which everyone can relate.

JetBlue's 4 True Blue Facts About Values

- Values reflect how people view themselves.
- Values touch people; values must have heart.
- Values don't change and are not wishy-washy. They are a constant.
- Values are how we behave—how we spend our time and our money.

Facilitated by Anne Bruce in JetBlue training program.

BEST COMPANY REPUTATIONS STEM FROM VALUES, TRUST, AND INTEGRITY

According to *Fast Company*, "The 'Fast Track Leadership Survey' on Business Ethics and Integrity," 95 percent of people surveyed answered "yes" or "absolutely yes," when queried: "Do the ethics of the CEO play a meaningful role in the way business gets done?" The report listed three main reasons why participants in the survey cited certain leaders as being great. They stated that the leaders:

- embodied entrepreneurship as they created a legacy—most of the leaders in this group had built successful global businesses from the ground up
- believed in something strongly and worked hard to get to a goal
- showed tremendous "personal integrity and tenacity."

Financial integrity is also important in leadership. *Forbes* magazine publishes a list of the "100 Most Trustworthy Companies" each year, based on research by Audit Integrity, which analyzes more than 8,000 corporations traded on U.S. exchanges. Each company is given an "accounting and governance risk score," or AGR, which helps assess factors that have statistically related to shareholder risk. In 2010, www .Salesforce.com topped this list, causing CEO and chairman Marc Benioff to state: "Business transparency is incredibly important to our organization, and I'm therefore incredibly proud of this accomplishment."

Authors James Kouzes and Barry Posner point out in their book, *The Leadership Challenge* (Jossey-Bass), that organizational leaders must rally around a key set of common values. Corporations that share such values exceed other organizations distinctly in their job creation, price of stocks, profits, and revenue expansion. These values, they state, also foster a sense of pride, loyalty, and effectiveness.

This is a good time to tell your leaders that if they are going to develop a winning reputation for leadership they will need to notice what America's best organizations are doing to set themselves apart. Remind them that managers in a values-led organization model the example and don't expect others to do anything they wouldn't do. When your leaders model this walk-the-talk style of leadership, their followers naturally will hold them in high esteem.

ENCOURAGING YOUR LEADERS' INTUITION

The final part of this chapter focuses on the importance of encouraging your leaders to hone their intuitive feelings, their gut instincts. Why is that important? Isn't intuition an illogical activity? It might seem so because gut feelings are difficult to intellectualize and explain, but in interviews with leaders, many acknowledge the value of their intuitive abilities and have learned to pay close attention to that inaudible voice within.

Albert Einstein once said, "The really valuable thing is intuition." This could also be interpreted for your leaders to mean that trusting their gut feelings will help them develop keener perception and judgment on the job. In fact, integrity and values-led leadership practices both stem from our deepest gut feelings about what is right and how best to treat people.

> **Key Point:** *Intuition is a leader's reservoir of vision and instinct. By definition, the word* intuition *has in its root form the Latin word meaning "to look at" or "see," to "imagine" or "picture."*

A leader's intuition brings together what is familiar through knowledge and experience. As years pass, we each gain our unique perspective on a variety of situations. We listen, feel, smell, taste, and experience our environment, and it is the combination of all of that input that helps us develop our intuition or inner vision as leaders. Intuition isn't some mystical process. It is simply our human ability to take relevant impressions, experiences, and comparisons and sift through them almost automatically, arriving at a conscious or unconscious solution or approach to a problem. Intuition is a leader's internal compass. The more experienced a leader is, the faster he or she will sift through input and select the right direction to take. In fact, according to a survey by *PRWeek* (Burson-Marsteller), 62 percent of the CEOs queried reported leaning toward making business decisions based on intuition rather than on hard data analysis.

Intuiting for Leaders: Maximizing Your Internal Compass

Use the following exercise to help your leaders to gain a clearer understanding of their own intuitive abilities and how they are using or might use them in the future in their leadership positions. For this exercise, assign a partner to each leader.

With your partner, respond to the following questions:

- When you have a hunch, do you usually follow up on it? Describe a time when you had a hunch and decided to pursue it. What were the circumstances? What was the result of following your hunch?
- Was there ever a time when you didn't follow up on a hunch and then wished later that you had? What were the circumstances? What was the result of not following your hunch?
- When making decisions, do you consider your gut feelings, or do you ignore them by overanalyzing the situation? What are the results of your actions?
- Describe a time when you relied more on your gut feelings than on your actual experience. What occurred?
- Do you think there is a connection between intuition and good management, judgment, and wisdom? Why or why not?

Have your leaders and their partners share with the class their personal experiences in using their intuition and how they might continue to hone their intuitive talents and use those skills as a leader.

Encourage your leaders to build their awareness of intuiting as a logical process, to act on their intuitive instincts, and to use them to their advantage whenever possible. In doing so, they learn to trust themselves and, more importantly, to trust the internal compass and use it to find their way when feeling lost or without direction.

THE IMPORTANCE OF ETHICS WHEN GROWING LEADERS

Karen Eriksen, PhD, is the president and CEO of Eriksen Institute and the author of *Perfect Phrases for Creativity and Innovation*. We got a chance to discuss with her the popularity of ethics courses that are offered at top business schools around the world. We learned that businesses have finally come to understand that if they want to be successful and increase profits, a good deal of achieving that end result will depend on employing and developing ethical leaders.

Ethics and Character—It Boils Down to Economics

Businesses headed by leaders with character consistently and substantially outperform those without. According to researchers at Harvard Business School and DePaul University, these businesses:

- show four times the revenue gains long term
- demonstrate eight times the increases in their workforce
- show 12 times the increases in stock prices
- indicate 756 times the net income
- evidence three times larger market value added
- rank 14.8 percentiles higher on rankings of financial performance
- obtain 6.7 points higher on overall reputation scores.

The businesses' profitability results from:

- increased customer referrals
- improved recruitment and retention; employee and customer referrals
- decreased recruiting costs
- reduced misconduct, employee fraud, and absenteeism
- more positive and fruitful working relationships
- decreased trust- and equity-destroying scandal
- improved communication—makes information available that's necessary for good decisions.

Other organizations whose leadership commits to character improve their functioning and productivity for the same reasons.

We asked Eriksen how understanding the importance of ethics might apply to managers who are creating leadership development plans within the organization. "Ethical values, like trust, trustworthiness, integrity, fairness, and respect, are fundamental to who we are and to how we treat other people," says Eriksen. Therefore, not only do managers and leaders need to operate from a clear ethical base because it is the right thing to do, but because the trickle-down effect means that if they don't operate ethically, their employees won't either.

"Managers and leaders not only need to model behavior that reflects ethical values, they need to speak about values, offer recognition and promotion on the basis of values, and plan training and meetings in which employees learn to apply ethical values to everyday situations. They must act to end unethical behavior and require employees to include growth in character as part of their leadership development plans," she adds.

Eriksen goes on to say that once a company had gone through some processes to become clear on the ethical values they were going to adopt, stand for, post, have discussions about, and so on, then managers and leaders could require employees to indicate in development plans how they would apply these specific values to their work.

For instance, Eriksen tells us that if competence, fairness, and integrity were included in the company's values or mission statement, the employee could be required to indicate how he or she would actualize these ethical values in the plan—much like Marlene Chism points out in chapter 1 of this book: *A Leader's Vow of Personal Responsibility*. Eriksen lists the following from her work as examples:

- Assess daily work tasks to determine where increased competence is needed.
- Increase competence by participating in relevant training programs or continuing education.
- Become more aware of how to treat reports fairly and with integrity, for instance, by assessing the degree to which others believe I am acting fairly and with integrity (anonymous survey of reports, colleagues, and manager).
- After listing daily work tasks, document ways to increase fairness and integrity, set specific goals and target dates for doing so, and revisit goals on target dates during supervision.

Studying Ethics

At a minimum, Eriksen suggests that leaders:

- become aware of laws and regulations that are applicable to their work
- commit to acting within these laws and regulations and to attending regular continuing education related to these laws and regulations
- commit to encouraging colleagues and requiring reports to act within these laws and regulations, to challenging unethical/illegal behavior upon becoming aware of it, and to blowing the whistle on anyone who fails to operate within the law and regulations
- participate in periodic discussions with colleagues and managers related to conscientiousness in abiding by the laws, particularly considering how to manage ethical dilemmas (different laws conflict; ethics and law conflict; and so on).

Optimally, leaders should also:

- know the aspirational ethical values of the company (or help the company to develop them)
- participate in training and discussions on applying these ethical values to the particulars of the job
- participate in regular ethical dilemma discussions in which employees struggle with how to apply aspirational ethical values to develop the best options in difficult cases
- aim to actualize these values on a daily basis, setting specific goals and objectives publicly and on a regular basis
- anonymously survey reports, colleagues, and manager as to success in actualizing these ethical values.

Eriksen promotes development of ethical decision making and inspires people toward optimal values and behavior, while transforming families and businesses alike. Visit www.erikseninstitute.com for more information.

Questions for Discussion: Integrity, Values, Intuition, and Stronger Ethics

1. Why is integrity considered to be an important part of a leader's character?
2. What are some nontraditional courses being included now in graduate school curricula?
3. Explain the statement "People do what they see their leaders do."
4. What is another meaning for the term ROI?
5. What is the definition of values-led leadership?
6. Why is it important that leaders stand for something or subscribe to a particular philosophy?
7. What is a leader's responsibility when it comes to shaping or enhancing the organization's value system?
8. Describe what is meant by the statement "Intuition is a leader's reservoir of vision and instinct."
9. What are some of the ways a leader can tune up his or her intuition?
10. Why do we refer to our intuitive ability as our internal compass?

Wrapping It Up

We've seen here that with values-led leadership, integrity, intuition, and ethics coming to the forefront of organizations and the larger society, there is a general understanding that the choice is between standing for something or falling for anything. The choice we make is reflected in how we do business, work with our customers, and develop our leaders. It is also relevant to the topic presented in the next chapter— building and leading turbo-charged teams.

What You Will Learn in This Chapter:

♦ Know what team leadership really means. Leaders must
- make team building a fulfilling and rewarding experience for all
- implement steps to build a leader's ideal team
- establish esprit de corps among the ranks.

♦ Synergistic teams and their functions. Leaders must
- retool teams
- create high-performing, self-directed teams
- manage virtual teams.

Let your leaders know that real leadership enables others to take action. It means that leaders don't hoard the power they've been given. Instead, they give their power away, trusting that the team will compensate for their weaknesses and areas of inexperience and make them look good. (See chapter 15 for more on empowerment.)

KNOW WHO THE FOLLOWERS ARE

It's much more important to know who the followers are than who the leader is. Successful leaders know how to assemble, empower, and draw from the strengths of their teams. They lead in the following ways:

- They achieve results through motivating and inspiring a winning team.
- They build a work environment where collaboration and continuous improvement are encouraged and where individuals collectively achieve their greatest potential.
- They provide team members ongoing opportunities to build loyalty and commitment to common goals, and they energize workers to seek and implement solutions on their own.

Being part of a successful team can be one of life's most fulfilling and rewarding experiences. Ask your leaders to think about a time when being part of a team made them feel extraordinary. Ask what it was about the team that made membership so memorable. Then ask them to describe the common goals that team members shared, the commitment they had to make to the team, and the trust that was established among its members.

That exercise helps your leaders recall the passion and excitement they once felt as part of a group. Point out that those are the feelings they will want to instill in others when building and leading their own dream teams.

TEAM TRANSFORMATION

High performance teams have it, successful leaders build it, and change initiatives thrive on it! What do you do when your team is not working? You have to transform it.

Today's teams are a new breed. Globalization, rapid technological progress, and the pressure to constantly innovate have created a new world of teams. They are functionally, geographically, and culturally diverse. They are under pressure to create results. They must rally behind one goal and figure out how to integrate into one corporate culture.

PeopleNRG Tells Leaders How to Quickly Turbo-Charge the Workplace

With years of experience helping thousands of leaders on five continents from more than 25 countries, PeopleNRG (www.PeopleNRG.com) is a change optimization and prestigious leadership company that provides speeches, workshops, coaching, and consulting in the United States, Europe, Eastern Europe, Africa, and Asia. Partners Lawrence Polsky and Antoine Gerschel say they have found four main problems with teams undergoing change and share their expertise in this chapter:

- **Lack of commitment to the new direction of the team:** PeopleNRG's 2011–2012 Global Research on Best Practices provided some astonishing data. States Lawrence Polsky, managing partner, "We asked 907 professionals in 51 countries about commitment. We found 81 percent said they 'say yes to the change but don't take any action.' 81 percent! When people are put in a new project team, or a company reorganizes, or a new leader comes to an existing team, they face the same lukewarm commitment."
- **Conflict:** High-performance teams can debate, argue, disagree, and create or stir up consequences without feeling bad about it. Teams get stuck when the leader or members don't handle conflict well. This lack of cohesiveness slows down productivity, reduces morale, and damages results.
- **Team fit:** "In every team project we do, we are asked if at least one person on the team 'should be off the team,'" states Polsky. "They don't seem to fit in. With implementation of change, not only are the skills of individuals changing, but also the team mix may need to be adjusted to succeed."
- **Distance and cultural issues:** Many teams today are spread out across regions and countries. They include members in different functions. They are diverse across age, gender, culture, knowledge, and experience, among others. The challenges of distance and culture can undermine any team, even with the brightest, most well-intentioned members.

How do you transform a team that is having problems? PeopleNRG lays out three steps to overcoming general problems among teams and preventing problems from arising.

Step 1: Understand the Team

Talk to the people on the team. "We ask teams these questions all around the globe," states Polsky. "Don't be fooled! They may look simple, but they will give you all you need to fix any team."

- What do you expect from the team? (And ask the team, what do you expect from your leader?)
- What does this team do really well?

- What doesn't work too well in this team?
- How does your team handle conflict? What happens when it doesn't handle it well?
- How, if at all, is clashing cultures a problem?
- What ideas do you have that can transform this team?

Step 2: Create a Fun, Solution-Focused Training Event

It's important to design a training event that is fun, and also provides valuable information for all the participants. Detailed below are some activities PeopleNRG uses to handle each team problem. To conquer the problem of a **lack of real commitment to the team**, begin with "party time," and also try out the other activities listed.

Step 3: Make It Party Time!

This activity will help the team focus on what they want to achieve together. The discussion will create a commitment to a desired future, which will create new behaviors today. Tell the team that one year from now, they are having a party. Ask the team to discuss, "What we will be celebrating? What great results will we have achieved? What kind of teamwork will we be proud of?" From there, have them decide on the party theme—where it will be, who will be there, what food they will have, what kind of music. Imagination is a powerful tool. Have them go wild and plan the ideal party.

Why Do I Care? Don't kid yourself. Work is very personal. Employees get up every day and spend their lives with you. How much more personal can you get? Polsky states, "We are continually blown away by the deeply personal answers employees give to this activity. At first we thought it was too personal for work. We have found the opposite. It sparks intense discussion. And there is nothing that drives commitment more than personal emotions."

Ask each person to answer this question "What does this team mean to me? How does it affect me personally—the good and the bad?" When one person is talking, the other person's job is to listen to understand what they mean. If they need to, they can ask questions to clarify.

Team Song. This activity is perfect for a retreat or after dinner at a training event. It will get everyone laughing and having fun, while at the same time discussing their team strengths and issues. Collect lyrics online of popular songs—any upbeat song can work. (See the sidebar for a list of some song ideas.) Have the team rewrite the lyrics as a team song. It can include lyrics about how they want to be as a team, what they are really good at, funny inside jokes, anything. Then the fun begins: Each group presents their song. Record it and store on mp3 and play it to kick off team meetings and events or when the team needs a boost.

When your team is facing **conflict**, try these activities:

Ideal Conflict Navigator. This activity will help the team identify the kinds of behavior they want from each other to handle conflict better. Ask the team to each think of someone they know who is excellent at navigating conflict. What traits, skills, and competencies does this person have?

Make a Team Song!

Collect lyrics online of popular songs—any upbeat song can work. Some examples of song titles and artists include:

- "We Are the Champions"—Queen
- "I Gotta Feeling"—Black Eyed Peas
- "Satisfaction"—Rolling Stones
- "Eye of the Tiger"—Survivor
- "We Will Rock You"—Queen
- "It's My Life"—Bon Jovi
- "Beautiful Day"—U2
- "What a Wonderful World"—Louis Armstrong
- "I Feel Good"—James Brown
- "I Can See Clearly Now"—Johnny Nash
- "Walking on Sunshine"—Katrina and the Waves
- "Live Like You Were Dying"—Tim McGraw
- "I Believe I Can Fly"—R. Kelly
- "You Gotta Be"—Des'ree
- "When You Believe"—Mariah Carey/Whitney Houston
- "Hero"—Mariah Carey
- "I Will Survive"—Gloria Gaynor

Have everyone share their answers. The team creates a flipchart list of all the traits. Next, each person individually assesses themselves. On a piece of paper, they put a line down the middle. On one side, they write down the traits mentioned that they are good at. On the other side, they list the areas they need to work on. Optionally, depending on the team trust level, you can have each person share their assessment and have a rich discussion.

Role Reversal. This activity is a great way for people to poke fun at each other and learn about conflict. Each person will pretend to be someone else on the team. Once they decide who they will be playing, give them a topic to discuss. It could be a work issue they are struggling with. It could be a current new topic. When you say "Go!" the team discusses the issue, but each person acts like the person he is pretending to be. Watch the laughter flow! People will have a lot of fun seeing how they are perceived.

When **distance and cultural issues** are plaguing your team, here are other activity options:

Let's Connect! Using a piece of paper, make three columns. In the first column, have everyone list all the points of contact they have with other members of team, including emails they send, meetings they have, phone calls they make, and so on. Explain to the

team that there are two aspects of any communication in the team: human aspects (building relationship) and business aspects (getting the work done). High-performance teams experience a balance of both. Remote or distributed teams have to pay special attention to the human aspect because that is the first to go.

Have them go back to their lists and title the second column "H" for human and the third "B" for business. Now have them go back to their lists and rank their items. In each column, "H" and "B," have them rank on a scale of 1 to 10 how much "H" and how much "B" exists for that point of contact. When they are done, have them discuss their lists with their table. "We have always found that people have much more B than H," states Polsky. "They discover that they need to consciously put more energy into making human contact with each other."

Finally, have the team brainstorm a list in two minutes of how they can create more "H" in their team.

Culture Clash: A Day in the Life. If cultures are clashing, this activity will bring out the issues in a safe way. Start with a short presentation on culture. You can use any model you know. Or you can simply look up the definition of culture and start from there. Split the team into two groups. One group has people who are from one of the cultures. The other group includes those from the other culture.

Each group makes two lists. One list is elements of the other group's culture that help the team. The second list is elements of the other group's culture that get in the way. Each group then takes their lists and creates a skit "Culture Clash: A Day in The Life." They create a fictitious situation to play act the culture clash.

If you want, after each skit, ask the group to explain what they were trying to say. Then facilitate a discussion about the issues. Sometimes the skits are so clear you don't even need the discussion!

And last but not least, a team is much like a human being: If they feel satisfied with what they are achieving, good about themselves, and recognized for what they are doing, they will be more productive! Here is a final activity PeopleNRG uses with great success to do all of these, while staying business focused.

Presents. Prepare anything you need to wrap presents (boxes, colored wrapping paper, strings and bows, scissors, tape, and so on). This activity consists of symbolic wrapping of *team achievements*.

First, have the team identify key stakeholders or customers with whom they work. These can be "traditional customers," and also internal customers (other departments, a leadership team, colleagues, etc.). Then pick the top three (or more if you have a larger group) stakeholders.

Define a time period: last month, last quarter, last year, or longer. Then, split the team in three groups, one for each stakeholder. Tell the group:

- Ask yourself, "What did you accomplish for your stakeholder in the time period defined above?"
- Discuss your answers.

● For each of the accomplishments you identified above, create a neatly wrapped gift. Use any and all wrappings you want to make it beautiful.

Each group then presents their gifts to the full group, explaining what they represent. Take a group picture holding all the presents. It makes a great keepsake and remembrance of the team's accomplishments.

Resolve Team Conflict

Sometimes despite your best efforts, your team members will be in conflict with one another. As Lawrence Polsky and his longtime partner and friend, Antoine Gerschel, point out in *Perfect Phrases for Conflict Resolution*, there are four easy steps to resolve any conflict among teams:

1. **Understand the issue: This is the hardest step to do well.** If you have an issue, raise it and explain the business impact of it. If your colleague has the issue, listen closely to understand before responding.

2. **Set the vision: This is where most people fall short.** Once the issue is clear, you need to discuss your new desired future. What kind of relationship, communication, or process do you want to have?

3. **Explore alternatives: Get creative and explore with each other ideas to reach your vision.**

4. **Agree on action: Any agreement will move you forward.** Decide what you are willing to do to make things better next time.

Remember, conflict is never as linear as these four steps. You will have to be flexible and creative to navigate the conflict together.

EIGHT HIGHLY EFFECTIVE PRACTICES FOR BUILDING A TEAM

Ask your leaders to imagine what the superstar talent on their teams will look like, and to describe the behavior of employees who have a burning desire to do a great job and the ability and discipline to perform at the highest level. Now let's consider eight critical practices for developing such teams.

Practice 1: Select and hire superstar players for your team. If you start with the right people, you're far less likely to encounter problems down the line. Look for players who share your passion for the project and have the ambition to follow through. Ask yourself, "Is this person a good team fit?" Remember, if members aren't bonding, they're not building. (See the section on attracting and retaining talent in chapter 7.)

Practice 2: Communicate openly and honestly with team members at all times. The key to your team's productivity will be in how well you communicate the goals of the team and how often you exchange information with team members. Be specific about what you expect the team to accomplish. Define your outcomes and deadlines and include team members in the goal-setting process.

Leading Over the River of Fear

PeopleNRG has implemented a process for leading through times of change called "The 19 Steps to Leading Employees Over the River of Fear." As Gerschel and Polsky explain, "Who in their right mind would try to jump across this divide? They see a great abyss of doom. They are happily heading down their current road, and then their leadership steers them toward this huge cliff of *change*. They hear the desires of the organization but have no idea how to get there. They know they cannot just leap across in one jump. They know if they try, they could die from the fall. Plus they don't see the value in taking the chance."

Leading the employees over this river of fear is in the hands of frontline leaders. Their challenge is to find ways to translate organizational plans that look good on paper into reality. PeopleNRG's process includes tips, techniques, and tools to succeed in this endeavor, such as:

- Increasing the Acceptance of Change
- Handling Denial, Fear, and Apathy
- Identifying and Stopping Threats to Change
- Building a Bridge to the Future

As they state, "The journey of change is filled with emotions: fear, upset, anger, and hope." Their method aims to equip leaders with the tools to guide their teams over the river of fear.

FIGURE 10.1 The River of Fear

Reprinted with permission of PeopleNRG.

Practice 3: Ask for and expect feedback from team members. Listen to what your team has to say and respond to their input. After all, they're the ones performing the jobs. They know what's happening, so listen carefully and respond in a reasonable amount of time. Some leaders call this getting upward feedback.

> **Key Point:** *Selecting the right team members from the start can ensure your organization's success up to 80 percent!*
> —**Source:** PeopleNRG Data and Research

Practice 4: Commit yourself to delegating decision making to the team. Don't make decisions for the team or restrict them to one decision maker. Push decisions down the line. Involve all team members and let those responsible decide how the job will get done. The challenge comes when you suddenly bring other people into the decision making process. That is when you will most likely need to approach decision making differently. Tell your leaders this may rely on a number of different factors, including the amount of buy-in required, the type of decision that is being made, deadlines to be met, resources available, and the sensitivity or nature of the task at hand. When you want to involve your whole team in the decision-making process, explaining to your leaders why and how best to organize the process will be key.

Practice 5: Care about your people. The saying goes, "People don't care how much you know until they know how much you care." If team members know that their leader has their best interests at heart, not only will they respect and trust that leader, but they also will want to work harder. When a leader cares about the team, that team will be inspired to care about what they are doing and how they are doing it.

Practice 6: Provide the tools and resources needed for success. Set your team up for success. Give everyone the tools and resources that are necessary to get the job done right the first time. Your team members will admire and respect you for making sure that they have what they need to ensure their success.

Practice 7: Coach team players at their own levels. Leaders can't afford to misjudge the level of competence in their team players. If you want your teams not only to succeed but also to learn and develop, then take the time to evaluate at what level each team member ranks, using the worksheet that follows these eight practices ("How I Will Lead My Dream Team.")

Practice 8: Promote *esprit de corps*! Establish for your team a group identity that makes them feel good and gives them a sense of pride. Build their group morale. Part of this effort involves instilling among the team's membership a feeling of being special. American Express has used this strategy successfully for years. When recruiting American Express card members, the company very effectively uses the slogan, "Membership has its privileges."

Now it is time to ask your leaders to complete a team building worksheet by describing how they plan to carry out the eight practices detailed above. Ask them to be as specific as possible when describing how they will lead their ideal teams. Use the exercise to prompt further group discussion on team building.

Worksheet: How I Will Lead My Dream Team

For each of the eight practices necessary for building your dream team, describe the specific actions you will take on the job.

1. This is how I plan to gather the most talented people for my teams:

2. This is how I will communicate openly and honestly with my team members:

3. Here are ways I will listen to my team members and ask for their feedback:

4. Here are ways I will delegate decision making to my team:

5. This is how I'll show that I care about my team and will always keep their best interests at heart:

6. Here's how I plan to go about providing the tools and resources necessary for my team's success:

7. These are the ways I will coach each team member at his or her own level:

 I have team members who have the potential to succeed, but don't know what to do and how to do it:
 - Team members who need coaching: _____
 - Team members who require support: _____
 - Team members to whom I can delegate: _____

8. This is how I will promote *esprit de corps* among my team members:

LEADING TEAMS THROUGH THE POWER OF INFLUENCE

A key element in effective leadership involves exerting positive influence within your team. While an informative leader may possess the right knowledge to point employees to the right path, an influential leader creates employees who are eager to listen, learn, and follow the example of the leader. No one knows the power of influence more than an attorney, whose job it is to influence clients, and ultimately, a judge. Linda Swindling, a self-proclaimed "recovering attorney" who is now a speaker, executive coach, and author/coauthor of more than 20 books (including her signature *Passport to Success* series—see www.LindaSwindling.com), knows firsthand what it takes to influence followers as well as fellow leaders.

Linda suggests that influencing a team takes more than a leader who "knows his stuff." She developed eight points to help leaders earn influence in a team environment.

1. **Delegate appropriately.** When a leader fails to delegate within the team, it sends a clear, unintended message: "I don't trust you to do it right." While some work cannot be safely delegated to others, influential leaders find a way to transfer tasks along with authority to team members whenever possible.

2. **Tame the ego and forget the perfectionism**. If you want to discourage yourself and your team, set goals that are unattainable. If you want to motivate them, let that mindset go. To best influence your team, practice the often-repeated words, "Value progress, not perfection."

3. **Stay in control of your emotions.** Influential leaders stay off the emotional rollercoaster. Why? It's hard for employees to trust a boss who may be Jekyll one moment and Hyde the next.

4. **Remain logical, reasonable, and consistent.** Influential leaders use their heads. Logic and reason win over resisters more than outbursts and tantrums.

5. **Honor confidences.** The quickest way to lose the confidence of every member of your team is to lose the confidence of one employee. If you cannot keep confidential matters to yourself, you should reconsider being in leadership.

6. **Help people avoid embarrassment.** It should go without saying that no one wants their embarrassing or humiliating moment pointed out. If you wish to influence others, be known for spotlighting their accomplishments, not their shortcomings.

7. **Avoid threatening or being threatened.** You might be able to get an employee to back down during a standoff by threatening. That will work only once. Threats re-establish relationships for the worst. If you threaten once, plan on having your bluff called. The same is true if you are threatened. Threats are a form of manipulation, not positive influence. Weak leaders manipulate; strong leaders influence.

8. **Keep your sense of humor.** Most jobs don't involve life-and-death situations. So don't be afraid to laugh at yourself or even chuckle about mistakes that your team makes. We learn more in environments where we laugh than in ones where we are tense and uptight.

Google Knows How to Build Talent in Its Teams . . . and It Shows!

Google is serious about its success in team building. And it shows. Google has consistently ranked on *Fortune* magazine's list of "100 Best Companies to Work For" (first in 2007 and 2008, fourth in 2009 and 2010), and their leadership principles back up this placement. Besides having one of the most innovative and intuitive online content management platforms on the Internet, Google takes its team building culture seriously too—although in a rather lighthearted and fun way. They are known for phrases such as: "You can make money without doing evil," "You can be serious without a suit," and "Work should be challenging and the challenge should be fun."

The vision fueling the Google machine that attracts and retains the very best talent starts at the very top. Google's founders, Larry Page and Sergey Brin, initially became personally involved in developing every professional job in the company. Additionally, the founders work to ensure that all Google employees have opportunities to work on exciting projects, learn continuously, and receive regular challenges to push the limits—all wrapped up in a culture that lets employees know that they are adding value.

Once hired, Google has a most unusual practice to continue employee talent development. Besides offering perks such as a climbing wall, free food, and free laundry, they implement something called "20 percent work" that allows most employees to spend 20 percent of their work hours pursuing their own interests and researching projects that interest them personally. And the company funds those efforts as part of business. Giving employees the empowerment to pursue new, creative outlets at work gives them transferable skills when they are on work assignments. But the greatest development benefit of this practice to Google is that it drives a culture of curiosity, innovation, and creativity.

In addition, employees are given the ability to award one another with $175 peer bonuses on the spot. This clever system keeps employees proactively promoting positive behavior, as well as modeling it—whether leadership is around or not!

HELPING LEADERS UNDERSTAND TEAM TYPES AND THEIR UNIQUE FUNCTIONS

There are many team types, each connected with specific organizational processes. Here are some of the different teams that function in organizations and the purposes they serve.

High-performing and self-directed teams: A high-performing or self-directed team does not have a manager supervising it. The team is responsible and accountable for everything the members are charged with doing. When such teams are in place and working well, they can provide great results for any organization.

Functional and cross-functional teams: A functional team comprises a group of employees who work together in one department and are responsible for generating some output

It's All Teamwork at Whole Foods

Whole Foods is the largest natural foods grocery chain in the United States. If you want to work there, you'd better understand that the entire Whole Foods culture is based on decentralized teamwork. Every store is an autonomous profit center composed of self-directed, self-managed teams. Team leaders from each store are a team, store leaders in each region are a team, and the organization's regional presidents are a team. The corporation is all teams. When most organizations pay lip service to popular management concepts like teamwork, empowerment, and trust, this undeniably radical company based in Austin, Texas, really puts their money where their mouth is by using teamwork, empowerment, and trust to form a highly profitable business model that is practiced daily.

Here are some Whole Foods examples of teamwork in action:

- Only teams have the power to approve candidates for full-time employment. It takes a two-thirds majority vote from the team to hire a worker.

- A model of egalitarianism, the CEO's compensation is capped at 10 times the average team member's pay.

- Every team member at every level has access to the organization's operating and financial data.

- The company promotes trust by removing rumors and misinformed conjecture with its open salary policy that lists the year's previous salaries and bonuses for every employee—by name!

- Their corporate mantra: All for one and one for all!

and improving functional processes in that department. Cross-functional teams come together from different departments in the organization in an effort to share information that will improve overall functions and processes.

Senior executive teams: Such teams comprise the CEO, president, and senior-level executives. They function as leadership groups that set organizational direction and goals and create mission and vision statements.

Middle management teams: These teams bring together managers from different departments within the organization, including the director who heads them up. They help ensure consistency among the workers who make up their departments and are responsible for disseminating new policies and sharing information.

Retooling teams or process improvement teams: These teams are temporary and are charged with the responsibilities of reorganization, re-engineering, or developing new processes to replace old ones. They often are cross-functional in nature because their efforts affect many different departments or divisions within the organization.

Project teams: Established on a temporary basis, they may be functional or cross-functional. These teams bring together all of the specialty areas within an organization

that are equipped to plan and execute a variety of special projects. Their efforts may be targeted toward the organization itself or toward its customers.

New product design teams: These teams pull together a range of workers within the organization who will be involved in the design, development, manufacturing, and rollout of any new product or service. They may be temporary or permanent, and their goal is seamless delivery of new projects and services.

Virtual teams: These teammates can be spread across the planet, connecting in cyberspace and sometimes never meeting or talking face-to-face with other team members or leaders. Virtual teams may be permanent or temporary, and they take on a variety of projects at all levels.

If they understand the various types of work teams and their functions, your leaders will be able to form the most appropriate teams to get a job done. They'll also be better equipped when selecting the best members for each group.

WORKING VIRTUALLY TOGETHER, APART

Teamwork can be done successfully over long distances, which is why we have included a separate chapter on the importance of leading virtual teams (chapter 11). Virtual teams are proliferating, and their members may never see or meet their colleagues. Although they may speak to their leaders rarely, they can function as effective and synchronistic groups working smoothly together on the Internet.

The toughest part of working with any team used to be getting together with other members. No more. Today, auditoriums and virtual conference rooms mean hundreds of people can meet without ever leaving their desks. These teams are able to hash out ideas with colleagues in the UK; meet with other team members in Burlington, Vermont, to go over some documents before a meeting; get the latest from a researcher in the Silicon Valley; and kibitz with a new member of the team in Melbourne, Australia—all without a single frequent-flier mile!

For your leaders to form a virtual team in your organization, they'll need a virtual conference room where team members can get together online. Increasing numbers of software tools are available to let team members swap messages, trade documents, edit handouts, and even see each other.

Ask your leaders to list the benefits associated with virtual teamwork. Then ask them to list some of the challenges of leading a long-distance team.

If you are wondering whether the eight practices cited earlier for building teams are effective in a virtual environment—absolutely. High-tech teams require the same kinds of high-touch human caring and guidance. Keep reading on to the next chapter, "Leading in a Virtual World—Leaders Will Require 'Telepresence,'" for more direction on this style of leadership.

Building a Dream Team Eight Ways

Use this job aid as a quick reminder of the practices for forming and developing successful teams.

Practice 1: Select the most talented people.

Practice 2: Always communicate openly and honestly with team members.

Practice 3: Ask for and expect feedback from team members.

Practice 4: Commit yourself to delegating decision making to the team.

Practice 5: Care about your people.

Practice 6: Provide the tools and resources necessary for success.

Practice 7: Coach team players at their own levels.

Practice 8: Promote *esprit de corps*.

Questions for Discussion: Building and Recharging Your Team

1. What is the meaning of establishing *"esprit de corps"* among teams?

2. How important is it for a team member to be a good fit? Why?

3. What is the purpose of a self-directed team?

4. What are some of the pros and cons of leading a virtual team?

5. Explain this statement: Real leadership enables others to take action.

6. Why do leaders have to be self-confident when creating teams?

7. How can being part of a team become one of life's most rewarding experiences?

8. Why are teams so important to an organization's overall success?

Wrapping It Up

Emphasize for your leaders that successful team building and leading require all of the interpersonal and communication skills and tools that they can employ—many of which are presented in this chapter. Understanding how to use these skills and tools when interacting with teammates will help them become stronger and more effective team builders. In the next chapter, it's all about leading virtual teams!

CHAPTER 11

Leading in a Virtual World—Leaders Will Require "Telepresence"

Telepresence products are being developed by companies like Cisco, HP, Apple, Mircrosoft, and others. The race is on! Large high-definition screens now line office walls of highly technologically savvy companies worldwide, where cameras follow you when you enter the room and leave the room, just like the eyes of people in a meeting do. Everyone is connected in "real time." There is no delay in transmission.

This is what you call the united virtual workplace of the future, where people actually feel like someone in a far-flung location, like Dubai or Singapore, is sitting right across the table from them. (The White House and Pentagon have been using this technology for some time now, by the way.) Keep in mind that top leaders worldwide acknowledge that although a virtual workplace of the future will be undoubtedly more efficient and ecologically sound, it will not replace the need to meet face-to-face with employees and customers, give someone a much-needed hug or handshake, or smell the scent of fresh flowers on the conference room table. However, it is evident, according to global high-tech gurus, that the ability to do the most human things virtually (touch, feel, smell) is just around the corner.

> **Measuring Telepresence at Hewlett Packard**
> *"When you can have two people sitting in the room on opposite sides of the planet and not feel like they're having a remote meeting, I think you've achieved telepresence. When you feel like the technology is getting in the way of a discussion, as it does during videoconferencing, then you don't have telepresence.* —Bill Avery, WW Strategy and Marketing, HP LaserJet and Enterprise Solutions, Hewlett-Packard (**Source:** *Managing the Mobile Workforce*, David Clemons and Michael Kroth, PhD)

What You Will Learn in This Chapter:

♦ Lead in a virtual world. Leaders must
- be flexible when assigning work (in some organizations, it doesn't matter where or what time the work is being done, as long as it gets done on time and correctly)
- schedule regular meetings to collaborate and stay on task
- understand that proximity to one's home doesn't automatically lead to harmony
- create specific job duties with measurable results and deadlines.

♦ Technology is key in an "officeless" company. Leaders must
- develop their "telepresence" to be successful
- become familiar with "intuitive" technology that is necessary to do the job
- communicate with team members electronically and frequently—this may be their only connection with you, and a speedy response helps people feel connected.

LET'S GET BACK TO THE FUTURE—HERE AND NOW

Your leaders will be looking to you for tools and strategies when it comes to training and supporting modern mobile work teams. At the start of 2012, it is estimated that there will be more than one billion mobile workers worldwide. It's your job to help your leaders cope with this reality. Leading in a virtual workplace brings advantages as well as challenges, and often requires a unique skill set.

Intuitive Technology

Mobile technology can be complex for some. But your up-and-coming leaders, especially your Gen Ys, will expect it all to be intuitive and organic in nature. Your customers just want it kept simple. In other words, the world wants technology that works the way humans think, while supporting the way they act and work in the real world. That's a tall order, but it's already being accomplished.

Case in point: New technology will be required to understand your leaders, more than your leaders understand the new technology available.

Leaders who welcome the power of mobile technology that is tied to a workforce that understands how to use it are creating a major shift in leadership thinking. The largest growth in mobile technology is expected to take place in a wide variety of online business apps, in mobile blogs, and through email. Mobile phone subscriptions are estimated to reach 5.6 billion by the year 2013, while **smartphone** shipments will exceed 390 million units. As this book is being written, there are more than 400 million phones with Wi-Fi capabilities in the marketplace.

ATTENTION LEADERS: BE FLEXIBLE; LEARN AS YOU GO

Traits like flexibility and communication become key, as you may have to create your own rules and grow your own virtual leaders along with your virtual work environments—one step at a time. The good news is that many leaders are not afraid to create their own unique and preferred ways to lead virtually as they go along. So get creative. Mobile technology shrinks the global workplace and continues to give your leaders new and improved options for leadership almost every day. At the same time, many leaders have already paved the way in this virtual world—creating proven methods for effective virtual leadership we can all learn from.

VIRTUAL LEADERS ARE TIED TO TECHNOLOGY

There are times when virtual leaders face challenges unlike those in a conventional work setting. Virtual leaders are tied to their mobile technology, keyboards, and databases, while more traditional leaders are often face-to-face with difficult people and difficult situations on site. When you're up close and personal, resolving conflict requires certain skill sets that leaders must learn and apply in the moment. But resolving the same conflict from 3,000 miles away (or farther) will require a different approach, creative thinking, good writing skills, and excellent questions to excavate what's really going on in a location you cannot see or observe firsthand. A lot comes down to trust and having your presence felt no matter where you are, or how you work. This is what ultimately makes a successful virtual leadership team.

LEADERS MAKE THEIR PRESENCE FELT

Virtual leadership is a mindset. It does not have to be harder than it is. Shift your paradigm on this very different leadership style and keep things simple.

A key to successful virtual leadership comes when you are teaching your leaders how to make their presence felt from a distance. And it's not that hard. Sometimes distance is a convenient excuse for *not* leading well or *choosing not* to face the hard issues. But the fact of the matter is, virtual management is getting easier to do, and leaders are discovering their own unique preferences for doing it and doing it quite well. There's no textbook solution, and there's no solution you can find quickly in this chapter. It's often a frame of mind and a willingness to try new approaches.

We can teleconference, teleseminar, Skype, text, tweet, email, videoconference, send instructions and graphics of how to do things, but then—oh yes, there's the option of actually picking up a phone and making a call to say something like, *"Hi John, I'm just calling to say hello and see how your weekend went at Yosemite with the family. I've always lived on the East Coast and have wanted to visit that area. What can you tell me about it? Where would you recommend I stay? Can you send the team a photo of that bear your son Stephen saw at your campsite, and maybe write a caption about bravery and leadership?"*

Again, it comes back to being an authentic person and genuine leader (chapter 1), being human, and making your presence felt. That is done with common sense, courtesy, taking time for others, and giving a bit of yourself in a personal way—not just being all business, or all technology, because you don't have physical interaction every day in an office together.

Managers who bring the human touch to virtual leadership are much more successful than those who strictly follow a rulebook or policy manual on the subject.

Your Attitude Will Determine Their Altitude

Remember in chapter 10, we used the term, "working virtually together, apart." Let that be your leaders' virtual leadership mantra! Leading from a distance is an attitude. And your attitude will always determine your altitude. Rise above the challenges and get creative on ways to "work virtually together, apart." Tell your leaders to ask the people being led from afar to offer up suggestions and improved processes. Remember that they are on the receiving end of your virtual leadership techniques; therefore, they will be the best people to address improving your organization's systems and processes on virtual management and tell you how to improve the way things are done. It's that simple!

When your leaders fail to ask for the opinion of those being affected by management's way of doing things, it's usually because they don't want to hear how they can improve. But in a virtual world, leaders need to ask their teams, more than ever, "How can we improve this process?" "How would you conduct these meetings more effectively?" "How can we improve efficiency when we cannot be together?" "How often do you think we all need to come together, in person?" "How can we maximize our costs and create a more powerful virtual workplace that sets the example for the entire organization? Please be specific."

Can You Hear Me Now?

Tell your leaders that once they get responses and suggestions from the team, they should respond right away with a big "thank you" (remember our pointers with Diana Damron on civility in the workplace, in chapter 2?) for taking time to propose their ideas. Then tell them, "I will be getting back to you by _____ (set a date)." Your leaders do not have to agree with the suggestions, or even implement one suggestion offered. But they do need to acknowledge everyone's input and time invested. When a leader does this consistently from a distance, the ranks feel they are being heard, even though they may not be on site or in the same time zone. No matter where someone is located, they want to feel valued, respected, listened to, and included. Also, how many times do your leaders stop to write a thank you note for a job well done, or send a congratulatory card to a new parent who works for them, or ask how Joseph's Bar Mitzvah went last Saturday? Being courteous, civil, and thoughtful can really help when it comes to leading across zip codes or oceans. The miles that exist between your leaders and their teams are often not the greatest issue of concern, although we make

it seem like it is. The issue is connectivity. Are your leaders connecting—whether that be near or far?

Your leaders are in control when it comes to their style of leadership, approach, and most of all, *attitude* toward virtual leadership. If they are complaining all the time that their teams are in other locations and they reside in Cincinatti, what message do you think that sends? Your leaders will be leading an entire group of up-and-coming leaders to think virtual leadership is one big pain! It's their call. Instead, inform your leaders that when the team in Vancouver "feels" that their leaders care and are in touch regularly, not just in times of crisis, their presence will be felt across many time zones. Tell leaders to change their approach, be positive, and lead effectively, and they will be training an entire group of leaders to follow.

> *Your attitude always determines your altitude as a leader.*
> —Zig Ziglar

VIRTUAL LEADERS AND THEIR ORGANIZATIONS ARE NOT BOUND IN THE SAME WAY

Often virtual organizations operate 24/7. And believe it or not, leading people virtually in this way can cut down some of the stress significantly for your leaders. How? All of a sudden, "when" you communicate becomes far less important than the fact that you just do it, get it right, and get the work done on time.

This Book's Editor Is a Role Model in Leading Virtually

As authors, we know how this virtual workplace operates firsthand. We may be finishing up a chapter for our editor Kristin Husak at 3 a.m. from a hotel in New Jersey, while we're on the road giving seminars and coaching, but does Kristin really care when we are doing the work, or from where we are actually writing the chapter? Not one bit.

Publishing is a "virtual" industry, and leaders like Kristin manage their authors and production efforts from thousands of miles away without even blinking. But as a leader, Kristin does care a great deal about the quality of our work, how well our chapters are written, and if they are completed in the timeframe required for her production team. The standard by which she leads and coaches her authors, even in a virtual workplace, is never compromised for a second. When you work viturally, you hold your standards of work high! Though most of her authors and some assistant editors are spread all over the country, even the world, Kristin's virtual leadership style is production oriented, high performing, and results driven at all times. Is yours?

The other critical element of our editor's virtual leadership style is that Kristin builds bridges and minds gaps when it comes to managing relationships among those she leads on a daily basis, no matter where they live, travel to, or work from. We look to Kristin for leadership guidance as we write our books, but when we need a helping

hand, or a friend to bounce ideas off of, day or night, she is right there—as if she were down the hall. (By the way, Kristin works in Alexandria, Virginia, and we work in southern and northern California.) This is a leader who makes her presence felt big time!

DIVERSITY AND DIFFICULT PEOPLE IN A VIRTUAL WORLD

When asked, many leaders have said that the issue of diversity and cultural competency can sometimes be much easier to address in a virtual work environment. The individual who might have extra needs working within the confines of an office building may be much easier to accommodate when working remotely. One of our clients told us that when they had a highly valued worker recovering from cancer and treatment, her ability to work from home remotely continued to give her a great deal of happiness and satisfaction. She said she no longer felt like the "sick person" in the office, and she always felt part of the team, even on those days when she did not feel her best.

When she later returned to work, she boasted about the opportunity to work virtually all those months, how her leaders trusted her, and the extreme compassion and understanding of her leadership team. Her loyalty to leadership and the organization never waned, and today she leads others using virtual leadership techniques her managers allowed her to benefit from.

And then there is the employee who is more difficult to work with, who may not get along with everyone in the office, and who may be much harder to sit beside, all day, on site. This person could indeed be the perfect virtual employee you'll want to lead as he or she works from a home office.

Virtual leadership is the perfect solution for managing those special people who can't seem to get along with anyone and yet, they can crank out a ton of work with precision and are highly productive. If you hear one of your leaders screaming, *"He's so productive, but working with this guy is killing me!"* it could be time to consider a virtual work setting.

THE FLIP SIDE OF WORKING VIRTUALLY—
READING BETWEEN THE LINES

The flip side of working from a distance means that a certain amount of intimacy and human touch is lost. Camaraderie may suffer when one group feels another is getting all the attention of the home office team.

Don't Get Lost in Translation

A good sense of humor and a funny joke about something going on with the team at work may lose something in (email and other electronic) translation. It's not the same as sitting in a team meeting where someone says something to crack everyone up

spontaneously and people roar with laughter, or when someone takes a moment to praise a co-worker and that individual smiles with thanks in return.

Virtual leaders complain of struggling with concentration, or maintaining full commitment to the team's new initiatives or plans to try something new. Leaders and team members may feel a sense of isolation. That's when the leader must make the team's presence felt by all—and come up with creative ways to engage workers overseas or down the street. That might mean holding contests, sending photos online, connecting with a group of high school student leaders in South Africa, or Indonesia, or New Zealand—anything to give you and your team a fresh perspective, and do so by helping others outside your own backyard. Learning something from afar, even from kids, can boost a virtual team to new and unexpected heights.

Virtual leaders have to read between the lines. They have to be extra-good listeners and try to pick up on tone and voice when talking to staff and colleagues miles away. A virtual leader does not have the benefit of using body language to gauge an employee's true feelings. This is sure to change drastically in the next decade as higher-quality digital high-definition videoconferencing will become a mainstay leadership tool for us all.

16 Fast and Easy Ways to Motivate and Drive a Virtual Team

1. Trust and engage your employees—create a turbo-charged environment of imagination and fun.
2. Provide cool tools and positively outrageous training necessary to do the job or project. Engage your learners.
3. Provide the exciting resources necessary to do the job or project. Find a way to make it happen.
4. Tell leaders to work toward their strengths, and let the motivation bubble up and overflow.
5. Give superstar commitment to the team or project.
6. Provide detailed expectations, boundaries, timelines, and consequences.
7. Outline goals and objectives in alignment with the organization, and do it with gusto.
8. Allow for mistakes—heck, you can even celebrate them—and learn from them quickly, then share them with others so the mistakes don't happen again. (Many people do not understand the power of celebrating mistakes. When you celebrate mistakes, you call attention to what was done wrong but from a human perspective. You say, that's okay, we will all learn from this. We're human! And most important—we won't repeat this same mistake again. Now let's celebrate!)
9. Share with your team your knowledge—remind them that knowledge is **not** power. It is what we do with our knowledge that makes us extraordinary!

10. Listen to your team, wherever they are, and collaborate a lot.

11. Show your team you care.

12. Recognize team members in front of the world. Share successes and accomplishments from Bozeman to Budapest, Denver to Dubai.

13. Communicate as often as possible via email, conference calls, or videoconferencing. Make your presence felt with a handwritten card sent in snail mail too, or an e-card for quick feedback. That's the human touch. People save handwritten notes because of the power of their meaning. They also save printed photographs and display them on bulletin boards or in frames in their office.

14. Expect your employees to do a good job and then empower them to do a great job. But when you say "empower," you'd better mean it. If you just delegate and then "tell" the team what to do, you'll lose all credibility.

15. Come up with creative ways to turbo-charge cyberspace—check out TED.com and YouTube for helpful ideas. Select video clips to watch for team meetings and discuss. Use Skype. Don't let distance get in the way. Distance is a paradigm shift—online professors motivate students from brick and mortar buildings to mountaintops on the big island of Hawaii!

16. Do yoga on the beach or in the park—this will clear everyone's head and likely provide creative solutions and answers to unresolved problems and unanswered questions.

VIRTUAL TEAMS CAN BE HYBRIDS

A team can be 100 percent virtual—or, as some companies have done, they can be built into a hybrid-type environment. These hybrid environments have a combination of open and enclosed work areas that can be used by team members on an as-needed basis.

Employees can work virtually at home or come into the office for collaboration, meeting time, or just work from the office on occasion to get a break from their normal routine or home office. The hybrid environment combines technology, face-to-face interaction, and virtual collaboration either within an office setting, remotely, or from what is known as a "third space." Hybrid workplaces offer lots of outside stimulation too.

Disengagement Costs the U.S. Economy $328 Billion Per Year

- 70 percent of American employees say they are not engaged on the job.
- 90 percent of American employees say they leave because they have no emotional connection with their leadership.
- 33 percent of workers view their managers as strong leaders who walk the talk.

Source: www.HumanResourcesSources.org

"Third Space"

A popular hybrid environment is called the "third space" (people working from remote locations or on site and then finding another location where they can meet folks, interact, and drink a tall latte while finishing up a proposal or working on an expense report). This is when virtual workers go to Starbucks, Barnes & Noble, or airport lounges and clubs (like American Airlines' Admiral's Club) to do their work and meet their deadlines. The "third space" is tomorrow's virtual workspace. Ever wonder why a bookstore would go wireless and serve food and drinks? Maybe they want you to stay and work there before and after you buy that magazine or book.

SEVEN HIGHLY EFFECTIVE HABITS FOR MANAGING A VIRTUAL TEAM

Managing virtual teams brings unique challenges, but with these tips it should be a smoother ride:

1. **Set expectations.** Just as teams you see every day need clear guidelines on what you expect of them, so do virtual employees. In fact, without the benefit of proximity, these expectations become even more important. Provide them in writing.
2. **Communicate clearly and often.** Use virtual work tools such as teleconference services, Skype, and IM in order to keep the lines of communication fluid. Make these tools universally used among your team, and train members on the technology behind your communications.
3. **Be available, and expect availability.** Just because your team has more flexibility working from home or on a virtual team does not mean that they should check out all day to shop and go to a moive, and then send emails only at midnight, when they finally check in to their office. A certain level of availability is needed among team members in order to communicate effectively.
4. **Set goals.** Since working remotely suggests more autonomy, be clear about the goals you expect your team to accomplish—including the timeline.
5. **Find out what drives your team members.** Just like you must know your employees in order to engage them, you also need to keep a line on who your remote team members are. Find out what they want from this position, and give them opportunities to grow.
6. **Build trust.** If you promise to deliver something, do it. Expect the same trust in return.
7. **Use the world clock on your computer.** Be considerate of other people's time zones. Send meeting notes a good day ahead of schedule so everybody has time to review and filter the agenda.

Keep in mind that companies save money on equipment and office space by allowing staff to work remotely. Another benefit of working remotely is that lots of workers are more productive working at home, since they do not have the typical office distractions going on around them, such as excessive chitchat or office machinery noises.

A Billing Company With Flexibility

MedAmerica Billing Services, Inc. (MBSI) is one of America's busiest and most successful medical billing companies. MBSI quickly discovered creative ways to retain top talent at their organization, and in a highly competitive industry, by allowing a large number of their employees to work from home. In one instance, when faced with losing their lead computer programmer, MBSI got virtual fast. By blowing up the box on traditional leadership, they were able to retain John Collins as their lead programmer when he decided to relocate his family to another state. This greatly benefited MBSI. How? They did not need to hire and train another lead programmer. John then joined many small niche programming groups in his new location and was able to find and recruit other top talent in the same geographic area where he was now located. Working remotely was a win-win for all involved. It not only saved money and time, but also generated greater efficiency in the process.

LEADING ACROSS INTERNATIONAL DIVIDES

When you are putting together a virtual international team, you want the best of the best and the brightest of the brightest working for you. Leaders in this situation need workers who have the capacity to understand the wide and varied differences that separate one country from another. You want people who can easily and quickly accommodate themselves to others' differences.

Leaders, Start Studying Customs Other Than Your Own

Knowledge of international customs is a huge asset in a virtual society. Local customers in faraway lands are integral to the fabric of the lives of the people you want to reach as customers and in helping your own people reach international team success for your company.

The Extensive International Puzzle

In Germany, a steel boilerplate can be no less than a certain thickness; in England, it has to be at least a certain thickness. So if your team of manufacturers is in London, but you have German workers at the same factory, what do you do? Use the minimum standard! Your German workers will continue to make their steel boilerplate thicker, because that is the German way.

Issues like this play heavily when you sit down with an international group of workers. Speaking different languages is only one piece of the international puzzle of leadership and communications.

Just about everything we've mentioned in this chapter is even more critical when your leaders' group is internally diverse and working in international circumstances. There is the norm that you are used to, and you now have to factor in different languages and translations, customs, legal structures, standards of performance, and oddities, such as different holidays and work rules.

On the other hand, there are some simple rules about working cross-culturally. We all have biases we refuse to acknowledge, but sometimes we freely admit to them when we are living and working among people who are clearly quite different from ourselves. Sometimes you have to live and let live, and that is certainly the case in a virtual workplace.

Get Leaders to Step Outside Their Comfort Zones

Working internationally is an adventure. Even the most seasoned travelers are often reluctant to work outside their comfort zones where familiarity, hearth, and home reside. If you're coaching and leading internationally, you are going to find yourself up against rules and regulations, customers, and even different "weekends" than what you may be familiar with (in the Middle East, Saturday and Sunday are not the weekend, it's Wednesday and Thursday).

There are more global virtual teams today than ever before, and their numbers are increasing rapidly. Get your leaders to step outside their maps of the world and think globally, not locally, for greater effectiveness when leading virtual teams.

Decision making from remote locales can also be a challenge in the virtual global workplace. Many cultures have different ways of facilitating their decision-making processes, and if the project or team spans outside the United States, then savvy managers should research cultural differences prior to engaging in major international leadership efforts.

HP and Virtual Management

In 2003, when John Monroe, the now retired head of Hewlett-Packard's Corporate External Standards organization, was given a challenge to "run a 16-country, multilingual team that operates on both sides of the International Date Line, make it capable of interpreting thousands of arcane and sometimes conflicting government regulations for product designers back home," all during a time when budgets for travel were smaller than ever, he knew that the team members would need to work hard to make it happen. Even though he wasn't happy about the lack of a travel budget, he decided to invest what he could in leading his team virtually. To do so, he built trust, worked to solve problems quickly, and demonstrated that he could succeed in saving the company money. In fact, his team saved HP $800,000 annually in compliance costs for consumer products in Argentina. In addition, they saved $200,000 a year in various aspects of business in Korea. Not every company leads effectively in a virtual setting, but HP proved early on that it can be done.

Questions for Discussion: Leading in a Virtual World

1. What are some of the advantages your virtual team may have over another office that is bound to one location?

2. What are some of the current challenges created by the distance between team members? Ask everyone on the team to contribute solutions to each challenge area.

3. Utilizing the tips in this chapter, how can you create clearer expectations for your teammates in their roles?

4. Which team members do you need to get to know better in order to find out what motivates them, what they enjoy, and what they want from the company and its leadership?

5. What technical tools can you implement, or do you need, to improve your communication and organization in the virtual workspace?

6. What changes can you make as a leader to motivate your team?

7. Are you being clear in setting your goals, roles, and deadlines?

8. How can you reward your virtual team for a job well done?

9. Specifically, how do you make your presence felt as a leader?

10. What does work look like at your office two years from today? five years from today?

Wrapping It Up

Encourage your leaders to be "boundary-less" thinkers and to keep looking for opportunities to be flexible and to learn what motivates each individual, whether that person is in Malaysia or Maine. As a final example to wrap up this chapter, consider the findings of this research project:

A San Diego–based research firm, Telework Research Network, and researcher Kate Lister offered up a rough guesstimate for an *Inc.* magazine project ("The Case and the Plan for a Virtual Office," April 2010) and took a shot at what the U.S. economy might look like if everyone who could work from home, did so, about half of the time. The stats are annual and may well signify that it's time to mail in your keys and join the ranks of the "officeless."

- $700 billion total estimated savings to U.S. businesses.
- $190 billion savings from office rent, electricity bills, absenteeism, real-estate costs, and employee turnover.
- 100 hours per person not spent in traffic or commuting using mass transit.
- $200 billion productivity gains by American companies alone.
- $276 million barrels of oil saved.
- 1,500 lives not lost in car accidents.

We think you may want to share these numbers with your leaders the next time someone teases you about managing the team in your PJs, while working from your dining room table.

Next, you'll learn about coaching for success and the talent management cycle.

Coaching for Success and the Talent Management Cycle

Coaching has quickly become a leadership skill required at all levels of an organization, and the title of coach has gained popularity. The title and its associated responsibility seem to reflect a new breed of leadership style—one that recognizes that the autocrat is no longer in a position to make better decisions than team members are capable of making collectively. This breed of leadership aspires to helping employees reach their full potential by adopting the age-old skills of coaching.

Here is where your leaders will learn ways to make a lasting impact on the organization through coaching others at all levels. Your leaders also will learn the various coaching styles most frequently practiced in organizations and how they can relate their own coaching personality to those in this chapter and then translate that style to a real-world environment. If your training does not include this element, here is your chance to supplement your leadership development program to emphasize this vital quality.

What You Will Learn in This Chapter:

- ◆ Primary leadership coaching styles. Leaders must
 - know exactly what kinds of coaches they are
 - appreciate the many different coaching styles that exist among leaders
 - understand that coaching is a requirement for the natural transition and success of any leader's career.
- ◆ Set up your own coaching program. Leaders must
 - provide onboarding for early engagement
 - prepare to meet the expectations of the people being coached
 - respect and value people's time
 - decide at the outset how they will measure their coaching effectiveness.

If you are developing leaders that your organization calls coaches, or if you are considering creating a coaching position or a structured coaching program in your organization, then this chapter will guide you in the process, providing you with powerful techniques and tools to influence the development and transition of leaders into coaches.

11 COMMANDMENTS FOR COACHING SUCCESS

Because the role of coach should be taken quite seriously, those who aspire to it should have behavioral characteristics and competencies that will set employees up for success. The following skills and behaviors are required for meaningful coaching to take place. We call them the 11 Commandments for Coaching Success.

1. Freely and frequently share knowledge and expertise with others and then ask for the same in return.
2. Respect and appreciate the differences in others and coach them accordingly.
3. Encourage employee suggestions whenever change is being implemented.
4. Make sure employees understand what is expected of them.
5. Be up-front and honest with people at all times.
6. Communicate openly and honestly.
7. Keep employees focused on the team's effectiveness and goals, and value personal contributions as well.
8. Give genuine praise and recognition for a job well done.
9. Look for new ways to help others develop their full potential.
10. Encourage team members to understand, respect, and support one another.
11. Walk the talk and model the standard of performance that is expected in others.

UNDERSTANDING THE PRIMARY LEADERSHIP STYLES OF COACHING

There isn't just one way or even a right way to coach. Instead, effective coaching can take on many styles, depending on the individual's personality and leadership style.

The first step to take when training coaching as a leadership skill is to build awareness of the primary coaching styles that people use. Ask your leaders to describe their personal styles of leadership. This will enable you to match coaches with compatible learners in class, or help coaches adjust their styles as needed.

Key Point: *Not all coaches are created equal, and coaches do not treat all others equally. Instead, they recognize and appreciate the differences in each employee.*

There are dozens of different coaching styles but we've chosen to focus on eight primary styles that people use most often. The objective here is to broaden the awareness and appreciation of these styles among your organization's leadership and to have each person identify themselves in one or more of the styles described.

THE EIGHT PRIMARY COACHING STYLES

1. **Key influencer:** A key influencer is a dominant figure, a person who leads by example and whom others aspire to emulate. This coaching style typically is practiced by people with tremendous influence and charisma.

2. **Formal and structured:** This style of coaching is seen in a system such as Big Brothers/Big Sisters or the Service Corps of Retired Executives (SCORE). Organizations like those do a wonderful job of coaching people through an established system that may include one-on-one support.

3. **Relaxed and informal:** Coaching like this might simply mean being available when support and guidance is needed. This coach is laid-back and usually takes an active role only when asked. His or her behavior is passive but meaningful.

4. **Hands-on:** If your dad taught you how to hit a baseball or bait and set a hook, or your best friend showed you how to hail a taxi the first time you visited New York City, you were coached hands-on. This style of coaching demonstrates how to do something not easily learned from a book.

5. **Hands-off:** Sometimes called coaching-on-the-run, this style might involve someone telling you where to find the photo copier manual and then expecting you to read it yourself and figure out the process. The hands-off coach will be glad to help you after you've first tried to do it yourself.

6. **Visionary:** This is, by far, the most frustrating of all coaching styles. This coach sees the big picture and talks endlessly about his or her vision. When it comes to putting legs on getting anything done, however, this style of coaching can leave employees without any specific directions. The visionary style of coaching has the greatest impact when the coach takes the time not only to describe the big picture but also checks to see that everyone understands just how that big picture will be painted.

7. **Group or team:** This type of coaching happens when an entire group or team of people band together to support one another and set goals. By sharing individual goals with a group of people, you're telling others what you intend to accomplish. Because this group revelation certainly can add pressure to follow through, employees tend not to give up or back out of their commitments. They've told everyone their goals, and they won't want to lose credibility.

8. **Coaches in disguise:** The most influential coaching experience of your life can show up in ways and at times you don't even recognize. It occurs when you're least expecting someone to influence you. Perhaps you're sitting in the airport waiting for your flight to be called when a stranger sits down beside you and shares some information that changes the course of your life, or turns out to be extremely beneficial a month later. You may never see this coach again, but he or she leaves you with a lasting impression.

> **Key Point:** *Coaching is a requirement for the successful and natural transition of our careers. Passing the baton becomes a reflection of all that we have become up to that moment.*

DEVELOPING A PERSONAL CASE STUDY

The most effective model we can use for understanding and developing our own coaching skills comes from our personal experiences. When training coaching techniques, no matter what the level of leadership, begin with the following personal case-study exercise.

What I've Learned From a Real-Life Coach

Have your leaders select a coach from their own lives—one about whom they can build a case study. Have your leaders choose a person who had great impact and influence on them. It may be someone in their personal lives (for example, a parent, best friend, sports coach, pastor, or rabbi) or someone related to their work (perhaps a supervisor, team leader, co-worker, or former employer).

Next, ask your leaders complete this case study worksheet:

1. Name of the real-life coach you've selected for this exercise:

2. What is his or her relationship to you?

3. What is this person's primary coaching style? (Refer to the eight primary coaching styles outlined earlier in this chapter.)

4. How have you specifically observed this person coaching others? How did he or she coach you?

5. Select one memorable circumstance in which this person demonstrated his or her coaching skills in the real world. What were the specific circumstances and specific skills demonstrated?

6. How did this coach communicate his or her expectations of others?

7. Describe in specific detail how this person provided valuable and honest feedback. What did you learn about this person's unique approach when offering constructive or helpful feedback?

8. When and how did this coach willingly accept and receive constructive or helpful feedback from others? What did you learn from how this person accepted and appreciated feedback?

9. When was a time you observed this person go beyond the call of duty in helping someone? What were the challenges he or she faced? How did this coach handle the situation in a way that made a long-lasting impression on you? What did you learn from this observation?

10. What techniques and interpersonal skills learned from this coach can you apply on the job?

11. Are there observable differences (personal style, background, culture, age, philosophies) that exist between you and this coach? What benefits can be gained from those distinct differences?

Use that exercise in the initial stages of developing and training coaches. When your leaders take the time to dissect the specific attributes of coaching that most affected them, they can begin to sculpt their own brands of coaching style with specific and finely tuned methods applicable to the needs of their employees.

Key Point: *Coaches affect eternity because there is no telling where their influence will extend.*

GUIDELINES FOR COACHING

Coaching is a vital skill for all leaders. Today they must be as adept at soft-skills development, which includes coaching, as at development of such hard skills as finance and inventory control.

However, developing the skills and taking the action steps necessary to implement those skills are two different things. Ask your leaders if they currently have a coaching program in place. If they don't, here are some guidelines and action steps to get them started.

You'll want to remind leaders that setting up a coaching arrangement does not replace other types of training. But it certainly can enhance it! To be successful, leaders require many different resources, from computer technology to employee learning and development. Coaching can be a great way to help employees use those tools more effectively while they receive valuable one-on-one guidance and advice along the way.

Leaders can select from the following coaching guidelines when implementing a program for employees.

- **Prepare to meet the expectations of the people you are coaching.** Have employees clearly define what is expected of you as a coach. It is also important to define for employees what you expect of them.
- **Respect and value your time.** Place a dollar value on your time as a coach. Sure it's subjective, but time is money and it's your right to say, "My time is worth X dollars," even if you're not actually being paid that amount. Did you know that some professional coaches get paid $250 an hour? By placing a specific dollar value on your time up front, you'll be less inclined to allow others to waste it. And conveying the value of your time will make others more respectful of your dedication and commitment to their development and learning.
- **Get employees to take action.** Be sure to emphasize the importance of follow-up and follow-through during the coaching process. Get employees to take action on your recommendations and suggestions. Be sure that employees understand that follow-through reveals a person's serious commitment to learning and improving. Make a list of action steps following each coaching session. Set a deadline for accomplishing those steps and then a date to meet again and follow up. For instance, if a coach suggests reading a book, the person being coached should follow up by getting the book, reading it, and then giving feedback to the coach.
- **Pass the baton.** Coaching requires empowering people and delegating responsibility. Give people responsible tasks to complete following each coaching session.
- **Decide ahead of time how you will measure your coaching effectiveness.** Determine at the start the best ways to measure your effectiveness as a coach and the success of the person you are coaching. What are the measurable outcomes you'd like to see take place? By what date?

- **Look beyond the walls to find a great coach.** Coaches are not only found at work. They can be found on the Internet, at church, through magazines and trade journals, through clubs and associations, and among peers.
- **Encourage peer coaching and teach-backs.** Peer coaching is an ongoing process, the pinnacle of team building. Partner new employees with an on-the-job coach, create a shadowing program, rotate partners as time goes on, or let employees team up with peers who possess strengths in areas they are trying to learn and enhance. Set up teach-back sessions at which employees teach their peers something they've learned that they think should be passed along. When we teach what we know, we become more expert at the task.
- **Encourage virtual coaching.** Coaching does not have to be done on the premises, nor does it have to be done in person. Coaching can take place via telephone, email, fax, regular mail, or on video and audiotape.

> **Key Point:** *Just as employees rely on ongoing feedback from their coaches, coaches rely on their employees to share the ultimate results of their coaching sessions.*

How to Measure a Coach's Success

- Conduct a baseline employee survey. Find out if employees have the support and skills necessary to do the job.
- Follow up in six months with another survey to see if the coaching program is taking effect.

COACHING DURING ONBOARDING CAN BE A STRATEGIC LEADERSHIP TOOL

Coaching employees as they come into a company can be incredibly effective in keeping them retained and engaged. Many organizations have put leadership onboarding programs on their lists of initiatives. The motivation for this as an area of focus can vary depending on the particular organization. Some have experienced painful turnover in a specific role or function, while others are seeking ways to speed their return-on-investment for the selection and recruitment processes. Research data shows that 40 percent of leaders hired into new organizations are out after 18 months, and 20 percent of internally promoted leaders are underperforming after two years on the job (Sessa, Kaiser, Taylor, and Campbell, 1998).

Based on this compelling business case, it becomes clear that effective leaders should participate in a purposeful onboarding program as they transition into new roles. Many leaders struggle with integrating the unwritten rules of an organization.

Onboarding provides a road map to understanding the culture and being successful with it. We reached out to experts and thought leaders, Brenda Hampel and Erika Lamont, of Connect the Dots Consulting (www.ConnectTheDotsConsulting.com). Brenda and Erika are the bestselling authors of *Perfect Phrases for New Employee Orientation and Onboarding* (McGraw-Hill), and Anne's co-authors on *Solving Employee Performance Problems: How to Spot Problems Early, Take Appropriate Action, and Bring Out the Best in Everyone* (McGraw-Hill). Brenda and Erika are experts on how to get today's best practices and tools for effective onboard coaching. The following is the result of an interview with our colleagues Brenda and Erika.

FIRST STEPS FOR ONBOARDING

It can be difficult to know where to start. Leaders and human resources professionals need to first understand that they do not need to reinvent the wheel. There are best practices that provide a good starting point that can be customized to meet the specific business case and culture of each organization.

Step One: Positioning and Defining Leadership Onboarding

After an organization has determined and articulated its business case for creating and implementing a leadership onboarding process, it may be difficult to know where and how to begin to build the process. The following is a road map for a leadership onboarding process that has been tested and used successfully in organizations considered small- to mid-sized, as well as Fortune 50.

The Connect the Dots onboarding model starts with a definition of leadership onboarding and its role and context in the Talent Management Cycle (see Figure 12.1).

Onboarding is positioned in an organization's talent management cycle to bridge the gap between the selection process and the performance management and leadership development processes. It allows both the new leader and the organization to transition and assigns roles and responsibilities for each participant. Onboarding begins upon job acceptance and usually ends around the four-month mark, when it is appropriate to transition to the formal performance management process. Most organizations do recognize, however, that it can take up to a full year for a new leader to be completely integrated, but best practices suggest a structured three- to six-month formal process.

Step Two: Inventory and Integration

There are probably many components of a leadership onboarding process that currently exist inside organizations, and it is important to recognize them and determine the ones that are working and the ones that are not. By comparing what is being done now with a best-practice model, it is possible to build your onboarding process for new leaders to fill the gaps.

Figure 12.1 Talent Management Cycle

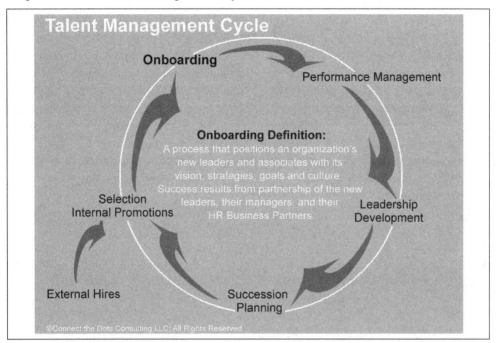

Things that may already be in place that you want to continue to use include:

- company information packet (or website or portal)
- relocation support process
- checklist for office setup
- meet-and-greet schedule
- new leader assimilation
- mentor or onboarding coach

Once the business case has been outlined and everyone is working from the same definition of onboarding, Connect the Dots lists three most important components of a successful onboarding program. Each time they work with a client organization to build or customize their program, they focus the roles, resources, and delivery around three main themes. Three pillars of onboarding success are **knowledge**, **relationships**, and **feedback**.

The first pillar, **knowledge**, refers to all the information that the new leaders need to acquire throughout their onboarding. It starts with a broad overview of organizational vision, mission, values, and history, and then builds to current strategies, processes, and culture. From there, new leaders need timely knowledge about their function, their teams, and their roles.

The next pillar, **building relationships**, is critically important to a new leader's success. This component is especially important for leaders who are brought into an organization to bring about change or lead through a crisis. But it is, of course, vital to any new leader's success as they execute their objectives through and with others.

Lastly, the providing of timely and actionable **feedback** is usually the missing link in most leadership onboarding programs. Organizations are typically not set up to give formal feedback, and the informal feedback on which they rely can be incomplete or missing entirely. Impressions and perceptions about the new leaders are formed very early, so it is important to incorporate both quantitative and qualitative early feedback into the onboarding program, usually at the 45- to 60-day mark.

These three components are the foundation on which organizations should build their leadership onboarding program, allowing them to see the results that are consistent with their overall objectives.

As with most programs, it is important to create a structure that provides consistency. This will help you to integrate these pillars into your actual onboarding program. At the same time, it is critical to allow enough flexibility to tailor the program for the unique parts of the business and particular needs of the individuals who are joining the organization or being promoted. To this end, Connect the Dots has created a best-practice model that accomplishes both.

Step Three: Building the Model

Once you have successfully 1) defined and positioned leadership onboarding in your organization, and 2) identified the parts and pieces that you are already doing and those that should be integrated into the leadership onboarding program, it is helpful to 3) create a time-based or phased approach to build out your process. This will create a road map for your new leaders, their hiring managers, and their HR partners so that each participant is contributing to the onboarding success of the new leader. Connect the Dots recommends a time-based process so that each part is delivered just in time and the new leader has context for the information that he or she is receiving at the time and reduces the "drinking from a fire hose" phenomenon that often happens in the first weeks and months on the job.

Starting with Pre-start, that period from when the job is accepted to Day One, help the new leader get all the information he or she can about the organization, its competitors, the business unit or function, manager, peers, and team. Next build a 90-Day Onboarding Plan that supports those key objectives that are laid out by the hiring manager. Included in every good 90-Day Plan is a list of people with whom the new leader must build relationships in order to be successful, as well as how they are connected to the new leader's onboarding objectives.

Month One should be focused on gaining information about the organization, function, and role. Also important are those "meet-and-greet" meetings with key stakeholders to start building critical relationships. The hiring manager's time with the new leader is vital during this period as things in the organization can often change, and the

job that the new leader accepted may not be exactly the same job that she has now. Role clarity for all new leaders cannot be underestimated.

Month Two brings more experience about the organization's culture and how to be successful in it. New leaders need feedback about how they are being perceived early on so that they can correct any missteps and get back on track. Formal feedback about how that new leader is onboarding (not performing) is critical and should take place by the 60-day mark. Then during Month Three, the new leader can focus on leveraging the things that he is doing well and work on the things that he must to improve perceptions. Too often, leaders are not getting the feedback they need until a year or more into the new role, and by that time, it is usually too late to make the necessary corrections, and derailment occurs.

Wrapping Up the Process: Transition to Performance Management

A best-practice onboarding process has a defined beginning and ending. Leaders cannot "get away with" being new forever, and organizations need to be able to transition them into their performance management or their leadership development process. Unfinished objectives are easily transferable into the leader's goals for the remainder of the year or are adjusted to address new priorities. Debriefing is also critical at the close of the process so that the organization can refine and improve its process. A new leader who has just completed a successful onboarding experience is one who is energized and is an advocate for the process. The HR partner has also successfully begun a relationship with an influential leader and can leverage that relationship as a business partner. With a well-integrated and sustainable onboarding process, organizations are able to not only transition their new leaders smoothly for quick productivity, but create raving fans for their business brand. No longer is there the gap between the recruitment process and the reality of the job if the new leader, hiring manager, and HR partner are aligned with the plan and the process.

A critical final step, once you know what needs to be done, is to decide who is responsible for each task. Clearly identified roles and responsibilities for each participant in the leadership onboarding process will affect the delivery of the program significantly. Begin by listing the participants in the program; a typical list includes the new leader, hiring manager, human resources department, and the mentor or coach. A useful approach to determining who does what is to ask the following **three Cs** of each participant group:

- What is **capacity** of the group?
- What is the **competency** of the group to deliver?
- What is the **commitment** of the group to the onboarding program?

The answers to the questions will help to surface the current state of each group and their ability to effectively deliver and facilitate the onboarding process, as well as the gaps between current state and desired state. An action plan can then be developed to address the gaps.

Delivery Methods

Onboarding best practices suggest that there are three main delivery methods of a leadership onboarding program: paper (or binder), online or web-based, and coaching.

Each method has its strengths and weaknesses, but the delivery method to the new leader should fall mostly into a coaching model, which is basically a series of meetings with printed, supporting documents provided to the new leader by the HR partner. Then the HR partner can facilitate conversations and assignments.

Lastly, every program must be structured and orderly, yet not rigid. A time-based program with specific milestones and checkpoints will provide new leaders a consistent experience without them feeling like they are going through a "process." It also allows the HR partners to use their knowledge and judgment to appropriately customize the program for each of their new leaders.

Human resources leaders are also responsible for measuring the success of an onboarding process—which is easier than you may think! Metrics of the leadership onboarding program should always reflect the original objectives of the organization. What was the business case for leadership onboarding in our organization? Which areas did we need to address? Cultural fit? Speed to performance? Retention? Engagement? These, then, are the areas that are measured. Facilitated discussions, individual conversations, feedback surveys, and onboarding assignments can be included in the leadership onboarding process to collect the data.

It is critical that the measurement tools collect two kinds of data: quantitative and qualitative. By asking for both, your organization will have richer information and be able to make improvements and adjustments to your leadership onboarding program, and to see trends in the challenges of your new leaders. It is again important to include all of the participants in the onboarding process so that the data is complete.

More and more organizations are recognizing the impact of a consistent and structured leadership onboarding program, describing the effects of it as:

- creating a level playing field for all new leaders, externally hired or internally promoted
- providing each process partner with a common starting point and resources
- giving each new leader access to the same experience and resources
- increasing the chance that new leaders will reach their objectives.

LEADERSHIP ONBOARDING IN ACTION

Organizations have experienced real success with this onboarding model. Below are a couple real examples presented as case studies.

Case Study 1: Growing Talent and Bringing in New Blood

A Fortune 50, global off-priced retailer discovered that it required a new approach to building its internal leadership "bench." It had historically relied on internal promotions; however, the changing talent pool caused it to begin to hire more leaders from outside the organization. To meet the demands of this business change, it used the Connect the Dots model to create a consistent onboarding process that integrates the

new leaders into the company culture and engages both the HR partners and the hiring managers.

And because they are a planning organization, they did their homework to build the business case. They did surveys and interviews of new leaders who did not have a formal onboarding experience, and then did the same for new leaders who did complete an onboarding program. Here is an outline of what they found.

Challenges and obstacles that the new leaders experienced in this organization *without* onboarding included:

- The physical environment was not set up (no offices, furniture, computers, etc.).
- They didn't know how to access information.
- There was no structure to transition—no formal objectives.
- No one would help them navigate culture—staff seemed apprehensive.
- It was assumed that they knew what to do—no real training in new position.
- For those relocating, personal transition issues overshadowed their early days.
- They were not able to contribute right away.
- They were told to put aside what they already knew and just absorb information.

A formal onboarding impact study identified these results of the program:

- Leaders said that the positions matched their expectations.
- They had a clear understanding of their roles and how it fits into the organization.
- Working with an HR partner was very helpful—it was valuable to have someone to think things through with and act as a sounding board.
- They felt supported by their manager and HR.
- They felt the environment was positive and welcoming.
- Their onboarding objectives clearly focused the first weeks on the job.
- Meet-and-greets were productive and led to stronger relationships.
- Early wins built confidence of new leaders and of the organization in the new leaders.
- Having structure during the first few weeks and months was effective.
- They felt the environment supports and encourages development on the whole.

Case Study 2: Rapid Growth and Culture Shock

Another example is from a leading pediatric health and research center that had been experiencing significant growth and change, including to its senior leadership team, during a two-year period. The organization's board encouraged this growth by recruiting nationally and internationally recognized clinical and administrative talent. The result was a significant culture shift, and the new leaders had to be integrated quickly and appropriately to be able to meet their aggressive objectives.

Using the Connect the Dots model, the hospital built its leadership onboarding process to make the new leaders feel like a valued part of the organization and the community while leveraging their diverse backgrounds and experiences.

Previous to implementing a formal leadership onboarding experience, the hospital's new senior leaders described the following "pain" in their onboarding:

- lack of understanding of who the key players were in the organization
- lack of access to these key players

- too many meetings without knowing the context or understanding of role
- pent-up demand for decisions and actions without enough information or experience to make good decisions
- not understanding the systems and processes to be able to navigate in first few months.

The results of putting in place a formal leadership onboarding experience included:

- better understanding of the new leaders' roles and the hospital's expectations of those roles
- just-in-time meetings and information provided context for decision making
- smoother personal transitions by connecting relocating leaders to community resources
- faster return-on-investment of the new leaders, payback to the hospital for the recruitment process
- reinforcement of cultural elements that needed to be preserved, and a reduction in negative culture elements or old ways of doing things.

The human resources team now has the tools to measure how well the new leaders are integrating (retention and engagement are up) and what parts of the hospital's selection and onboarding programs need improvement.

Successful leadership onboarding is a true partnership between a new leader and the organization. It has been a useful tool in the engagement and retention of new hires in an uncertain economy. Onboarding will continue to play a key role in the talent management process as the climate starts to shift from decline to stabilization, then to growth. It will be more important than ever to get and keep the right leaders in the right jobs through this powerful coaching and engagement tool.

Coaching at American Express, Disney, and Bell Atlantic

At American Express, there's an informal buddy system whereby financial advisors select learning partners. Each person agrees to support and encourage the other by meeting regularly for lunch, giving advice, or just listening like a best friend. The process continues for several months.

At Disney, following the first few days of recognizing and respecting Disney traditions in what is called the "Disney Traditions Class," new employees are introduced to Magic Kingdom–style coaching. For as long as two weeks, Disney HRD managers conduct training and coaching for cast members on the job—breaking traditional corporate training molds by taking coaching to the real world.

At Bell Atlantic, reciprocal learning comes naturally in coaching arrangements called mentoring cycles. In mentoring cycles, mid-level executives are paired with more senior-level executives to talk and work through a variety of on-the-job challenges. Executives talk about their personal experiences, and as a result, everyone broadens his or her knowledge quickly through the sharing of techniques and solutions that have been honed with time and experience.

Case in Point: Coaching the Microsoft Way

Without exception, Microsoft dominates the high ground of the information superhighway. The corporation owns the operating systems and basic application programs that run on more than 170 million computers worldwide. With such success, you might expect that coaching isn't needed at Microsoft, but it is. Founder Bill Gates's philosophy is that growing employees benefits them, their leaders, and the company. Coaching is one way that Microsoft helps employees get to the next level of performance in an extraordinarily fast-moving and competitive industry. The following leadership practices are active at Microsoft:

- Walk a mile in someone else's shoes. Let employees spend a day in another department to see what goes on.
- Lead by example.
- Give employees opportunities that expose them to upper-level management.
- Encourage continuing education and intentional learning.
- Set up lunches for teams with upper-level managers.
- Let someone go to a meeting in your place—what a morale booster!
- Challenge people's weaknesses by giving them new responsibilities.

THE POWER OF COACHING

By implementing practical coaching techniques like the ones covered in this chapter, you will be providing managers with the power and ability to tap into an unlimited resource: their people. In addition, your organization will continue reaping the enormous benefits that only coaching can bring. It's pretty clear that successful leadership requires successful coaching.

Coaching Self-Assessment: 11 Commandments Checklist

On a scale from one (lowest) to three (highest), assess your successful coaching characteristics. Use this tool for ongoing self-improvement evaluation in any of the characteristics you rate as two or lower.

	1	2	3
1. Freely and frequently share knowledge and expertise with others and ask for the same in return.	☐	☐	☐
2. Respect and appreciate the differences in others and coach them accordingly.	☐	☐	☐
3. Encourage employee suggestions whenever change is being implemented.	☐	☐	☐
4. Make sure employees are clear about what is expected of them.	☐	☐	☐
5. Be up-front and honest with people at all times.	☐	☐	☐
6. Communicate openly and honestly.	☐	☐	☐
7. Keep employees focused on the team's effectiveness and goals, and value personal contributions as well.	☐	☐	☐
8. Give genuine praise and recognition for a job well done.	☐	☐	☐
9. Look for new ways to help others develop their full potential.	☐	☐	☐
10. Encourage team members to understand, respect, and support one another.	☐	☐	☐
11. Walk the talk and model the standard of performance that is expected in others.	☐	☐	☐

Questions for Discussion: Coaching for Success

1. Why are coaching characteristics important leadership qualities?
2. Are there any coaching characteristics or behaviors that could be added to the list of coaching styles?
3. How does identifying individual coaching styles help leaders become more effective coaches?
4. How can a leader's coaching style be adapted to meet a worker's specific needs?

Wrapping It Up

In this chapter, we've learned that the role of coach carries great responsibility because coaches intervene in their employees' lives and job functions. And wherever intervention takes place, there is not only profound opportunity for influencing someone's personal and professional development, but there also is a great opportunity to mess things up unintentionally. Be certain your leaders understand both the duality and the serious nature of the role they will undertake in coaching.

In the next chapter, we'll study performance management techniques, and your leaders will enhance their understanding of the coaching process and how to develop their communications excellence.

Performance Management—Using Communications Excellence

Right now, in some organizations, a leader is meeting with an employee to discuss his or her performance. Some leaders would rather have a root canal than hold an employee performance review! But that's because leaders often focus on the wrong issues when it comes to performance management. For instance, a leader may focus more on filling out the company's evaluation forms correctly than on using effective communications tools to help that employee succeed.

Here is where your leaders will learn that the only way to improve the overall performance levels in the organization is through a stronger development of performance communications skills. The skills covered in this chapter will drastically affect your leader's ability to manage performance at every level. If your training does not include this element, here is your chance to supplement your leadership development program to emphasize this vital quality.

What You Will Learn in This Chapter:

♦ What performance management requires of you. Leaders must
- implement feedback early in the onboarding process
- know that performance management is a people process
- accept that performance management encourages ongoing communications between leaders and their people
- implement the practical application of performance communications techniques that will raise levels of performance.

♦ Real-world leadership performance scenarios. Leaders must
- learn to handle an array of performance issues when they come up
- stop poor performance issues from recurring
- establish a leader's performance strategy for a successful outcome.

PERFORMANCE COMMUNICATION—IT'S AN ONGOING PROCESS

Airplanes can fly on autopilot—organizations can't. Many challenges will arise for your leaders every day, so teach them how to think on their feet and how to use their communications skills to remove barriers to their employees' performance—either before or as they occur, not later when irreversible damage has been done. That is what we mean by the "ongoing process" of performance communication. It's the daily challenge of maintaining employee performance at its optimum level.

> **Key Point:** *Performance management is a people process that encourages ongoing communication between a leader and his or her employees. It involves establishing clear expectations while maintaining the level of work to be performed. The process is a system with a number of moving parts, all of which are critical to the overall performance and productivity of the organization.*

Performance communications techniques that will be practiced by your leaders are a two-way process that should accomplish the following objectives:

Objective 1: Quickly identify and uncover obstacles to an employee's performance.

Objective 2: Quickly give both parties what they need to eliminate the obstacles that stand in the way of an employee's improved performance and success.

Dos and Don'ts of Performance Communication

Do focus on:	Don't focus on:
• The future and a positive outcome	• The past
• Performance issues	• Personality conflicts
• Setting goals and planning	• Evaluations
• Finding solutions	• Blaming and criticizing
• Dialogue	• One-way communication

> **Key Point:** *Performance communication is an ongoing process between a leader and his or her employees to ensure that performance challenges are identified early on, before they get out of hand and interfere with an employee's success.*

The methods and processes your leaders use to foster their communications excellence may include some of the following:

- MBWA, or "management by walking around" and observing what is going on (observation is your most strategic tool, and it's free; use it)
- weekly meetings at which employees report on the status of their projects
- monthly meetings with each employee to evaluate overall direction and review what has been accomplished to date
- providing lots of helpful and corrective feedback
- one-on-one communication when employee performance issues arise
- written status reports from employees received on a regular basis.

After you've reviewed these communications processes with your leaders, ask them to share what specific methods or processes they find most useful or effective on the job.

THE IMPORTANCE OF EARLY FEEDBACK

Leaders typically do not get meaningful, actionable feedback during their first months in a new role, or at a new organization. This leaves much to chance for both the leaders and the organization. Effective communication includes early feedback in managing performance. Brenda Hampel and Erika Lamont (see chapter 12 for their coaching onboarding for leaders guidelines) have consulted, coached, inspired, and developed operational and human resources leadership teams for more than 25 years, creating onboarding strategies and coaching leaders in top organizations through their company, Connect the Dots Consulting. We caught up with them to discuss early feedback, including how it is different from the more common 360-degree leadership feedback, and how to successfully implement early feedback. They also provided case studies of how other organizations have leveraged this tool. Below is a summary of some of their strategy and feedback.

One question you may have is, "Why should organizations pay attention to giving leaders early feedback?" Many people think you have to "wait and see" how the person does in his or her first year. While this may be true in some cases, you also have heard the scary statistics about new leaders and their failure rates.

The Center for Creative Leadership reported in 1998 that 40 to 50 percent of new leaders fail during the first 18 months in their new roles. The numbers being reported continue to hover around the 40 percent mark according to studies by the Alexcel Group and Monster.com. The impact, of course, is the cost to the organizations that lose these new leaders. Brad Smart, author of *Topgrading*, conducted a study that found that failed leaders cost each organization 24 times their base salaries. For a conservative example, this would mean that a leader with a $120,000 annual salary costs her organization $2.8 million if she leaves and must be replaced.

The business case is pretty clear. New leaders are at risk, and their failure costs organizations millions of dollars each year. But what is being done to address this issue? More and more organizations are implementing formal leadership onboarding processes that include formal early feedback to smooth these transitions for new leaders and increase their chances of success. They not only are able to integrate into their roles and the culture of the organization, but can usually do so more quickly than their counterparts without such support. They are able to "pay back" their organizations quicker and help them realize a more substantial ROI.

So the answer is easy, right? Create and deliver a leadership onboarding process that supports all the new and transitioning leaders. This will enable leaders to access critical **knowledge** about the organization, learn about their functions and their roles, build key stakeholder relationships, and get timely **feedback** on how they are integrating in order to be successful. The missing component in many leadership onboarding programs is the final one: **timely feedback.**

An important component of this is that not just any feedback will do. "We have seen the typical feedback that an organization gives new leaders falls into four common categories and they usually get it (or not!) from their managers, direct reports, or peers in a very unstructured and hard-to-manage way," states Hampel. She and Lamont explain that this typical feedback is usually one of the following:

- none
- "drive-by"
- second-hand
- humorous.

It is most common for leaders to get the "sink or swim" approach to transition, or the "she's a smart person, she will figure it out." In this case, no news is not good news. Unfortunately, this approach is not very successful because impressions and perceptions are formed quickly and sometimes are difficult to change if left unchecked. The new leader who is not aware of his missteps will continue to make mistakes that no one is pointing out to him. The result can be lost time, bad decisions, damaged relationships, and even derailment.

"Drive-by" feedback is also prevalent and is found mostly in hallway conversations or other informal settings. This may be a short comment by the new leader's manager, or a peer without context or further explanation as to why a particular behavior or action didn't fit. The new leader is left with more questions than before she received the feedback, and may be unsure as to what to correct or how.

Secondhand and humorous feedback are just as ineffective as "drive-by" because they also lack context, or examples to help the new leader understand why something he did may have been out of line. One example might take the form of "I heard you really let them have it in that budget meeting!" Is that a good thing or a bad thing? The leader is left to figure this out alone, and doesn't always come to the right conclusion. The most common results of these typical kinds of feedback for new leaders are confusion, frustration, disillusionment, misperceptions, and performance issues. All can contribute to the alarming failure rate of new leaders.

Early feedback as part of a formal leadership onboarding process is different. It allows the new leader to see specifically how he is or isn't integrating into the culture of the organization. It is data-driven and delivered by a qualified coach so that there is context and discussion around each point. The key difference also is that this type of feedback is not performance related but onboarding specific.

The Model for Early Feedback

This model represents a best-practice early feedback process for new or transitioning leaders. It shows when to collect the data, who to include in the process, and what will be measured. It allows both the new leader and the organization to get an accurate snapshot of what the new leader needs to stop doing, start doing, and continue doing to be successful in her new role.

FIGURE 13.1 The Model for Early Feedback

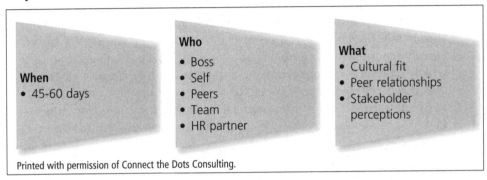

Printed with permission of Connect the Dots Consulting.

Process vs. Integration

Many organizations use surveys to measure their leadership onboarding programs. However, these are typically "process related" and are not indicators of the actual integration of their new leaders. They will ask questions such as "Was your office set up?" or "Did you receive your ID badge and parking pass?" or "Was the comp and benefit paperwork completed on time?" Although these are important logistical details of a new leader's transition, they do not indicate whether that new leader is actually integrating and behaving in a way that is consistent with successful transition in this new organization. Following are the seven indicators that Connect the Dots has identified as the key areas of focus when measuring whether the new leader is truly integrating into her new role, function, and organization.

The Seven Onboarding Indicators

Connect the Dots has identified seven onboarding indicators that when measured can predict the success of a new or transitioning leader. New leaders who receive positive

FIGURE 13.2 The Seven Onboarding Indicators

Printed with permission of Connect the Dots Consulting.

and constructive feedback, both quantitative and qualitative, from key stakeholders in these core areas are more likely to succeed.

1. **Cultural fit:** How well does the leader understand the culture and adapt his style to fit in?
2. **Stakeholder perceptions:** How do the key stakeholders (manager, peers, direct reports, customers) perceive that the new leader is doing everything she should to get up to speed and integrate?
3. **Personal transition:** Is the new leader's relocation going smoothly? What family or personal needs does he have that could distract from focusing on onboarding?
4. **Organizational knowledge:** Is the new leader more focused on learning about the organization than proving herself?
5. **Peer relationships:** Peers can be the toughest stakeholders to win over, yet provide the best insight to the culture and how to navigate the organizational politics.
6. **Business/market knowledge:** Often leaders are brought into organizations from different industries (manufacturing to healthcare, for example) to leverage their successes. It is critical that "Business 101" knowledge, acronyms, and processes are shared and not assumed.
7. **Team alignment:** For new leaders, it's all about assessing their new teams and getting them aligned around common goals. Early warning signs from team members can help leaders get back on track before it's too late.

Collecting and Delivering Early Feedback

"It is important to collect feedback via both formal and informal channels," states Lamont. "What we have seen work best is to include both formal and informal collections tools into your onboarding process. The formal tools are usually surveys that ask specific questions about each of the seven indicators. The surveys are distributed to key stakeholders such as the boss, peers, direct reports, human resources partner, and any other relevant participants. A self-assessment is also critical to be able to measure perceptions against what the new leader is thinking. Next, it is also important to collect data through conversations and observations. The boss, human resources partner, and the new leader himself can solicit feedback from several sources to get a good picture of what that new leader needs to start doing, stop doing, and/or continue doing in his onboarding."

Once the feedback data has been collected, Lamont explains, it is important to have it reviewed by an experienced and qualified participant in the process. This could be the boss, the human resources partner, or an external coach. It is important to extrapolate themes and help the leader understand both how to leverage strengths and how to bridge gaps and make adjustments. Timing is also critical in the delivery of the feedback. There should be no big gaps in time between when the feedback is collected and when it is delivered. If there is, the feedback loses its relevance and the new leader may disregard it.

Here are the key steps to implementing early feedback:

1. Match metrics to objectives.
2. Collect quantitative and qualitative data.
3. Include all participants.
4. Report results both for individuals and organization.

Hampel and Lamont created a multi-rater survey tool, *Are You Connected?*, with 27 questions that measure the seven indicators and report both quantitative and qualitative data for the individual leaders and their organizations. The survey process is designed and works like a 360, multi-rater tool. It has proven to be an invaluable source of information that allows new leaders to understand how their behaviors are being perceived and make adjustments accordingly. The survey is sent to key stakeholders including the new leader, his or her manager, peers, direct reports, and HR partner. The questions both require a numeric score and allow for comments. The results are compiled into an easy-to-read report with supporting resources and an action planning guide. A qualified facilitator guides the discussion and reviews the data with the new leader and sometimes includes the manager.

When early feedback is collected and delivered properly, the entire organization benefits.

New leaders get:
- timely feedback against the seven onboarding indicators and an action plan to address gaps
- opportunity to make adjustments before derailment.

Hiring managers and HR partners get:
- a "snapshot" view of how that new leader is doing
- specific quantitative and qualitative data to facilitate conversation.

Organizations get:
- data that show any common onboarding challenges/themes
- data that reflect needs in the selection and/or onboarding processes.

HR's Role in the Early Feedback Process

This is the best part! HR adds tremendous value in several ways: to the new leaders, to the hiring managers, and, of course, to the organization.

- The HR partner is a contributing partner to the actual feedback. He or she can provide a great perspective to the new leader from someone who is inside the organization but outside that new leader's immediate workgroup.
- HR partners act as internal consultants or experts who can help the new leaders by
 - identifying opportunities and addressing issues
 - coaching new leaders to make timely adjustments
 - speeding the "pay-back" of the new leader to the organization.

- The HR partner and the new leader build a strong and trust-based relationship from the very beginning and can better sustain it as they continue to work together going forward.

Benefits for the Organization

The real measurement of success is the overall impact to the new leader, his or her team, the department, and the organization. Hampel and Lamont have found five consistent themes in the results of their clients who use this type of feedback model.

Organizations have new leaders with:

- increased speed to performance
- increased engagement and retention
- alignment with culture and objectives
- stronger and better relationships with key stakeholders
- higher rates of achieving performance and onboarding objectives.

The following are two examples of some of Hampel and Lamont's clients who have used the early feedback process to literally "save" some of their new leaders.

Case Study 1: The Difficulties on a Multicultural Leadership Team

A foreign-based luxury brand automotive manufacturer with a large U.S. presence fills its leadership roles both from its global locations and from its U.S. offices. This multicultural leadership team presents a unique challenge for leaders joining the company. The U.S. human resources leadership team was struggling to retain new leaders who were being hired into one specific, high-profile role. The hard and soft costs of turnover were becoming obvious and painful. The culture of the organization is strong and expects new leaders to "hit the ground running" and produce quickly—without support or feedback. The HR team knew the turnover would continue if something was not done to support these new leaders.

Connect the Dots worked with them to implement Hampel and Lamont's onboarding coaching and early feedback models. To accommodate the organizational culture, they coached the OD partner, as he coached the new COO. In addition, the *Are You Connected?* early feedback survey was used to provide the COO with critical data regarding how his stakeholders experienced him during his first 90 days.

The leader onboarding coaching model and early feedback survey provided both the new leader and OD partner with the tools and resources at the right time throughout the onboarding period. Connect the Dots advised the OD partner on which resources to use, how to deliver messages and tools, and when and how to include the hiring manager. The *Are You Connected?* survey provided the COO with valuable feedback about how successful his stakeholders perceived him to be. Connect the Dots Consulting coached the OD partner on delivering the feedback and coaching.

Case Study 2: Giving Feedback While Being Nice

Another one of Hampel and Lamont's large retail clients had a similar issue with not providing any feedback to their new leaders. Their culture was to "be nice," and they were uncomfortable giving any kind of constructive feedback. However, the HR leaders knew that the new leaders needed feedback in order to be successful in their complex culture. Additionally, the HR team did not have the expertise to determine the appropriate behaviors to measure.

Connect the Dots implemented the *Are You Connected?* early feedback survey with this organization's new leaders as an extension of their leadership onboarding process. They used the seven onboarding indicators and customized the survey tool to match the organization's culture and communication style. Training for the HR partners was conducted to certify them to use the tool and deliver feedback. The new leaders now have a clear view of where they are hitting and missing the mark. One VP said, "The early feedback survey has literally saved some of our newest top leaders."

A Final Word on Early Feedback

With the sustained failure rates of new and transitioning leaders, it is fair to say that most are probably not receiving or acting on early, relevant feedback during their onboarding periods. Organizations are missing the mark by not providing a structured and formal process for collecting and delivering this critical feedback. Even if your organization lacks a full-blown leadership onboarding process, your leaders can still benefit tremendously from participating in an early feedback process. There is payback and impact to the feedback process as a stand-alone, and it can also be a way to gain some traction and success if you have not been able to engage your leaders in any type of onboarding activities. Feedback is powerful and, when done correctly, can speed success or prevent failure.

A DAY-IN-THE-LIFE FOR LEADERS: PERFORMANCE MANAGEMENT SCENARIOS

This section of the chapter offers hard-hitting, real-world scenarios of performance management. They present the six most common and most challenging situations that take place in almost any work environment. Performance topics featured here include

- dealing with peer-to-boss resentment
- managing conflict and resistance to change
- productivity affected by personal problems
- raising the bar on complacency
- dealing with the rumor mill
- handling defensive attitudes.

As the developer of this program, when you use these scenarios in leadership training and development, you will equip your leaders better to handle their daily challenges. They will learn to deal with a variety of performance issues when they occur, prevent performance issues from recurring, and establish a strategy for producing a successful outcome. The scenarios also are powerful tools for you as the trainer of leaders because of the specific ways that solutions to each problem are easily outlined in a bulleted format.

How to Use the Performance Scenarios

Group your leaders into teams and assign each team a performance scenario and communications challenge. Ask them to brainstorm their own solutions and recommended tools for each of the six scenarios. After teams have presented and discussed all of their solutions and ideas, distribute the "suggestions for leaders" that appear after each scenario. Those answer sheets can serve as feedback tools to help them measure the strength of their own answers. The suggestions offer additional fast tips, tools, and techniques for their leadership tool kits.

Performance Scenario #1: Dealing With Peer-to-Boss Resentment

Susan is a newly promoted customer service manager. She knows that a co-worker really wanted the same position. Susan used to enjoy working with that person because she was always easygoing and cooperative—that is, until Susan was promoted. Since that time, Susan's co-worker has been a constant obstacle to everything Susan has tried to do. She is uncooperative and sometimes antagonistic. It's been two months since the promotion and the co-worker has begun speaking badly about Susan. In staff meetings her body language is defensive and cold. When Susan asks her what is wrong, she rolls her eyes and says, "Nothing" or "I don't know what you're talking about."

Communications challenge: How does a leader coach a former peer who now clearly resents and challenges her supervision?

Suggestions for leaders:

- Try to understand that this co-worker's resentment is not about you but about him or her. This person probably feels he or she did not get a fair chance, and because you are now in a leadership position, you are a convenient target.
- Try to find out why this person doesn't feel respected or acknowledged for his or her contributions.
- Don't apologize for having been promoted. This is an opportunity to demonstrate self-respect as a leader and coach.
- Be humble. A dose of humility on your part can go a long way. Be savvy to ego-driven behaviors.
- Take a direct but caring approach. Talk about the resentment honestly. Get the issues out so that they can be dealt with and you can really coach this person constructively.
- Finally, ask what the employee's plan is for moving forward.

Performance Scenario #2:
Managing Conflict and Resistance to Change

Jenny is a frontline supervisor. She has a great team with the exception of one senior employee who always resists Jenny's initiatives or ideas. It seems that no matter what Jenny tries, this man undermines her or pokes holes in the process in front of others. Jenny is not certain if this person is resisting her personally or is resisting changes taking place within the organization overall. What makes this particularly difficult is that this man's performance on the job is fine.

Communications challenge: How does a leader handle a top-performing employee who continually resists change and bucks authority?

Suggestions for leaders:

- You're the leader. You've worked hard to create an environment for honest feedback, so use it. Don't avoid the problem. Get it out on the table.
- When resistance to change and authority exists and is not dealt with openly and honestly, it will stay bottled up and rise again and again. Dealing with it directly could avoid possible sabotage or much tougher issues in the future.
- As the team's leader, remind yourself that resistance to your authority or to change is usually a sign of someone's negative energy needing to be expressed, but it has nothing to do with you personally.
- Take an authentic approach. Welcome the resistor and ask for his or her input. Consider it valuable information that you can transform into positive results for the group.
- Never argue or attempt to sell your point of view. Just explain it.
- Summarize the other person's point of view to ensure you have understood it correctly.
- Ask for support, or at least ask that the worker not block your efforts in doing your job to the best of your ability.
- Be brief. Communicate clearly and take the time to explain your thoughts and intentions. Give answers to questions. If you don't know, find out.

Performance Scenario #3:
Productivity Affected by Personal Problems

Steve is a new team leader. He never realized how involved he was going to become in his team members' personal problems. Although he doesn't feel comfortable counseling them, he knows that as a leader he has to take action when he senses that problems at home are affecting on-the-job performance. Currently, Steve has a team member who is getting a lot of pressure from his family to spend more time at home. The employee is upset about this, and it is clearly affecting his job performance and productivity.

Communication challenge: How does a leader effectively counsel an employee whose family pressures keep him or her from traveling or working the hours necessary to do the job?

Suggestions for leaders:

- Ask meaningful questions. Ask why this is happening. You can start the conversation with an observation that you've noticed a change in performance and then provide examples.
- Take the time to look carefully at past performance. Is there a pattern, or is this something unlike this person's usual performance on the job?
- Listen carefully. Demonstrate patience.
- Make a commitment to coach and work with this person to build a plan for effective change.

More help:

- Prepare yourself when counseling an employee for the possibility that you will uncover significant personal issues that are preventing effective performance. Know your organization's employee assistance program and other resources that might be available.
- Be clear about your objective: What are the expectations? What job needs to get done? Resist becoming entangled in your employee's personal life. This does not mean, however, that you should not be compassionate and understanding and take the time to listen.
- At some point, you will have to discuss the negative consequences of repeating the performance problem. Be honest and direct.
- Protect the employee's privacy. Never repeat something about an employee's personal life without his or her permission. Your credibility as a leader is on the line.
- Set a time to meet again and review a plan for change. Place the responsibility on the shoulders of the team member. Offer your support and monitor progress just as you would any other performance goal.

Performance Scenario #4: Raising the Bar on Complacency

James is a senior-level regional manager who greatly enjoys his job. His team does good work, and turnover is relatively low. But James can't seem to motivate his people, and they lack enthusiasm. When he asks for new ideas, they just shrug. None are really high achievers, but they do their jobs consistently. James is frustrated because no one requires discipline, but none are good enough to reward for outstanding performance on the job. It seems that complacency has set in.

Communications challenge: How does a leader motivate people who are marginal to perform at a higher level? How does a leader raise the bar?

Suggestions for leaders:

- The employees in this situation are probably saying, "What's in it for me?" As a leader, you need to answer that question for yourself as you analyze your people's resistance to change and the desire for personal and professional improvement.
- Because things are running smoothly, you should ask yourself, "What's in it for my employees if I ask them to do more?" Anticipating likely obstacles or difficult situations is important.

Tips for leading employees to improve performance:
- Raise the bar. When a leader raises his or her expectations for achievement overall, people are held accountable for those new standards.
- Provide a positive reason (or reward system) to move everyone in this direction.
- Provide an undesirable prompt that moves people away from the old version of complacency and the status quo.
- As leader, you also should be asking, "Can I, too, meet these standards?"
- Determine beforehand whether anyone in the group is meeting some of these standards already. Leaders learn to harness examples of high energy in the workplace and turn them into impressive internal benchmarks.
- Be clear on what the new standards you set will ultimately provide for everyone. Describe the benefits to everyone.

More help:
- Be sure to make clear what you expect of everyone. The clearer your expectations of others, the greater the chances that they genuinely will be motivated to achieve them.
- Think it through. How will you measure and reward success?
- Let the team set its own standards. Help define what raising the bar looks like, and ask how each person will choose to participate. Include everyone.
- Build in small successes and wins along the way. Celebrate with the team.
- Identify the individual needs of the group. People are motivated when they believe their needs will be met and they will receive something they want and need.
- Coach esteem and self-confidence. Provide helpful feedback and natural praise. Taking the time to say "Super job!" can go a long way.

Performance Scenario #5: Dealing With the Rumor Mill

Shawna is a supervisor and coach who can't seem to get a handle on her team's participation in the rumor mill. She's a good coach and leader who assumed she was communicating information effectively to her employees, but now she's not sure. It even appears that her employees get wind of the rumors before she does.

Communication challenge: How serious is the rumor mill? What, if anything, should a leader do about it? Should a leader only concentrate on rumors that are true and ignore the rumors known to be untrue?

Suggestions for leaders:
- In virtually every organization, people want to know what's going on. Be aware that if people don't get the information they want quickly enough, they will find other means (usually rumors) to do so.
- As a leader in the organization, you will more than likely be removed from the rumor mill. Some employees no longer trust a person who's been promoted beyond peer status.
- Leaders must learn how to use the rumor mill in a beneficial way. Here are some suggestions:

○ Take the first step. Go to the people with information before the people can come to you.

○ Develop good habits among staff and ask that people come to you first before going to outside sources to verify information they've heard elsewhere.

○ Take what you hear seriously, but don't react until you know the facts. Think about how you will respond.

Performance Scenario #6: Handling Defensive Attitudes

Manuel is a mid-level manager. His greatest challenge thus far has been communicating effectively with other members of management who seem to be reacting inappropriately to his new position of authority. He is confronted with one excuse after another whenever he questions someone or offers constructive feedback. He is starting to lose patience and is confused about how to work with his peers.

Communications challenge: How should a leader handle fellow managers' defensive behaviors? And how can a leader sharpen his or her own interpersonal skills with their management team?

Suggestions for leaders:

• Try to understand where the defensive behavior is coming from. Most people are protecting themselves from others whom they fear will make them feel or look incompetent or unproductive. This defensive mechanism also can come from a basic insecurity about a person's own status or power.

• Seek common ground among the management team.

• Convince peers that you really do care about them, that you are not an adversary, and that you want to grow and learn from your fellow managers.

Leaders' tools for building rapport:

• Use body language to convey that you are comfortable to be with and that you are neither on the attack nor a threat to anyone. Do this by studying the communication styles of the people with whom you seek rapport.

• Don't become defensive. Stay calm and in control.

• Make "I" statements such as "I'm concerned" or "I asked you about this and I have lost track of the status."

• Summarize and clarify to the best of your ability any defensive remarks you hear at the time they occur. Ask questions. Don't judge, and don't argue. Encourage accountability. Ask for and expect respect.

Objectives for Successful Performance Communications

• Quickly identify and uncover obstacles to an employee's performance.

• Quickly give both parties what they need to eliminate the obstacles that stand in the way of an employee's performance and success.

Questions for Discussion: Managing Performance

1. How do you demonstrate to leaders that early, meaningful, and actionable feedback is important?
2. What does early feedback for a new hire look like in your company?
3. What is performance management?
4. What is performance communication? Why should it be an ongoing process?
5. What should leaders focus on and what shouldn't they focus on during the performance communication process?
6. Describe some methods leaders use to foster the communications process.

Wrapping It Up

Remind your leaders that performance management, just like performance communication, is an ongoing process. The more they practice using the tools and techniques in this chapter, the sharper and more proficient they will become. When leaders learn the intricacies of managing performance through communications excellence, they will be better poised to become influential leaders in the organization. (For more on coaching and delivering feedback, see Appendix B.) Developing and wielding influence is the topic of the next chapter.

CHAPTER 14

Becoming an Influential Leader

Sometimes when people think of leadership, they think of a position, a title, or the status of a job. That can prove to be a dangerous way of thinking because employees may focus on rank and title rather than concentrating on what it really takes to become a leader.

It's important that your leaders understand that the essence of their leadership skills should encompass the talent and ability to obtain and attract followers. Simply put, leadership requires followers, and attract-

> **Key Point:** *Influence is the one-word definition of leadership.*

ing followers cannot be accomplished without one important trait: influence. Everyone talks about the trait; most people want it, and few actually understand it.

Here is where your leaders will learn the vital importance and use of influence, along with a step-by-step process for developing more influential techniques. In this chapter, your leaders will better understand how the most successful leaders learn to influence people and create desirable outcomes in a variety of situations and leadership scenarios. If your training does not include this element, here is your chance to supplement your leadership development program to emphasize this vital quality.

What You Will Learn in This Chapter:

- ◆ Influencing others to follow your leadership. Leaders must
 - model the behavior they seek in others
 - offer ongoing coaching and feedback
 - reproduce more influencers like themselves.
- ◆ Expand your sphere of influence. Leaders must
 - tap into the influence of other leaders to grow engagement efforts
 - ask for and welcome employee input on every level
 - write broader job descriptions and expand responsibility
 - eliminate as many rules as possible.

To start your leaders toward a clear understanding of the value and power of influence when it comes to effective leadership, let's begin with a case example.

EVERYONE HAS INFLUENCE

At Georgia Power Company, Don Swinford, corporate facilities manager, believes that everyone has influence. "Influence rises and falls with leadership at all levels," says Swinford. "A person's ability to influence is not dependent on his or her position." Swinford says he's learned three important things about influencing others as a leader:

- Mentor others continuously.
- Connect with your people so that you understand their needs and so that they will want to follow you.
- Enlarge people by making them feel important and by acknowledging their contributions.

Swinford suggested using a powerful tool when one of his employees sought to influence management about a specific project he'd hoped to launch. Swinford urged the employee to create a business case for his project. "I told him to make a business case that would be compelling enough for management immediately to want to hire 10 people to carry out the project."

Swinford's advice to create such a tool was taken seriously, and the employee built a dynamic case for his project. It included the following components:

- an outline of the project and all of its responsibilities
- a cost/benefit plan
- a list of the overall benefits of the project if completed
- specific deadlines for measurement.

With Swinford's advice and using the detailed case, the employee convinced management to back the project. Ten people were hired immediately to implement the project, which to this day continues to be a success.

INFLUENCE DOES NOT DEMAND AUTHORITY OR A HIGH PROFILE

Speaker, author, and leadership consultant Scott Carbonara (see www.scottcarbonara.com) recalls some early lessons he learned when starting in the corporate world.

"I had been an award-winning crisis counselor before taking a mid-level position in the human resources department of the largest non-investor-owned insurance company in North America," he states. "Back then, I had no problem describing myself as a *grunt*," says Carbonara, adding, "A *grunt* in title and position. But I was *not a grunt* regarding leadership influence."

Carbonara, who is coauthor of the *Go Positive: Lead to Engage* training program, explains, "I came to the organization with an entirely different skill set than my peers, but a skill set required to address the needs of the business. For example, one division suffered from skyrocketing attrition. We couldn't hire and train service reps fast enough to fully staff the customer service division because employees kept quitting."

"The 'obvious' solution was to pay people more. I questioned that as the solution to the attrition problem," Carbonara recalls. "Beyond questioning that to myself, I questioned it with the people who mattered most: the service reps. I interviewed hundreds of employees who had quit the company to find out what they could tell me. And guess what? I may have been a low-level *grunt*, but I learned some very powerful, dynamic information, information that allowed me to influence the executive vice president of operations, who later hired me as his chief of staff."

People Leave People, Not Companies

What Carbonara discovered was that people didn't leave the company because of the pay. They left because of how they were treated.

Carbonara heard and recorded the responses from former employees. Their comments made him cringe, and they told a very different story from the one about pay being the issue. He heard:

- "It was a sweatshop with air conditioning!"
- "If only they treated us like we were human. . . ."
- "I was so upset and stressed out that it nearly ruined my marriage."
- "When I voiced my concerns, I was told, 'You can be replaced tomorrow.'"
- "I wouldn't have stayed for any amount of money."

"This information enabled me to influence the way people were managed. And it took me from a title-less grunt to a grunt with title," he laughs at himself. "Seriously, by using influence, I created a job for myself that allowed me to scrap and then rewrite leadership job descriptions and training as well as the way management got incented for performance."

You Don't Need the Title to Have the Influence

"In 1999, our service rep attrition had climbed to 38 percent in the division and over 50 percent in certain offices," Carbonara shakes his head. "By our most conservative figures, our turnover cost us $10 million dollars in that one year. And that was just hiring and training cost—not the loss of reputation or lost customers. By 2001, though, our attrition rate hovered at 6.5 percent, a rate unheard of in customer service within any industry," Carbonara says proudly.

Carbonara believes that "Leaders have influence. A title is to influence as a fork is to being a world-class chef. You can have any sort of fancy title, but influence provides your real source of power. Title is merely a small tool. Some of the most influential leaders I know started off with no title, but when you were around one of them, you

had no doubt that you were in the presence of a leader," he concludes. "Long before I became the executive director of strategic communications or the chief of staff of internal operations, I was a low-paid, no-title leader who influenced the organization. The title came later."

EVERYONE CAN BE AN INFLUENCER

Every one of your leaders is an influencer of other people. And every person he or she influences is an influencer as well. Remind your leaders that being influential is not an aspect of any particular occupation or job title. A Sunday school teacher influences her students on issues of morality, but a rock star like Madonna influences entire generations of people on the culture of music all over the globe. One's influential impact on others is as unique as the individual influencer.

Teach your leaders that they don't have to be high-profile members of an organization to be influential. They also don't have to wield any special authority to effect change either. Consider Mother Teresa. No one bestowed on her the "authority" to try to change the world and its treatment of the poor and helpless. Nevertheless, she went about building a global organization that influenced and helped tens of thousands of underprivileged people.

It all comes down to this: Any person who touches the life of another person in any way is a person of influence. If a leader is a supervisor or a manager, for example, his or her success will depend on the ability to influence employees, just as a coach influences his or her players or a parent influences a child's upbringing.

HOW LEADERS INFLUENCE

It's important that your leaders understand the step-by-step process they will need to follow when developing their influential techniques. Help them understand that influence is a growing process—something that happens in stages, not overnight. There are five crucial steps to developing influence. After covering each step in the process, ask your leaders to share their thoughts on how these steps manifest in their own development processes.

A LEADER'S FIVE-STEP PATH TO DEVELOPING INFLUENCE
Step 1: Take a Good Look in the Mirror

Carbonara suggests that you ask yourself this simple question: What if everyone in the organization acted just like me?

Some leaders would be thrilled by that outcome because it would mean that the entire organization is staffed by leadership rock stars who would

- come in early and stay late
- intuitively balance the needs of the customer with the values of the organization

- treat company money like it was coming out of their own pockets
- greet each other with a warm smile
- communicate with directness and honesty, but also kindness and compassion.

Sadly, though, some leaders might find a different experience. Those leaders may wonder

- Why is the office empty from 11 a.m. to 1:30 p.m. each day?
- Everyone is on the phone, but I don't see any business taking place. Are those work calls?
- Are we near a bus depot? Because across the office I hear one person bad-mouthing another and throwing someone under a bus!
- Is everyone here reading the same two books, *How to Make Excuses* and *Looking Busy When You're Really Doing Nothing*?

Answer the following questions: What behaviors of mine do I want others to copy? What behaviors do I need to change so that others *do not* adopt these behaviors themselves?

Carbonara cautions leaders that followers will likely go only as far as they are led. Leaders can't point the way. Leaders have to *lead the way*.

Step 2: Model the Behavior

Someone is always watching and taking his or her cue from a leader. People are most influenced by what they see going on around them. It's basic human nature. The behavior you model as a leader will set the stage for how your followers will behave. Do you think Jacques Cousteau had any influence on his sons when they decided to enter the field of marine biology? Do you think a parent who pressures his child to enter a field that is of no interest to the child ultimately influences the child's actions and responses? A leader's actions are influential, whether those actions prove to be good or bad.

Answer the following questions: As a leader in your organization, how will you build influence among your followers? What behaviors will you model for them? What impact do you anticipate your behavior will have on others?

Step 3: Communicate on an Emotional Level

Communicating with people on an emotional level means being motivational, speaking from the heart, conveying passion for an issue, and believing strongly in something. It is the part of influence that builds a bridge between the leader and his or her followers. It also creates confidence in others and builds self-esteem. When you communicate on an emotional level with people, you influence them to want to listen to you and to be a part of your leadership plan.

Answer the following questions: How will you communicate more effectively with your people on an emotional level? How will this communications process look on the job? What are the benefits you can expect as a result?

Step 4: Offer Continuous Coaching and Feedback

Once you've mastered communicating on an emotional level, it's time to focus on continuous coaching. Coaching is the key to establishing long-lasting and truly profound influence on people. This step is so incredibly powerful because it allows you, as a leader, to witness the transformation of those you are influencing. Continuous coaching is the means to prompting a significant difference in your employees forever. (Refer to chapter 12 for additional tools and tips on developing a coaching program.)

Coaching can be soft and passive, like modeling the right behaviors or providing challenging development opportunities. Sometimes the work itself becomes the coach as people learn by doing. But Carbonara reminds us that "Ongoing feedback is part of an active, intentional process for continuous improvement."

"When you go on a diet, you have to get on the scale to know your starting point *and* how much improvement you're making," Carbonara reminds us. "That scale serves as invaluable feedback. Leaders are only halfway there when they point out the way. The real cement for developing people of influence is to give them feedback along the way so they know when they are improving."

Answer the following questions: How will you influence your employees in both their personal and professional growth? Why must the influence of coaching be continuous for a leader? When has a coaching experience influenced you?

Step 5: Reproduce More Influencers

Producing more influencers is the most important step on the path to developing your influence. As a leader, over time you will become an increasingly active influencer, and it is then that you will begin to see the enormous value you are bringing to other people's lives. For example, the leader who empowers his or her employees helps them broaden their horizons and take risks, just like the parent who reads to a child encourages a love of books and of reading. But this fifth step goes beyond these obvious occurrences to the highest level of influencing—producing other influencers.

By creating influencers like yourself, you will not only become a more important influence in the lives of others, but you will be helping others become influencers in the lives of the people they touch as well. This is the ultimate power of influencing for every leader: to have your people pass on what they have learned from you by continuing to influence others to their full potential. Remember, everyone is an influencer.

When Carbonara was asked to create and staff a strategic communication team, he admitted that it took a couple of years before his group turned into a high-performance team. "I remember being thrilled when I finally recognized that my team and each of its members was absolutely outstanding," Carbonara recalls with excitement. "That feeling was short-lived. I got a call I hadn't really expected," he laughs.

Linda, a corporate vice president, called Scott to ask him if he had any employees he'd be willing to let interview for a couple of new positions. "Linda told me, 'I want only the best. That's why I'm calling you first,'" Carbonara recalls.

Carbonara talked to two of his employees and encouraged them to apply. He assured them both that he wanted them to stay on his team, but he let them know that the other job would present a fantastic growth opportunity for their professional careers.

After the interviews, Linda called Carbonara again. "Bad news, Scott," Linda joked good-naturedly. "Of the seven people we interviewed, your two employees tied for first place. Can I have at least one of them? I don't want to gut your team by taking both," she said.

Carbonara counteroffered. "I told her to take them both," he says. "I was honored to have had the chance to develop such great employees, and I was thrilled to share them. But I knew something else," Carbonara says, looking back. "I knew that those two employees would be game-changers for the entire company. As much as they made a difference in *my division*, I knew that they would have so much more influence at the *corporate level*."

Was that a good decision? Carbonara says yes. He's quick to point out that in the years that followed, those two employees evolved into friends and eventually peers. "They had audiences with executives across the organization, some that I didn't even know. But whenever I needed anything, my requests went to the top of the list," Carbonara smiles. "By influencing and developing those employees, it paid me back tenfold."

THERE IS PLENTY OF ROOM AT THE TOP

"Have you ever met a leader who tempted you to say or think, 'That person is in it for self?'" Carbonara asks. "It's hard to feel committed and engaged to a selfish boss, isn't it?" he asks rhetorically. "Imagine the exponential impact of having positive press spread about you across the company! I had people in other states reaching out to me for a job. And I had peers ask me to help hire and train their management teams," Carbonara says with excitement. "Using your influence to develop other leaders of influence creates an environment of highly engaged individuals because it lets people know that they are valued and that there is plenty of room at the top."

Answer the following questions: How do you plan to create other influencers? What will this process look like for you on the job? How will reproducing influencers in your workplace benefit the organization?

> *A life isn't significant except for its impact on others' lives.*
> —Jackie Robinson, baseball legend

EXPANDING THE SPHERE OF INFLUENCE

Developing influence is just one part of the skill base necessary for leaders at every level. A much larger and more important part of creating influence is in showing your leaders how to expand the sphere of influence within the organization. When your leaders learn how to expand their sphere of influence effectively, they will be building a cadre of people throughout the organization who will be helpful to them in garnering the support necessary for almost any project. For that reason, influence taught as a leadership technique and dovetailed with a comprehensive leadership program will become the essential tool used by your leaders at all levels of your organization. Carbonara says that there is an untapped engagement-expanding reservoir in each company.

There Is No Room for Immaturity in Leadership

"Immature leaders believe falsely that they have to do everything themselves," Carbonara says with a shake of the head. "Which is silly. Maybe I'm lazier than others," he says with a laugh, "But I want to find a way to let everyone in the company help engage and develop my team."

Carbonara would invite his boss and peers, HR professionals, or corporate thought leaders to speak at brown-bag lunches held to develop his team. Often, he would outline for his guests the topics he wanted covered, but he also informed them about the work of his team and individuals on the team.

"Me saying nice things about my employees to my employees is like your mom saying that you look nice and that you are very smart," he chuckles. "Yes, maybe you are those things, but moms *have to say that*. But when a boss or another leader comes up to your team member and says, 'I hear that you did this. Great job! I appreciate you!' it makes you look good and it makes that leader look good. More importantly, it makes your employees feel special and valued. You want to increase your influence as a leader? Engage your employees by letting them know, and letting others know, how valuable they are to you and the organization," Carbonara concludes.

Ask yourself this question: Who can I tap into inside my own organization to increase the influence and engagement levels of my employees?

Ask your leaders to describe in specific detail how they would expand their spheres of influence within the organization. After you have gathered input from your group, add to some of their suggestions by offering the following means for expanding the sphere of influence.

- Increase signature authority at all levels.
- Write job descriptions more broadly. Expand responsibility and don't define a job just by the tasks performed.
- Eliminate unnecessary approval steps. Empower people to make their own decisions.
- Encourage each worker to be flexible.
- Think leader, not boss.
- Think teams, not subordinates.
- Ask for and welcome employee input at every level.
- Communicate consistently and continuously.
- Take away as many rules as possible.

Broadening the Sphere of Influence the Nordstrom Way

Nordstrom sets world-class standards when it comes to expanding leadership's sphere of influence. The well-respected retailer is also famous for its aversion to rules and policies. In its non-traditional employee handbook, this is rule number one:

Use your good judgment in all situations. There will be no additional rules.

Another effective way Nordstrom expands its leaders' sphere of influence is through its strong philosophy about entrepreneurial thinking. "Every employee is told to think like an entrepreneur," says Diane Elliott, department manager in cosmetics at the chain's Sacramento store. "If you help your employees feel as if they own the business, they will put more of themselves into their work. Entrepreneurial thinking is a powerful way to spread leadership's influence throughout our stores," adds the retailer's 11-year veteran.

If you want your leaders to feel influential and empowering, teach them to expand their sphere of influence early on. When your leaders expand their sphere of influence, they not only empower others, but also feel more powerful themselves.

DEVELOPING AND EXPANDING YOUR INFLUENCE

Review with your leaders the five steps to developing influence:

- Step 1: Take a good look in the mirror.
- Step 2: Model the behavior.
- Step 3: Communicate on an emotional level.
- Step 4: Offer continuous coaching and feedback.
- Step 5: Reproduce more influencers.

Remind them to broaden the range of their influence in the following ways:

- Increase signature authority at all levels.
- Write job descriptions more broadly to expand responsibility beyond the tasks performed.
- Eliminate unnecessary approval steps and empower people to make their own decisions.
- Encourage flexibility in workers.
- Think leader, not boss.
- Think teams, not subordinates.
- Ask for and welcome employee input at every level.
- Communicate consistently and continuously.
- Take away as many rules as possible.

Questions for Discussion: Developing the Power to Influence

1. What is a one-word definition of leadership?
2. What constitutes an influential leader?
3. What is meant by "everyone has influence"?
4. Why isn't a leader's high profile or authority necessary for that person to be influential?

Wrapping It Up

It is made clear in this chapter that job title, age, marital status, ethnicity, and religion will not be common denominators in your leaders' success. Their ability to influence others, whether for good or for bad, is what unites them as a group, and their values and integrity determine the direction their influence takes in others' lives. The ability to influence carries enormous responsibility, and so your leaders must work to build hope and trust among their followers and create a path to empowerment for all of their employees. Building hope and trust is the topic of chapter 15.

Hope and Trust Start on the Path to Leadership Empowerment

This is one of our favorite chapters in the book, because it is chock-full of real-world examples on how to empower leaders and instill hope and trust in the process—one of our favorite topics!

Far too often, empowerment is seen as an empty concept. Are you surprised? Think about it: Organizations toss around the word *empowerment* as some sort of flavor-of-the-month solution to getting more work done, but few companies treat empowerment as the important leadership tool it is meant to be.

Here is where your leaders will learn what real empowerment is all about and how to use it as an effective leadership tool. This chapter will demonstrate to your leaders how they can transform empowerment from an empty concept to a practical skill that continues to influence behavior in a positive and rewarding way. If your training does not include this element, here is your chance to supplement your leadership development program to emphasize this vital quality.

What You Will Learn in This Chapter:

- ♦ Synergy that comes from empowerment. Leaders must
 - • assess their current empowerment skills
 - • unleash synergy among people
 - • couple the gift of power with the authority to get the job done.
- ♦ Entrepreneurial thinking for the twenty-first century. Leaders must
 - • make everyone feel like a partner in the organization
 - • convey that entrepreneurial thinking is a by-product of empowerment
 - • understand that hope and trust are the milestones of empowerment.

AUTHENTIC EMPOWERMENT KEEPS IT REAL

Employees are eager for a chance to have more input and responsibility, but management too often endows them with more responsibility only for the most trivial jobs. When teams' recommended solutions to organizational challenges are vetoed by senior management, what message does that send? What happens when the so-called empowered employee takes a risk and makes a decision to do something bold, then screws up, makes a mistake, or acts human? He or she is reprimanded or fired. So where's the empowerment?

Here's the perspective of one middle manager in the hospitality industry: "Senior management keeps telling me to empower my people, but then they don't support the initiative, or they renege. Almost every time my people make a recommendation or try to take action on something, I have to go back to them and tell them they can't do it. The word *empowerment* has zero credibility in our organization."

Empowerment, or the lack of it, has cost many a leader his or her credibility and the trust of staff and peers. As someone in the organization who is responsible for developing a leadership program that trains leaders to empower others, you have a unique and powerful opportunity to prevent empowerment from coming back to bite your leaders because they never really learned how to do it. You can show them how to transform empowerment from a flimsy concept to a hard skill and an influential behavior with teeth.

REAL-WORLD EMPOWERMENT EXAMPLE

Accountability and empowerment are the foundations upon which the Ritz-Carlton's leaders manage their people. Power is shared. Every Ritz-Carlton employee, whether a bell person, room service supervisor, front desk associate, or housekeeper, is fully empowered to spend up to $2,000 on the spot to correct any problem for any customer whatsoever. And why not? The Ritz-Carlton would not have hired a person they didn't believe was capable of using good judgment! You could say that empowerment at the Ritz-Carlton starts with the hiring process.

Ask yourself what kind of message your organization's management team sends when it comes to giving away its authority. Does your organization act like the Ritz-Carlton and say, "Go for it. We trust you and have confidence that you'll do the right thing"? Or does your organization practice the Dilbert comic strip mentality—us versus them—making people feel small and incompetent? Here's an example of one company that takes power away from its people.

At a West Coast grocery store chain, a former manager says of her experience supervising grocery cashiers, "Our organization's management style was really quite hypocritical. At management meetings, we were told to empower our frontline people, but as soon as a cashier was given an out-of-town check or a check without proper identification, he or she would have to call management to verify and approve the check right in front of the customer. There was never a reason why our cashiers

couldn't have verified and approved the checks themselves. Calling us to the line only accomplished two things. It told our customers that we didn't trust our people to handle a simple process like approving their checks and, more importantly, it sent a clear message each time to the cashier that he or she wasn't capable or competent to do this on their own."

CAUTION: AVOID A RECIPE FOR DISASTER AND COACH IN THE MOMENT TO BUILD EMPOWERMENT

If you want to completely de-motivate and embarrass your people, first tell them you're empowering them to do something, and then take back the responsibility and tell them exactly how to do it. No questions asked. Don't laugh. This happens all the time.

The key here is that if you empower someone with a task and they fall short of the mark, for whatever reason, you don't snatch away the chance to make it right. Instead, practice coaching in the moment by providing honest feedback and helpful advice. Maybe you have to demonstrate or provide an extra example for the leader.

Remind the leader that he or she has what it takes and that there is often a learning curve involved. Maybe you can share your own experiences about a time when you were learning something new and how tough it might have been, the mistakes you made, and ways you overcame the hurdles. This approach inspires a leader to get back on track and try again.

To prompt your leaders to identify true and false empowerment, ask them to describe ways that management can empower people effectively. Urge them to be specific in their examples. Then have them describe the ways that management disempowers its people, intentionally or unintentionally. This exercise will provide a good opportunity for your leaders to share and discuss the various effective and ineffective ways that empowerment is practiced on a day-to-day basis. By better understanding the far-reaching effects of empowerment on the job, your leaders will begin to define their own individual styles of empowering others to learn and grow.

THE SYNERGY THAT COMES FROM EMPOWERMENT

Empowerment is synergistic. When practiced correctly, it can unleash tremendous synergy within the organization. When your leaders learn to empower their employees by giving them real responsibility coupled with the authority to get the job done their own way, the results can be phenomenal. If the idea of "giving away power" bothers some of your leaders, have them think of the process as acknowledging or releasing the power in others so that they may demonstrate their best work.

In chapter 14, we discussed the importance of your leaders' expanding or spreading their spheres of influence. This concept dovetails nicely with the idea of a

> It's surprising how much you can accomplish if you don't care who gets the credit.
> —Abraham Lincoln

leader giving away his or her power, or releasing the power in others. Ask your leaders to do the following quick self-assessment to determine their level of management skill when it comes to empowering others.

To understand more fully your present approach to empowering others, read the following statements and then rank your behavior by placing an X on the scale somewhere between *seldom* and *almost always*.

Leader's Self-Assessment on Empowerment

When it comes to empowering others . . .

1. I give my people exposure to senior management so that they may enlarge their circle of influence within the organization. Seldom——|——|——|——Almost always

2. I often give others responsible and important tasks. Seldom——|——|——|——Almost always

3. I resist trying to tell someone how to do the job I've empowered them to do. Seldom——|——|——|——Almost always

4. I don't get bogged down in creating more rules and policies when it comes to giving people flexibility to accomplish their jobs. Seldom——|——|——|——Almost always

5. I actively and regularly support good judgment and commonsense behavior. Seldom——|——|——|——Almost always

6. I help employees take control of and responsibility for their lives. Seldom——|——|——|——Almost always

7. I help create an environment where it is safe for employees to make mistakes. Seldom——|——|——|——Almost always

8. I don't restrict people by titles and job descriptions. Seldom——|——|——|——Almost always

After your leaders have completed the self-assessment, have them draw a vertical line through the center ticks on the scales. Point out that any Xs that fall on the left side of that line indicate areas needing greater awareness and improvement. Encourage them to repeat the assessment in three months and to compare their results over time to measure and prompt continuous improvement.

EMPOWERMENT IS THE TWENTY-FIRST CENTURY METHOD FOR BUILDING ENTREPRENEURIAL THINKING

Successful empowerment techniques require making everyone feel like a partner in the business. World-class organizations and their leaders make their people feel like owners and partners, because people who feel like they own the business will protect it, look out for it, and pour themselves into it. For example, at Starbucks, all employees are called partners, whether they brew Frappuccinos part-time or serve as CEO. This form of empowerment encourages employees to act like entrepreneurs.

Ask your leaders to suggest ways they successfully can instill entrepreneurial thinking among the ranks. To get things going, offer such general topics as risk taking,

Empowering Tool: Retitling Employees

World-class organizations that retitle their employees help create workplaces alive with entrepreneurial thinking and a sense of ownership. Here are some real-world examples to share with your leaders:

- Starbucks and TDIndustries (an employee-owned construction company) call their employees *partners*.
- Guidant, maker of pacemakers, uses the term *employee-owners*.
- Lenscrafters, Marriott, W.L. Gore, Publix Super Markets, and Capital One refer to their people as *associates*.

understanding how the organization operates and generates income, how to read an annual report, and ways to stay ahead of the competition. Teach your leaders that entrepreneurial thinking is a by-product of empowerment. Then have them evaluate their own entrepreneurial behaviors. Do their actions reflect the best interest of the organization as if it were their own? Do they go the extra mile to get the job done regardless of their job title or description? Are they self-motivated and do they take responsibility when things don't go as planned? Those questions can help your leaders determine their existing levels of entrepreneurial thinking and their attitudes about empowerment.

THE IMPORTANCE OF HOPE AND TRUST

Hope and trust are the milestones on the path to empowerment. Leadership can only succeed on the basis of hope and trust. Even before empowerment became a management buzzword, successful leaders knew the value that hope and trust added to their relationships with others. Teach your leaders to trust their instincts and to rely on these basic principles.

Every relationship that your leaders have will depend on the hope and trust they establish with others, and those feelings must travel in both directions. For example, it's not enough for leaders to trust their employees; those employees also must trust their leaders. Convey to your leaders that their workers want to trust them, want to believe and have hope that they really are serious in their concern for employees' well-being. That desire to believe is a basic human desire.

> *Technique and technology are important. But building hope and trust is the issue of the decade.*
> —Tom Peters, *The Circle of Innovation*

Leaders Hold Hope High

If anyone has ever honored the value of hope, it was Winston Churchill, England's former prime minister. Following World War II, he was asked by a reporter what Britain's greatest weapon had been against the Nazi regime. Without hesitation, Churchill proudly responded, "It was what England's greatest weapon has always been: hope."

The point that Churchill was making was that people will continue to persevere, struggle, and strive against all odds if they have hope. Why? Because people's morale and expectations partly are based on a vision of hope—the hope for achievement and success from all of their efforts and for a better tomorrow. When employees believe in the power of hope, all sorts of possibilities present themselves.

Explain to your leaders that it is their responsibility to hold hope high within the organization. Ask for their thoughts about how this best can be accomplished. Then ask them to describe times when hope sustained their quests to achieve a difficult or seemingly impossible goal.

Leaders Hold Trust High

Trust is the guardian of your organization's integrity. It probably is the most important factor when it comes to building both personal and professional relationships. Employees first must believe in and trust a leader before they consent to follow him or her. Trust is the essential component your leaders will need to build a high-performing organization.

According to Tom Peters, managers must take a "high-tech, high-trust" approach to leadership, putting trust at the top of the agenda. Peters also recommends treating trust like a "hard issue," not a "soft issue." Too often trust in an organization is viewed as something "touchy-feely." In fact, the issue of trust is as important as the work skills required to do the job.

The glue that binds followers and leaders together. —Warren Bennis, on trust

Ask your leaders what the word *trust* implies. You'll likely get responses such as reliability, dependability, and accountability. Now ask them to name some of the ways that leaders betray trust. Responses you can expect include failing to communicate, not telling the truth, breaking promises, and being two-faced.

Now give your leaders time to answer the following questions about trust. Let the answers prompt a discussion of how precious the gift of trust can be.

1. Can you think of a time when trust was lost in your work environment? What was the situation?

2. What were the consequences of trust being lost in the workplace?

3. Was trust ever regained? If not, why not?

4. What do you think trust has to do with respect and credibility?

Drive home the point that trust is something that is built day by day. When a leader's actions destroy or break trust, it is almost impossible to regain it. The lesson here is that leadership can only perform on the basis of trust.

How Hope and Trust Fuel the Engine in Times of Change

When a business goes through a change, hope and trust become the vital energy that keeps the organizational engine moving ahead. Napolean Bonaparte said, "A leader is a dealer in hope." Hope is the element that leaders must dole out as the fuel of change, and trust is the structure by which leaders continue to drive a company and team onward.

Jocelyn Godfrey, founder of Spiritus Communications, Inc., a marketing, publishing, and consulting firm that aims to offer inspired communications (see www.Spiritus Communications.com), recalled in a recent interview the catalyst that formed her business: "I was 24, and the advertising agency I had worked for was forced to shut its doors. Rather than see this as a reason to cry defeat, I chose to invest in the hope that this was a golden opportunity to do something greater." With that mindset, she secured her first account on a freelance basis, simply by putting together a proposal and asking for the business—and has been successfully building her business for the past 15 years into a nationally recognized source for leaders wishing to define and brand their messages.

"A lot of people come to me when they are trying to get their new business off the ground, or take it to another level. There is no room for hopelessness in the heart of an entrepreneur, or a leader setting off towards a new goal. Hope feeds trust, and those two elements have to take root before you see any tangible evidence of success," states Godfrey. "Without hope, an entrepreneur won't likely take the first step to start a business or implement a new idea. Similarly, as a leader of an organization, hope is the trait that propels you to create a plan, and through trust in your plan and your people, you act on those goals."

Jeff Bezos, founder of Amazon.com, took large risks when he left a comfortable job on Wall Street to start a risky venture selling books online. But it paid off in droves. He

had hope that he could do something, and he put it into action through trusting that his efforts would pay off—or that he'd survive even if they didn't. He is quoted as saying that if he were to look back on his life later, he would have fewer regrets over having tried something and failed, than over not having tried at all.

Amazon.com

Amazon.com began as an online bookstore and is now the world's largest online retailer. It is a multinational electronic commerce company headquartered in Seattle, Washington. Its founder, Jeff Bezos, was spurred on to start Amazon by what he called "regret minimization framework," his personal quest to fend off regret for not staking a claim in the Internet gold rush.

The Marathon Margin of Leadership

How can leaders have more hope and trust when they lack it, and how can they use it to fuel those they lead through times of change? Godfrey, who is also an amateur runner, recommends what she calls "The Marathon Margin," which is her proprietary business consultation processes to achieve both personal and business success. When marathon runners are training for a race, they are taught to determine their maximum heart rate, so that they can design their training regimen. Then their program is designed around this personal threshold—one that pushes them just enough that they will increase stamina and fitness, but not pushing them so hard that they burn out or endure unnecessary stress injuries. This is the "margin" in which they must remain to train for optimal growth. "Similarly in business, we have an optimal margin," states Godfrey. "Our goal is to push ourselves enough each day that we are growing, without burning ourselves out or allowing ourselves to go down paths that are not healthy for us simply because we lacked the time or ability to focus on making wise choices. If we remain within this margin, then we will progress. We would not go from the couch to running 26.2 miles in a day. But we can go from the couch, to walking one mile, then running two, and so on. We do it by pushing ourselves just enough each day to progress, but not so much that we experience counterproductive results."

One of the biggest keys to maintaining the Marathon Margin, states Godfrey, is to embody hope in your ability to succeed, while also trusting that you will learn and accomplish everything you need in order to meet your goals. "I've talked to many runners who told me that the first step in their 'training' was to sign up for a marathon. This doesn't surprise me. The act of signing up demonstrates runners' hope that they can finish the race. Hope and trust keep them engaged in this margin of success and growth, which compels them to condition themselves to go further than they thought possible. What's true for a runner is true for any entrepreneurial business leader. Hope—that is, belief in yourself and in your ideas—is the essential first step to success."

"You have probably heard that success is not a sprint, but a marathon," states Godfrey. "When a marathon runner starts the race, she must hold on to one belief: *'I can do this!'* That belief is the hope and trust that her legs will get her to the finish line. Similarly, you achieve your dreams by having the hope and trust that you can succeed, by developing an challenging yet obtainable plan that strengthens you, and then by taking action each day within your optimal margin." (For more on the Marathon Margin, see Appendix C.)

Are You Modeling Hope for Future Leaders?

Part of progressing in leadership involves demonstrating trust in others and modeling success for them. "If you are mentoring other leaders, you don't want to be operating without trust in the group's ability to 'finish the race,'" states Godfrey. "For an entire group to feel like they can follow your leadership and join you at the finish line, you need to model hope in their ability to run with you, and trust them as they put forth their best effort."

HOW LEADERS CAN BUILD HOPE AND TRUST IN THE ORGANIZATION

When your leaders put their trust in others, they will be sending a strong message that says, "I believe in you. I believe that you are trustworthy. I respect you." These kinds of messages build confidence and self-esteem in workers and demonstrate true empowerment.

Urge your leaders to demonstrate their trust in others, by listening closely and empowering people to make important decisions on their own. These are the expressions of trust your leaders can use to build a stronger organization. Caution them to avoid patronizing comments such as, "Now, Jane, I'm trusting you can handle this project." *Translation:* "Well, Jane, you'd better not blow it!" Or, "Okay, Tom, the project's yours. I trust you'll do the best job you can." *Translation:* "I guess you're the only guy I can give this to. I sure hope you know what the heck you're doing."

Below are 10 leadership tenets of hope and trust.

- Respect and honor others.
- Be aware of what you say and how you say it.
- Practice what you preach and do what you say you're going to do.
- Be true to yourself. Be authentic. Don't hop the fence for popularity.
- Listen and appreciate another person's point of view.
- Avoid using put-downs and zingers.
- Look for the good and reward the positive.
- Appreciate others' uniqueness. Embrace diversity and cultural differences.
- Acknowledge that hope and trust go two ways.
- Don't be afraid to show your human side and acknowledge your mistakes.

Motivation is partly based on a vision of hope—the hope of finding meaningful purpose and reaching greater success from our efforts—hope of a better future for ourselves, our families, friends, and co-workers. In other words, hope is like an ocean of possibilities and represents *what life could be*. When we are motivated to believe in the possibilities, a brighter tomorrow often surfaces. However, for this concept to gain traction in the workplace, first there has to be a strong level of trust between managers and their employees.

Riding a Wave of Momentum

Trust is the wave of momentum that carries an organization and its people with force and grace to unpredictable heights, at unimaginable speeds, from an ocean of hope and belief.

If you think about it, levels of trust among teams and within organizations big and small often come in waves—and like the organizations themselves, some waves are big and some are just ripples. Trust is the perpetual wave of management upon which all great leaders feel compelled to ride and navigate.

As Tom Peters and other management gurus have predicted over the years, more than technology or training, trust is going to be the core leadership value and soft-skill competency of the decade that all managers must learn to instill and navigate if they are to survive and thrive! So get ready to ride the varying waves of trust when you see them coming, learn to navigate others to trust in themselves in choppy waters, and then start building trust throughout the organization as one of the most important leadership initiatives and competencies you'll ever implement. We believe that trust is everything.

A Surfer-Leader Brands Trust at MedAmerica Billing Services, Inc.

"Trust is how we roll," says James V. Proffitt, the engaging and high-energy COO and president of MedAmerica Billing Services, Inc. (MBSI), based in Modesto, California.

Proffitt is not only a beloved and trusted leader at MBSI, he's an avid surfer and skateboarder. When Proffitt talks about his extreme passion for inspiring motivation and trust in teams at MBSI, he often refers to navigating the ocean's waves on his surfboard or while riding his skateboard—"It takes trust!" says Proffitt. "Trust in yourself and trust in others."

Proffitt's leadership empowerment advice is to hire the best, trust your people, or wipe out. "MBSI hires active, intelligent, motivated, and trustworthy employees to make things happen day in and day out," says Proffitt. Trustworthy employees blow up the box and do amazing things because they, too, are trusted by their managers and feel empowered to make decisions that change the course of the company. "It's highly motivating!" emphasizes Proffitt.

"It's just not enough anymore to develop and train employees on the basics. "We need to develop their emotional intelligence (EQ) as well, by making trust a core competency for leadership success—a competency that expands everyone's knowledge-base because they feel empowered to get out there and innovate, create, be flexible, and ride the varying waves of leadership success."

Just like in surfing or skateboarding, managers can make mistakes. "If you mess up, who cares? It doesn't mean you wiped out. Get back up on your board and ride!" says Proffitt. "Trusted employees are not afraid to learn from their mistakes. They know the organization trusts that they'll correct the problem and do the right thing, because it's the right thing to do. They don't get stuck or afraid. They know it all comes down to movement and momentum and that they've got to keep going forward to keep the respect and support of top management at all times. Respect the process," says Proffitt. "Hire and empower the best people you can and then trust those people, or you'll wipe out!"

Real-World Example

MBSI has a strong and credible reputation as the most successful industry leader among medical billing companies in the nation. The reason? Its management staff and teams are known for exhibiting high levels of trust in the workplace, says one colleague. Here you have an industry leader that could easily get locked down in the daily details of precision auditing, compliant coding, hospitalists practices, custom data analysis, and electronic submission of claims. But instead, leadership at MBSI encourages creativity and innovation, supported by mutual trust as one of their core leadership competencies.

"It's something I believe in strongly," says COO and president, James V. Proffitt. "Companies that succeed do so, in my opinion, because they exhibit high levels of trust in their people. I believe that innovation and positive change come from trust, and that's when you get to see individual wins that lead to organizational wins—talk about empowering!"

Proffitt offers more examples to leaders: "Building trust means that you have to be out in front, focus, mentor, and be real with people!" This, he says, leads to relationships with high levels of trust. Once you're there, just allow your employees to do their own thing. Employees need the latitude to make it happen, and with the right relationship in place, learning, growing, and excellence are going to be the result.

How Trust Will Help Your Leaders

"To really be able to help everyone," says Proffitt, "people first have to trust your motives and believe in your advice. At that point, it's easy to discuss what's important, develop career plans, give constructive and honest feedback, memorialize action plans, and track progress via review sessions. Then, if you need to have the 'tough love' discussion, it's more likely to be accepted."

REINFORCING THE MESSAGE OF EMPOWERMENT TO YOUR LEADERS

Reinforce to your leaders the truth that even though their employees may possess enormous amounts of talent, creativity, intelligence, and skill, it all will lie dormant and eventually wither if they do not empower their people ambitiously and deliberately build hope and trust.

When all of these elements begin to overlap, a dynamic synergy will develop and employees will be energized like never before, ready and willing to unleash their full potential. This is what results from true empowerment.

Below are two key empowerment actions that your leaders should remember:

- Give away your power and the total responsibility for achieving something of significance.
- Give away complete authority and allow people to accomplish the task their own way.

Questions for Discussion: What It Means to Empower

1. Empowerment is the twenty-first century method for building what?
2. The secret weapon of empowerment comprises two parts. What are they?
3. Why is building hope and trust within the organization critical to real empowerment?
4. Why is empowerment synergistic?

Wrapping It Up

In this chapter, we come to understand that the spirit of hope will come alive when your leaders start empowering others to be all that they can be. Next up: managing knowledge faster than the competition.

Managing Knowledge While Learning Faster Than the Competition

There is a saying that "knowledge is power." It is not. What is powerful about knowledge is *how it is used.* Your leaders can be trained, they can study and acquire enormous amounts of information, they can be hotshot Gen Ys who know everything about mobile techno groups, but if they don't apply what they've learned and pass that knowledge along to others right away, what is the purpose? We've come up with a new mantra for this chapter. Share with your leaders this improved version of the old saying: *"Lifelong learning and applying knowledge is positive power!"*

Here is where your leaders will learn the importance of knowledge management as a leadership tool and powerful means to create a world-class learning environment. If your training does not include this element, here is your chance to supplement your leadership development program to emphasize this vital quality.

What You Will Learn in This Chapter:

◆ Manage knowledge daily. Leaders must
 ● become the innovator in educating the workforce
 ● recognize the shelf life of the organization's knowledge
 ● focus on lifetime learning, not lifetime employment.
◆ Learn faster than the competition. Leaders must
 ● create a "future learning" environment
 ● use their existing training departments to gain a competitive advantage
 ● align the organization's employee development with its most important goals and required competencies.

ASTD—YOUR ANSWER TO BETTER, STRONGER KNOWLEDGE MANAGEMENT

ASTD (American Society for Training & Development) knows that knowledge management is key to leadership development. This is why they have developed several tools and programs to assist leaders in honing their knowledge management skills, including a certification program aimed at enhancing employee performance and fostering innovation. (Go to astd.org to find endless ideas, tools, job aids, books, and other resources to build your brain on this subject.)

ASTD also realizes that knowledge management involves more than just storing and disseminating data; it also goes hand in hand with workplace performance. Knowledge management involves providing employees with access to experts in their field, facilitating the exchange of information among leaders, networking via social media, sharing ideas via web and mobile web channels, and more. Successful businesses build such knowledge management into their corporate culture in the form of **online discussion boards, robust record keeping, company blogs, training on how to enhance the sharing of information, and even corporate culture books**.

Consider this excerpt from an ASTD blog: "Essentially the idea is that one of the most valuable assets an organization has is the knowledge of its people, and that knowledge can walk out the door at any time. But knowledge management is more than just a way to hold on to its assets, it's a way to disseminate knowledge consistently throughout an organization. It allows employees to find out what they need to know fast and to find information that's accurate and up-to-date. If done right, it also ensures that employees get the right information."

CREATING A WORLD-CLASS LEARNING ENVIRONMENT

Chances are good that you purchased this book because you are a performance and learning professional—learning officer, learning manager, facilitator, HR professional, chief of people, VP, instructional designer, course developer, employee development coach—someone who's been charged with the responsibility of creating a learning environment for your leaders. If that is the case, get ready to wake up to the new reality of having not only to develop leaders but to develop them in a way that

- manages knowledge
- trains them to competencies
- recognizes the short shelf life of knowledge
- focuses on lifetime learning, not lifetime employment
- sustains a competitive advantage while learning faster than the competition.

Asked what constitutes a world-class learning environment, Chuck Lynch, formerly a leadership facilitator with Continental Airlines, and later a learning consultant with Achieve Global, offered the following opinion: "It all comes down to creating a learning organization that believes in training from the ground up—that means the front line to

the president and CEO. Everyone should be expected to develop themselves to their full potential, no matter what their level in the organization. When this credo is practiced, an incredibly strong message is sent out, not just to the organization as a whole, but to potential new hires and customers around the globe."

MANAGING KNOWLEDGE

This book offers you numerous ways to develop and train your leaders at every level, but how you ultimately decide to manage the knowledge available here is what will make the greatest difference. Remember, having this book, or the knowledge, is inconsequential. How you apply it in developing your leaders is where managing the knowledge comes in.

A learning professional's ability to manage knowledge is critical to the success of his or her leaders. You are the innovator in educating your workforce. But wait. Did you know that organizational learning is undergoing a seismic shift throughout the global marketplace? It is, and that will continue for some time. Managing knowledge effectively is the first step in providing your leaders with the skills, knowledge, and competencies that they will need for success.

What is the best way to manage all the cutting-edge lessons and practical applications of the latest tools in leadership development? Remember that you are the best one to identify your leaders' learning needs. With that perspective clearly focused, you select the most appropriate sections of this book to address those needs. Adapting, modifying, expanding, and working the material effectively to meet your organization's learning objectives and strategies are the first steps you should take in managing the knowledge you have to share with your leaders. Refining the process further for the greatest impact, follow these steps:

Step 1: Take into consideration your leaders' skill levels and competencies before you try to develop them. Are your leaders novices, masters, or somewhere in the middle? Match the learning and knowledge you have to share to your leaders' levels of competency. If you match masters with novices and expect the same learning results, you will inevitably squash the confidence of the less experienced learners.

Step 2: Assess your leaders' real-world experience. Just because some of your leaders have learned certain skills along the way doesn't mean that they actually have practiced using them in the real world. Assess just how much exposure and on-the-job experience your learners have had in the specific areas in which you are developing them.

Step 3: Fire up and continually challenge those of your leaders who have "been there and done that." Leaders with a great deal of experience who have fine-tuned many of their skills over the years will need to have their passions and enthusiasm for the job reignited. Encourage them to share their stories and coach others. Those leaders are looking for ongoing challenges. Manage the knowledge by keeping them on their toes.

Grow Your Leaders by Expanding Their Knowledge of the World Right at Home

Statistics show that leaders who have been involved with various international exchange student programs offer fresh and unbiased views of the global workplace and economy. They gain communication skills that can't be learned in a college classroom. In short, they are more effective, tolerant, and aware.

Therefore, many organizations today are encouraging their leaders to open their homes to international exchange students. Autumn Mostovoj, West Coast Operations Manager for non-profit EF (Education First) Educational Homestay Programs, confirms that more and more leaders in organizations are volunteering to host international students and that leaders who do this find that they are the ones who often learn and benefit the most from this unique multicultural experience.

Help Your Leaders See the World From a New Perspective

"I've worked with many leaders in well-known organizations here in California, who all of a sudden see the world from a new perspective when they volunteer to host one of our international students. Let's face it, today all leaders are worldwide ambassadors because our business world has shrunk and we all work in a global society. In my opinion, there's no better way to learn about other cultures or behaviors and to sharpen your leadership skills than to share your home with an international student for two to four weeks a year," says Mostovoj. "People are so surprised at what they learn about leadership from these amazing young people coming into their homes."

Mostovoj adds, "When professional workers choose to host a student through EHP, they fling open the doors of worldwide awareness in their personal and professional lives. Many leaders who are hosts with us have shared with me that they have learned so much from our students in terms of culture and politics, or that they've become better and more tolerant communicators, because they are now faced with breaking down language barriers, often like they face on the job. There's no doubt in my mind that programs like this build better leaders for companies, because they now see the world from a new perspective."

EF's Educational Homestay Programs conduct leadership workshops and ongoing training for its staff. "We look at our people's strengths and we focus on the best possible experience for everyone involved," says Mostovoj. "In a way, we are managing and growing the knowledge of the host families and the students all at the same time. We use tools and techniques to help us build leadership examples from within our own organization so that we can set an example. The bottom line is that good communication is the foundation of all successful relationships, on the job and in the home. We know that nonverbal communications skills are powerful, especially when we live and work in a multicultural society. Leaders who get involved with our homestay programs learn an abundance of successful relationship skills, better body language, how to control tone of voice and gestures, even eye contact, and posture. All of these lessons are critical skill builders for leaders. We'd like to think that our programs are a unique way to grow future leaders, here at home and from around the world," Mostovoj says proudly.

For more information on how your organization can get its leadership involved with international homestay programs like EF's, email Autumn Mostovoj at Autumn.Mostovoj@EF.com, or call 1-800-521-0083.

THE IMPORTANCE OF TRAINING LEADERS TO COMPETENCIES

According to competency expert and consultant Joan Smith, it is essential for learning professionals to establish focus groups before training begins. Smith suggests that focus groups comprise a variety of representatives from inside the organization, such as sales and marketing representatives, regional managers, and senior vice presidents. The groups assume responsibility for identifying the competencies required for each of the areas represented. When that has been accomplished, the training division can move on to developing what Smith calls "a competency, strength-based curriculum for learning in a performance-driven organization."

Smith, who also serves as vice president of Reid Publications, based in Ontario, Canada, suggests the following approach to developing a competency-based curriculum: "There are three approaches necessary. First, the curriculum must be content specific. Second, there have to be built-in learning opportunities for the participants. And third, there's got to be a functional framework for linking learning to performance."

There is no substitute for learning by doing. The more opportunities your leaders have to serve the organization in an action capacity, the more likely they are to develop the skills and competencies necessary to lead successfully.

Disney's Performance Learning Cycle

At Disney University, they call this the performance learning cycle. According to Disney's representatives, most companies unfortunately practice the "spray and pray" method of training their leaders. That is, they spray training on people and then pray they will absorb it. Instead of that ineffective approach, trainers at Disney ask themselves, "Are we giving our employees the right kind of training?" That means providing workers with on-the-job learning techniques that offer them a chance to practice what they have learned. When learners are trained to the competencies required for the job, that question becomes moot. The performance learning cycle at Disney goes from training, to focused experiences that directly address required competencies, to results, and finally to recognition and praise.

RECOGNIZE THE SHORT SHELF LIFE OF KNOWLEDGE

In the past decade, the umbrella of organizational learning, which incorporates training divisions, corporate universities, conference training centers, and other educational facilities, has experienced an increasingly shortened shelf life of knowledge and information. In many industries, the shelf life of knowledge is no more than a few months. And in high-tech industries, it's much shorter than that. It's important for you and your leaders to know the shelf life of your organization's knowledge. Think of your training programs as having expiration dates stamped on them. Managing knowledge requires that you keep your information not only current but ahead of the curve.

Organizations no longer can depend on formal learning institutions to retool the workplace. Organizations everywhere are finding that now it is up to them to educate and train their own leaders. That means you! Your role as a developer of people has never been more vital to the success of the organization. Droves of companies are entering the education business at a phenomenal rate. The remarkable growth of corporate universities is an example of that. In the past 10 years, we've seen the number of such universities rise from around 500 to well over 1,000, setting the stage for organizational survival and competitive vigor.

The terms *corporate university* and *training facility* can be misleading. In today's learning environment, many corporate universities have no physical location at all. They are virtual and they comprise a best-practices effort to develop all levels of employees in a variety of skills and competencies needed to be successful and to prepare for the requirements of future job opportunities.

Once organizations began acknowledging the short shelf life of information and knowledge, organizationally driven training systems were created. That launched distance learning, e-learning, collaborative efforts with international universities, and desktop "storefronts" for learning and computer-based training.

Corporations spend more than $100 billion each year for all kinds of corporate education and training. A sizable chunk of that money is wasted on travel and outdated methods to deliver the programs. It's obvious that learning techniques and the future education of leaders are rapidly moving well beyond the walls of the traditional classroom—as in online or e-learning, for example (see www.MindLeaders.com, where Anne is a featured author of several distance learning programs).

Therefore, now might be a good time for you, as a developer of leaders, to consider how you might use the information and knowledge in this book in a less traditional, more cutting-edge venue. In other words, how can you adapt your existing training format to a more innovative learning format?

Successful leadership programs aren't an accident and don't just happen. They result from considerable planning and innovation. The following questions will help you step outside the traditional training box and consider the vast array of learning options.

- By incorporating the information in this book into a distance learning program, would I be able to train more leaders more often?
- If I were to develop and use computer-based learning programs, could I add more students to the program without incurring the extra expense of more facilitators?
- Would a more self-directed leadership program give my students the option to pace themselves and choose the style of learning interaction he or she prefers?
- Would alternative teaching methods, such as distance learning, deliver a more consistent message with greater immediacy companywide?
- Am I offering my leaders access to the enormous amount of learning resources available, and by the same token, am I offering remote subject matter experts easy access to my leaders and to our organization?
- Would alternative training methods help reduce my training costs?

Managing Knowledge Workers Who Are Leaders

Knowledge work is sometimes referred to as "the source of new ideas." In order to receive the most from your knowledge worker leaders, you can help create an environment where new ideas are widely accepted and harnessed. www.MindTool.com recommends a few ways to go about this.

These ideas help build trust and strengthen the bond between your knowledge workers' performance and your organization's success, helping to create a competitive advantage.

Link technology: Find ways to provide the most current technology you can to leaders, and then train people how to use it.

Manage knowledge: Develop a strategy to manage knowledge within your company. Create a knowledge database, enhance learning possibilities for everyone at every level, and encourage your employees to share knowledge. Set up a special area for collaboration and give employees time to share ideas with everyone. Encourage industry-leader benchmarking when possible.

Be a "coach," not a "boss": Bosses are **not** required! Leaders are! To maintain leaders' trust and respect, be aware of the work they're doing, and coach them as needed on an ongoing basis. Give praise in progress. Develop a coaching relationship in which you give knowledge workers the freedom and support they need to do their work.

See the big picture: People want to know "why" as much, if not more, than "what." Don't ask your knowledge workers to improve a product's design without telling them why it needs improving and how the improvements will benefit the performance of the company. When workers understand "why," they will offer solutions that are innovative and insightful. They get jazzed to be part of something big.

Get creative with performance metrics: What gets measured is what gets done. In managing knowledge work, it's the final output that matters most, and the steps along the way are sometimes less important. By examining what is most valuable in terms of output, you can usually identify key performance indicators up front and start designing your own matrices for checking improvement processes. Tie indicators to the big picture outcomes you desire most.

FOCUSING ON LIFETIME LEARNING, NOT LIFETIME EMPLOYMENT

Help your leaders to understand the major paradigm shift that has taken place over the past 20 years. That shift has been from a mantra of "Work hard, be on time, do your job well, and you'll be guaranteed lifetime employment," to "Take responsibility for your learning, sharpen your skills, acquire as much knowledge as possible, and you'll be ensuring your marketability in the workplace for the rest of your life."

In a way, today's learning organizations have replaced the old notion of job security—a strategy that organizations are using to remain competitive in the global economy. The result of this has been what is called the "intentional learner." In other words, the responsibility for learning has now shifted from the training department and its facilitators to the individual employee.

The organization's training function also has shifted from a simple training event to learning as a lifelong commitment. Consider this comparison of the two approaches.

Yesterday's Training Department	Today's Learning Organization
Training as a one-time event.	Learning as a lifelong process and commitment.
Training scheduled at a physical training site.	Learning is immediate—available anywhere in the world at any time, offered virtually.
Learning from lecturing.	Learning by doing, and from a distance.
Learning from in-house facilitators and external university professors.	Learning from internal senior staffers and a consortium of online professors; or self-directed learning.

What other comparisons can you suggest that further signify this dramatic shift in organizational learning? Add them to the list above and be prepared to share the concept of intentional learning and shifting perceptions with your leaders.

IS YOUR ORGANIZATION READY TO BECOME THE PRIMARY EDUCATOR OF ITS WORKFORCE?

Education no longer stops when leaders graduate from traditional schools and universities. In yesterday's work world, an employee's life was split into two parts—one part represented a person going to school and graduating, and the second part represented a person getting a job and going to work. Today's organizations expect their workers to build continually on their knowledge and skill development throughout their lifetimes. As a result, the forward-focused organization has become the primary educator of its workforce, so that it more effectively can meet the needs of its customers in an increasingly competitive business environment.

Acknowledging the need for businesses to become educators, many organizations, like Disney, have initiated strategies beyond their own workplaces and are offering them, for a fee, to their suppliers and outside customers; for Disney this is through Disney Institute training. The corporate university now has become a profit center in many organizations.

THE FUTURE OF LEARNING

As a learning professional, now is a good time to imagine what the future of training will look like in your organization. Here are a few significant suggestions to consider in planning ahead for the ongoing education and development of your leaders.

Align all of your organization's training and employee development programs to its most critical business goals and competencies. One way this is being done in companies is by

creating some variation on the position of chief learning officer. The position is accountable for linking employee learning and development to the overall organizational strategies and goals. In many cases, this position reports directly to the CEO or president of the organization. Learning professionals who align their organization's training with its goals and competencies are ahead of the curve.

Implement teach-back methods of training by using your organization's existing leadership as faculty. When the organization's leadership gets involved in the learning process, they send a strong message that they seriously are committed to developing their people. Plan to recruit top management to help with your learning programs. This is sometimes referred to as a teach-back method because leaders who have learned a particular skill or competency are in the best position to teach others what they have learned. Let your leaders know now that you intend to involve them as faculty in the future.

Use your organization's corporate university and training programs to gain increased competitive advantage in the marketplace. Use your organization's brand-name presence to leverage its competitive stance in the marketplace. One way of doing this is to place an official name on your organization's training. Remember, a corporate university does not have to hold an actual physical location to function or to create branding. If your organization has a facility people can physically visit, that's great. But if not, use the virtual university approach for branding your organization's reputation in business excellence. Then, if your organization ever decides to market its reputation in the training arena to outsiders for a profit, you will have established a solid foundation for doing so.

Corporate Trainings With Brand Clout

- Second City Communications (the corporate arm of the Second City Comedy Theater)
- Xerox's Document University
- Southwest Airlines' University for People
- Toyota University
- Google Code University
- Apple University
- Dell Learning
- Hamburger University
- Disney University

Build strategic partnerships with higher-learning institutions worldwide. More and more organizations are granting degrees to their employees in partnership with accredited higher-learning institutions. Those degrees are offered at both the undergraduate and graduate levels in such areas as engineering, HRD, computer science, and business

administration. Also on the rise are joint degree programs in which organizations can specify to their leaders the exact types of skills and competencies needed for their future success.

Combine technology with traditional training for increased learning solutions. Learning that combines both high tech and high touch can offer your leaders the best of both worlds, not to mention highly entertaining, engaging, and fun training programs. The efficacy of technology for learning is increasing daily, with the greatest areas of growth occurring over an organization's intranet. It is predicted that corporate intranets will account for more than one-third of all training delivered in the near future. In addition, technology offers organizations easy and fast methods for measuring, tracking, and accelerating learning. (For more information on alternative training methods like e-learning, visit www.annebruce.com/e-learning.)

HOLISTIC LEADERSHIP DEVELOPMENT AND TRAINING

Employee learning and development now is being viewed in some organizations as a holistic concept—that is, learning no longer is considered a one-time training event. Instead, a more whole-person approach is being used. Because all leaders are lifelong learners and their learning is connected to the organization's strategies and competencies, holistic development creates a more successful and self-assured, self-gratified leader who discovers fulfillment through his or her meaningful purpose within the organization.

By taking such an approach as you develop leaders at all levels within your organization, you not only will be managing knowledge effectively and sustaining a competitive advantage, but also preparing the organization to refill its talent pool with future leaders.

To create a world-class learning environment, leaders must:

- manage knowledge
- train to competencies
- recognize the short shelf life of knowledge
- focus on lifetime learning, not lifetime employment
- sustain a competitive advantage while learning faster than the competition.

In order to manage training knowledge:

- Consider your leaders' skill levels and competencies before you try to develop them.
- Assess your leaders' real-world experience.
- Fire up and continuously challenge your seasoned leaders.

Questions for Discussion: The Power of Knowledge Management

1. Why is it important to take into consideration your leaders' skill levels and competencies before trying to develop them?

2. How long is the typical shelf life of knowledge in most industries?

3. What are some of the organizational advantages of alternative learning formats such as distance learning?

4. What is the most significant paradigm shift taking place in organizational learning?

5. What are the advantages to employees when the organization builds strategic partnerships with higher-learning institutions?

6. What is meant when training is referred to as a holistic concept?

7. If training is no longer seen as a one-time event, then what is it?

Wrapping It Up

A learning organization focuses less on transferring skills through training and more on improving human performance through various means, including distance education, self-directed and virtual learning, distance career development methods, and more. This shift in focus will help your leaders keep the organization's competitive advantage over time.

In the next chapter, we'll study the importance of your leaders developing an inspirational shared vision among their followers.

Vision and Purpose Build Confidence and Excitement in Leaders

Most athletes have to keep their eyes on something beyond their own feet. Skiers, for example, focus down the mountain as they traverse the moguls. Jockeys look up and around the bend as they navigate their horses' moves through the sea of flying hooves. Even ballerinas keep their heads up and their vision at one spot in the distance as they pirouette.

Similarly, leaders must look beyond what is right in front of them. They must keep their eyes on the larger picture and on their desired destination, as they strategically plan how to direct their teams onward. This long-distance view becomes a leader's vision.

The impact and influence that a leader's vision has on the organization's eventual success and ultimate future can be staggering. Take a look at Bill Gates, for example. He and his organization still maintain the same well-publicized vision as when he founded Microsoft in 1975: a computer on every desk and in every home. Talk about the power of vision! The Microsoft organization remains committed to the vision of Gates, and it's been that specific, singular focus that has revolutionized the way people all over the world live and do business.

Here is where each of your leaders will learn about the long-lasting impact that his or her visionary talents can have on the survival and success of the organization, as well as how to inspire shared vision among employees. This chapter will help guide your leaders through a point-by-point visionary process of creating a better future fueled with possibilities. If your training does not include this element, here is your chance to supplement your leadership development program to emphasize this vital quality.

What You Will Learn in This Chapter:

- ◆ Leadership vision creates the future. Leaders must
 - inspire shared vision in others
 - learn to ask the critical questions that inspire vision
 - start a vision quest.
- ◆ Envision the future of all projects. Leaders must
 - stretch creativity and envision the future
 - create job titles that inspire vision
 - cast the net of participation beyond their wildest dreams.

VISUALIZATION EXERCISE

Ask your leaders to find a quiet place to sit for a few minutes and close their eyes. Tell them to let their minds get completely still. Have each leader imagine they are sitting at their desk. All of a sudden the president of the company walks in and commends him or her for a job well done! Visualization is also about "hearing." Have your leaders imagine they are hearing a specific compliment: "Your revenue-generating idea about the Johnson project in today's meeting, Greta, was terrific! I am excited to get the numbers and meet again on how we might launch this new project in the fall."

Suggest that each leader actually "hear" the praise in this imaginary voice. Then they should allow themselves to "feel" the proud satisfaction of this praise run through their bodies—tell everyone to sit up straight and accept this compliment with a big smile!

Vision and purpose builds confidence and excitement in leaders. So show your leaders how to make it happen with this exercise.

VISION CREATES THE FUTURE

Without vision there is little or no sense of purpose in leadership. Every moment of importance, every crusade, every project, and every organization begins with a dream or a vision. It's at this point that a leader's vision becomes the powerful force that not only invents, but creates, the future.

What Is Vision?

Ask your leaders to share their definitions of vision. You're likely to get a number of responses, including some of the following:

- a powerful mental picture of what we want our future to look like
- a future message harmonious with our values and sense of purpose
- a unique and ideal image of the future
- a picture of how we see our destiny unfolding
- a way to explore the possibilities of what could be
- a result of head and heart working together to create the ultimate dream
- a way of picturing excellence.

Debrief your leaders' definitions by suggesting that leaders experience visioning in many different ways. Some leaders see vivid mental images, some experience sensations, and others have an unspoken sense or intuition about what their visions are or should be. Most commonly, however, visions are perceived as strong mental pictures. After all, the word *vision* comes from a word literally meaning "to see." It perfectly describes a leader's capacity to be forward-looking.

Your Leaders' Vision Quest Begins

To inspire vision in others, your leaders must have a strong desire to make something happen, to change the landscape of the organization, or to create something no one's ever created before. Ask any entrepreneur or successful leader what he or she

envisioned for the organization at the outset. All of them probably will tell you that they imagined an incredibly exciting experience and that they had recurring dreams of what could be. More than likely, they also had complete conviction about making those dreams possible and therefore the confidence to make extraordinary things happen. In other words, their vision became the powerful force that fueled the possibilities and created the future. The leadership lesson you want to drive home is this: It all starts with a vision.

> **Key Point:** *Visioning isn't a plan. It's a mind stretch.*

Make All Your Leaders VPs: Visionary Persons!

Once in a while, you get a chance to meet and work with a true visionary. For Anne, that was her experience working with Ann Rhoades, bestselling author of the book *Built on Values: Creating an Enviable Culture That Outperforms the Competition* (Jossey-Bass, a Wiley Imprint, 2011). Ann Rhoades and her team helped create and were instrumental in the super-high-performing leadership cultures of companies like JetBlue, PF Chang's China Bistros, Southwest Airlines, DoubleTree Hotels, and many other trailblazing organizations.

Ann is known as PRES (Person Responsible for Extraordinary Service) of Albuquerque-based People Ink, which through the years has gained big points with prestigious clients when it comes to helping leaders to lift the fog that can sometimes build up around their organizations, often clouding the ability to maintain clear vision in tough times. People Ink provides full-service "People Systems" for building outstanding organizational cultures for startups or retooling existing service-based organizations, helping them create thriving and engaged workforces. At People Ink, the title VP stands for Visionary of People. (Go to www.peopleink.com for lots of great information).

In an interview with Ann Rhoades' former co-worker, Visionary of People Jeff Sullivan, Jeff shared with Anne Bruce (for the first edition of this book) some of his creative strategies on how he's gone about facilitating the vision quest of some of People Ink's clients.

"Most start-up companies have at least one strong thing going for them. At this point in their existence, they possess the most profound clarity of vision. However, as they grow their businesses, it's not unusual to see that vision become more and more diluted, or less clear, often muddied by lots of hiring and multiple locations," says Sullivan.

"Bringing vision to crystal-clear imagery again, especially for the organization that loses focus along the way, becomes an opportunity for us to say, 'Take a look at all of your organization's moments of truth and all of the opportunities that come with that to once again define yourselves.' In order for a client to get clarity of vision, it's sometimes necessary to facilitate them through the process in order to get them to really start thinking outside the box, like they did in the beginning," adds Sullivan.

So how does a dubbed "visionary person" like Sullivan facilitate such a process? "It's something called the radical application of common sense," he says. "And it often requires getting leaders to really stretch their creative thinking processes to the max. I have a five-step visioning exercise that I like to use."

FIVE STEPS TOWARD FACILITATING A
LEADER'S VISIONING PROCESS

Read the sidebar about People Ink and share Jeff Sullivan's perspective on visioning with your leaders. Then take them through the following exercise based on his visioning process. The exercise will get them thinking and imagining creatively in no time.

1. Start by having your leaders take a close look at a business unlike their own—a business they know very little about. For our example, let's choose a taxi company.
2. Ask them to envision what would be necessary in order to launch a taxi company. Their initial answers probably will include things such as cars, drivers, a dispatcher, special licensing, and permits to carry passengers.
3. Next, request that they crank up their visioning techniques and describe what would be needed to have the most successful taxi company in the world. Here you can expect answers such as exceptional customer service, clean and brightly painted cars, airbags in the front and back, beautifully appointed interiors, no charge for extra passengers, and so on. Point out here that everyone's vision is beginning to get a little clearer, but it's not yet strong enough to fuel the required passion, excitement, and unlimited possibilities that would create an unprecedented experience in ground travel worldwide.
4. Have your leaders really stretch their creativity and envision what might seem like the impossible. Have them look into the future of their taxi company and come up with a vision that blows the doors off what anyone might even begin to imagine at this point in time. This is what is known as divergent thinking, and it involves opening your leaders' minds to unbelievable possibilities and unusual ways of thinking. Explain that there are no rules and that it's okay to be crazy, creative, and radical in visioning for the company! Examples from this part of the exercise that leaders often come up with include taxis that turn into helicopters and fly over gridlocked traffic, money-back satisfaction guarantees on every fare, heated seats in the winter with individual massage controls, and taxi fares that are paid for with a simple thumbprint on an electronic payment card. Point out to your leaders that this is exactly the kind of visioning that Bill Gates used almost 37 years ago. At the time, his vision of a predominantly high-tech world where there would be a computer on every desk and in every home was almost unimaginable—but it's that kind of creative visioning process that has created our present reality. That's the creativity and passion every one of your leaders needs to use when developing his or her vision for a project, a new division, or an entire organization.
5. Finally, stress to your leaders that among all the dozens of out-of-this-world creative ideas that come from this exercise, there are probably two or three that with special adaptation and the radical application of common sense can be used in a vision statement. This is what is called convergent thinking, and

it brings together wacky ideas with trends and helps analyze their potential impact to create a format for realistic actions.

To place this exercise in the here-and-now, have your leaders apply the same process they used to create a vision for their imaginary taxi company to a real-life work project. Observe the newfound ease in each leader's ability to create a truly passionate vision.

When Envisioning the Future, It Helps to Know Who You Are and What You Are Not

People Ink helps organizations envision and create people-centric, legacy cultures that accomplish the extraordinary. The People Ink team has a wide range of experience and is grounded in knowing who they are and what they are not.

For example, the company states loud and clear "Who We Are" on their website: *We are experienced culture creators who believe "you cannot force culture . . . you can only create environment."* Next, they are equally proud of "What We Are Not": *Traditional Human Resources, Conformists, Enforcers, Rule Makers, Inside-the-box Thinkers, Command and Control Freaks, or the "Inc." in a big company.*

And although they've all grown up to become successful professionals, these Visionaries of People never steer far from the creativity of their youth—or a box of crayons for that matter!

> **Key Point:** *A leader's vision is the powerful force that fuels the possibilities and creates the future.*

INSPIRING A SHARED VISION AMONG LEADERS

Your leaders will need to enlist others in their vision because a leader without constituents is not a leader. And employees will not follow someone else's dream unless they also see it as their own. Your leaders cannot demand buy-in from employees—they can only inspire it. If the people believe that the vision is theirs, they will follow. Here are some effective methods for inspiring shared vision.

Casting the Net of Participation

Have your leaders think about the people they want their vision to inspire. Then ask them to group those people and define each group with a title. Have them write down each group title and, under that, write what motivates those group members to action. Here's an example:

Name of Group: Stakeholders	Name of Group: Customers
What motivates them:	What motivates them:
• Profits	• Consistently great service
• Competitive advantage	• More value for the money
• Growth	• Quality
• Diversification	• Variety

When all of the groups and what motivates them have been listed, ask your leaders to identify and write down what all of these groups have in common. What are their shared motivations? Point out that the answers they find will tell them how they best can appeal to each group's overlapping interests.

In addition, encourage your leaders to initiate a vision discussion with each of the groups listed. What do their customers, stakeholders, vendors, and team members envision for the organization's optimal future? Have your leaders collect this feedback and use it in the visioning process where appropriate. Leaders forge unity of purpose by demonstrating that the vision represents the common good for all.

Eight Effective Techniques for Leaders When Inspiring Shared Vision

- Speak positively and enthusiastically about your vision.
- Share your thoughts and feelings from the heart.
- Describe your vision vividly so that others can see it too.
- Take the intangible and make it tangible by describing sensations and smells.
- Encourage others to be intuitive.
- Breathe life into your vision and keep it alive.
- Listen to everyone. Ask for feedback.
- Demonstrate your passion and excitement for your vision.

Beyond Their Wildest Dreams—Envisioning the Future of a Project

To enlist others in a vision, your leaders must know what their constituents are thinking. When the people believe that their leader knows and understands their interests and needs, they will follow willingly. Here are some starter questions that help initiate that dialogue by identifying what inspires vision in others:

- What gets you excited about this project? What inspires you most?
- Forget the business connection for a minute. What higher meaningful purpose will you derive from this project?
- What specific things do you think will influence the direction of this project, such as available resources, people, technology, geographic location, trends, etc.?

With those questions, your leaders will create an effective way for both parties to communicate their dreams to one another.

Now have your leaders respond to the following questions and picture themselves at the end of their project. Be sure to remind your leaders to be specific in their responses.

Describe what you see when this project has been successful beyond your wildest dreams.

What are people thinking?

What are they doing?

What are they saying?

What are they feeling?

STRUCTURING A VISION STATEMENT

Your leaders are almost ready to write their own vision statements, but before they do, have them complete this exercise. By describing the following, each of your leaders will be putting together the basic structure needed to write his or her own meaningful vision statement.

Steps to Structuring a Vision Statement

Step 1: Describe the passion that inspires you as a leader about this project.

Describe what inspires your people about this project.

Step 2: Describe the uniqueness of this dream and what makes it almost magical.

Step 3: Describe in detail the magnificent future you see for your people and for the organization as it relates to this project.

Step 4: Describe how this vision serves the common good of all the people involved.

Step 5: Describe your vision with tangible images and visual descriptions that will appeal to everyone involved.

Communicating the Vision: Writing a Vision Statement

Your leaders now should be ready to write compelling and passionate vision statements for projects of their own. Remind them about the important objectives of a vision statement that were described in chapter 6. Unlike a mission statement that defines who people are, often using their beliefs and philosophies, a vision statement says where people are going and provides inspiration and hope for what the organization is capable of becoming.

Leader's Vision Statement

Now instruct your leaders to pull together their notes from this chapter—and specifically their responses from the Steps to Structuring a Vision Statement exercise—and have each leader write his or her own statement. Then ask them to share them by reading aloud to the group.

Remind your leaders that vision statements serve as excellent measures of our success. Also, check to see if their statements meet the criteria described earlier: Do they tell you where they are headed? Do they provide inspiration and hope for what the organization is capable of doing? If some of your leaders' vision statements do not include these critical components, make sure they revise them accordingly.

Dressing Up a Vision or Mission Statement

At Levi Strauss & Co., they dress up their statements by printing them on blue denim paper stock. Other companies find equally creative ways to present their vision and mission statements—from credit card companies that print them on plastic cards to organizations that print their messages on the backs of employee business cards. You'll also find vision and mission statements on magnets, bookmarks, and posters.

How your leaders ultimately regard their own statements probably will be reflected in the presentation style they choose and where they opt to display them. It's common to find framed statements in company lobbies, employee cubicles, managers' offices, break rooms, and cafeterias.

Real-World Expanded Vision the Amazonian Way

Jeff Bezos continues to expand his vision for Amazon.com (world's largest bookseller), going beyond being a successful online bookstore destined to change the economics of the book industry, to being a virtual bookstore with the world's largest selection. That's the Jeff Bezos dream—in motion and expanding daily. Bezos uses the word "compelled" to describe his drive for attaining and expanding his vision.

Maintaining an organization's vision, like Amazon.com, requires setting a foundation for the future in order to achieve its long-term goals. The Amazonian process looks something like this:

- Clarity about your purpose: Top management must be able to answer the question, "Why are we here?"

- Know where you are going: Long-term strategies should come from the top.

- Ask where you are now: What are the strengths, weaknesses, opportunities, and challenges?

- Practice strategic and tactical planning triages: Identify the three most important areas in the business in which to excel.

- Develop core outcomes: Identify short-term goals for the business consistent with the purpose and vision of the company.

- Develop strategies for each outcome: Strategies are broader efforts for achieving each of the core outcomes.

- Develop tactics: Step-by-step actions to be taken to achieve each strategy.

I say to you, my friends, that in spite of the difficulties and frustrations of the moment, I still have a dream. It is a dream deeply rooted in the American dream.

I have a dream that one day this nation will rise up and live out the true meaning of its creed: "We hold these truths to be self-evident; that all men are created equal."

I have a dream that one day on the red hills of Georgia the sons of former slaves and the sons of former slave-owners will be able to sit down together at the table of brotherhood.

I have a dream that my four little children will one day live in a nation where they will not be judged by the color of their skin but by the content of their character.

"I Have a Dream" Speech—Dr. Martin Luther King Jr.

INSPIRING VISION

Dr. Martin Luther King's "I Have a Dream" speech is one of the most instructive examples of passionate and inspiring presentations ever made, and you can use it as a powerful way to conclude your "Leading With Vision" leadership training program. The example is not merely memorable; it has withstood the test of time as a remarkable example of compelling human inspiration and personal conviction. After showing your leaders a videotape (the DVD can be purchased through Amazon.com) of the speech, ask them for their observations about Dr. King's ability to inspire vision in others. Here are a few of the observations you can expect:

- Dr. King used lots of vivid images.
- His references to the Constitution and the Bible gave the speech credibility.
- His audience related to his examples.
- Dr. King made it easy for a listener to see his vision and feel his passion.

VISION AND HIGH PERFORMANCE GO TOGETHER

One of the common threads found among high-performance organizations is that they have a crystal-clear picture of where they are going and what they are trying to create together. Employees must believe in their hearts that their leader's vision is their vision too. The responsibility for conveying the feeling falls on the shoulders of your leaders. Inspiring passion and commitment aligned with the organization's goals and objectives is a critical competency that your organization's leaders must have when managing people in a fast-changing environment.

Inspiring shared vision means doing the following:

- Speak positively and enthusiastically about your vision.
- Share your thoughts and feelings from the heart.
- Describe your vision vividly.
- Take the intangible and make it tangible by describing sensations and smells.
- Encourage others to be intuitive.
- Breathe life into your vision and keep it alive.
- Listen to everyone and ask for feedback.
- Demonstrate your passion and excitement for your vision.

Ask yourself:

- What are people thinking?
- What are people doing?
- What are people saying?
- What are people feeling?

Questions for Discussion: Leading With Vision

1. Why is creativity an important part of leading with vision?
2. What is the difference between a mission statement and a vision statement?
3. How will your leaders know when they've written a vision statement correctly?
4. In addition to Dr. Martin Luther King Jr., what other well-known leaders have inspired throngs of people with their compelling visions and dreams?

Wrapping It Up

This is a good time to have your leaders address the toughest part about leading with vision: living it. Living a vision is a daily process and a commitment to action, not merely a declaration or a poster. Explain to your leaders that it can be a long way between the vision they've created and its realization. Vision is a visceral experience and is felt emotionally. In the next chapter, we'll provide you with the three Ps—purpose, passion, and performance of leadership—guaranteed to kick up your visioning lessons and learning a full notch!

Purpose, Passion, and Performance: The Three Ps

In today's workplace, those who lead with purpose and passion typically increase the performance of their teams. In our fast-paced environment, businesses are moving at lightning speed, and leaders need to motivate and challenge their employees to keep productivity and quality at their highest while igniting a burning passion in their employees to strive for their highest potential.

We can learn more about instilling passion and purpose for increased performance when we study some of the most successful companies of today. Tony Hsieh, CEO of Zappos, has demonstrated a method of instilling passion by "delivering happiness" to his employees. Hsieh's forward-thinking business model has been studied and infused into many corporations. This chapter will include a mini case study on Zappos to demonstrate how defining and sticking to your company's core values, allowing workers to be themselves, acting with transparency, and encouraging relationships outside the workplace can foster passion and even joy among your employees—which in turn increases your odds of creating happy customers and thus a productive and profitable workplace.

You also will learn to use the three Ps—purpose, passion, and performance—to lead your team in achieving company goals as you tap into your employees' highest potential.

What You Will Learn in This Chapter:

- ◆ Instill the three Ps in the workplace. Leaders must
 - deliver each employee a clear purpose and goals
 - ignite a burning passion to reach the goals through following the mission statement and vision
 - be enthusiastic and believe in the purpose and goals
 - model some of the best companies that are great, and then strive for that greatness.
- ◆ Maintain passion in the workplace. Leaders must
 - greet their employees
 - celebrate failures
 - know and disseminate the company's core values
 - have a little fun.

ZAPPOS, AN INTERNET SALES LEADER

Zappos was founded in 1999 by Nick Swinmurn. Realizing he needed help, he later asked Tony Hsieh to join him as CEO. Hsieh, having embodied an entrepreneurial spirit since he was an adolescent, had already learned a lot of lessons along the way.

By the time Hsieh joined Zappos, he had already run and sold his previous company, LinkExchange, to Microsoft for $265 million. LinkExchange started with just 10 employees, but grew to 100 under Hsieh's leadership. Hsieh's main reason for selling LinkExchange was that he no longer had the passion to go to work at his own company. Microsoft offered the opportunity for him to get out and try a new challenge. Hsieh left large sums of money on the table in order to leave to pursue his next challenge because he wasn't driven by the easy paycheck. Instead, he was driven by his passion—to create, inspire, and achieve.

Get Quirky

Quirky is good in this culture. The famous e-tailer believes in the "psychic gratification" employees get from helping others. Call center customer care reps are given tons of freedom—they are allowed to chat as long as they like with customers, write thank-you notes, or even send flowers to a customer. Their top priority is making "emotional" connections!

Zappos hires positive people and then places them where positive thinking is reinforced. CEO Tony Hsieh gives employees a list of his 10 Core Values, two of which state: (1) create fun and a little weirdness; and (2) pursue growth and learning.

Today, according to Hsieh, "Zappos is among the world's most successful, progressive, and forward-thinking companies as created by its incredibly visionary leaders."

In fact, Zappos has made *Fortune* magazine's "100 Best Companies to Work For" over the past three years, and has also enjoyed tremendous job growth.

In addition, Zappos experienced the following gross sales record in its first five years of operation:

- 1999: Almost nothing
- 2000: $1.6 million
- 2001: $8.6 million
- 2002: $32 million
- 2003: $70 million

In 2008, they earned $1 billion in gross sales—two years ahead of the goal they had set.

Zappos Believes in Company Culture First

In Hsieh's book, *Delivering Happiness: A Path to Profits, Passion, and Purpose*, he illustrates the story of how he led Zappos. For Hsieh, running a successful business isn't all

about the money; it is about happiness. In fact, he was reported to earn just $36,000 as his annual salary, even after Amazon acquired Zappos.

Hsieh has said in numerous interviews and keynote speeches that he figured out how to be successful in business: Make "*people*" happy, and allow their individuality to shine through. He also believes that if the employees are happy, the customers will be happy too. It's all about building the right company culture, and the rest will follow. In an interview with Henry Blodget of *The Business Insider,* Tony answers the question on how past failures led to future successes. Tony responded, "In my previous company, LinkExchange, . . .we hired people that had the right skill sets and experiences, but weren't necessarily great for the company culture. And that's how the company culture just went completely downhill."

In a later interview, Hsieh stated: "At Zappos, our number one priority is our company culture. Our belief is that if we get the culture right, most of the other stuff—like delivering great customer service and building a long-term enduring brand and business—will be a natural by-product of our culture."

Core values are key in creating culture. Zappos publicizes and follows its core values, which include:

1. Deliver WOW through service.
2. Embrace and drive change.
3. Create fun and a little weirdness.
4. Be adventurous, creative, and open-minded.
5. Pursue growth and learning.
6. Build open and honest relationships with communication.
7. Build a positive team and family spirit.
8. Do more with less.
9. Be passionate and determined.
10. Be humble.

Zappos has taken its values integration to the level of almost becoming part of its marketing strategy. In fact, its employees are expected to hang out with one another after work, have fun, think outside of the box, and share their ideas openly—all examples of Zappos values in action.

Performance Evaluations and Core Values Go Hand in Hand

Hsieh in fact states in his book: "As we grow as a company, it has become more and more important to explicitly define the Zappos core values from which we develop our culture, our brand, and our business strategies. With so many new employees joining the company as we grow, we want to make sure that everyone is on the same page and acting consistently with what we want Zappos to be all about. Over time, we will be restructuring performance evaluations so that a part of every employee's performance evaluation is based on the Zappos core values."

Do you think it is a coincidence that Zappos' commitment to values and level of success parallel one another in driving them off the charts? Today's top companies are

demonstrating that it's highly advantageous, if not necessary, to lead through clearly defined core corporate values. And the best leaders are leading not by selfish values to serve only themselves—but by values that will propel their entire organizations toward expansion and greatness. Guess what? In the process, everyone wins—including the leaders!

Passion vs. Paycheck

How does Zappos give its employees purpose and passion, and increase their performance? Hsieh says it best himself: "You know, it really just comes down to not feeling like a number. To that personal and human connection, and when a customer calls us, they're going to talk to someone that really, truly wants to provide great service and isn't there just for a paycheck. There's not . . . a list of . . . 10 magical things that we do. But it's really, a customer has a question or an issue, or whatever and we basically just tell our reps 'just use your best judgment' and just do what you think is right." Now that is empowerment!

WHAT ARE PURPOSE AND PASSION?

Webster's dictionary defines purpose as

- the reason for which something exists or is done, made, used, and so on
- an intended or desired result; end; aim; goal
- determination; resoluteness
- practical result, effect, or advantage: to act to good purpose.

How does this definition relate to your workplace, you might ask? You can instill purpose by helping your employees believe in something bigger than themselves and by focusing on the desired result and vision of the company. In the Zappos case study, the passion is built from empowerment and allowing employees to act like themselves at work, and be a "little weird."

In fact, some consider love synonymous with passion. Passion is something you have a deep desire to obtain or achieve in life. What would happen if your employees developed a deep desire to achieve greatness in your workplace—to be passionate about the work that they do? What would happen if your employees didn't think work was work anymore because they were so passionate about what they did? Passion for success leads to greatness. By instilling purpose and passion into your workplace, increased performance happens naturally.

HOW TO INSTILL PASSION AND PURPOSE INTO EVERY TEAM WITHIN THE ORGANIZATION

Motivation is the key to creating purpose and passion and superstar teams within the organization. Superstar teams thrive on the passion of their leaders, and their leaders

know how to nurture and instill great passion in their people. Great leaders pull out all the stops and create a game plan with the ideas below.

Create a Vision of the Future
As a leader, it is your role to develop a powerful vision for the team. It should be simple yet profound and achievable. This vision should be created by the team to get their buy-in. Creating a vision board and a team motto can help move the vision into fruition and empower the team to reach for the stars.

You May Not See the Whole Story
One of the best leadership lessons are in people's stories. Many times, we judge people without knowing the background behind the behavior. Some people are good at keeping their private lives separate and compartmentalized, but in the workplace, there is not some magic switch that can be turned off to leave outside factors out of the workplace. Savvy managers always remember the whole person approach and, although leaders are not counselors in training, they can listen nonjudgmentally, offer kindness and compassion, and if necessary, let their employees know about EAP (Employee Assistance Programs) benefits. Just remember that there may be more to the story than you can see, and by treating all employees with dignity and respect, you gain trust.

Sometimes You Need to Break the Rules on Purpose
Many times leaders are rigid, follow policy books to a "T," and never deviate. One quick spontaneous team booster would be to break a minor rule every now and again to ignite some passion. The team members would feel that their leader went out on a limb for them (and she probably did!), and they will feel that the leader cares about the happiness of the team. This deviation from the norm should consist of something simple, such as a quick cupcake party where you celebrate a small success of the team and allow people to eat at their desks instead of a break room. The team will love this mini booster, and it will ignite even more passion when they realize that their leader is willing to take some risks for them. Basically, the leader is taking one for the team, and they will usually do it for the leader in return at a later time.

Put Them on a Mission to Reach for the Stars
To reach a state of passion, the team needs to feel as though they are on a special mission to reach the ultimate team goal. This empowers them to greatness and gives them the energy and drive for success. As their leader, you should make great strides to keep reinforcing the mission to the employees. For a new mission, this may mean throwing a mission launch party, as well as planning what will be done when the mission is over (keep them looking forward to the reward!).

Overcome the Mission Buster
Every team has a mission buster—some force that throws obstacles at the team in an attempt to make them unsuccessful. Every team should strive to eliminate the mission

buster. If there isn't one, you may want to initiate an exercise by introducing a fake obstacle to eliminate, so that the team can overcome the enemy, build their confidence, and be motivated to greatness.

Have Some Fun Along the Way

Leaders should add some fun to break up the monotony and alleviate some of the pressures at work. If the team is having a little fun, they will support the mission and vision to give them passion to do an excellent job. You can try a scavenger hunt, or hide lottery tickets in secret spots that will be discovered by workers throughout the day. Make the rewards random, and your efforts will boost morale and lighten the mood for the day.

Stop, Look, and Listen to Your Team

Most decisions involving in a team should be democratic, but for the ones that cannot be, be sure to listen to all feedback. Everyone wants to feel as though they have a part in their future, and they need to be able to visualize themselves in the bigger picture. Once a decision is made, get out of the way and let the team members work at their best pace, so they are able to perform their absolute best. Great leaders surround themselves with great people, engage them in key decisions, and then get out of the way.

Flexibility Speaks Volumes

Smart leaders understand that their employees have more to life than their work at the company (children, parents, spouses). Leaders who are flexible can build an alliance with their teams that cannot be broken.

By following these guidelines, you as a leader will instill purpose, ignite passion, and increase performance in your teams.

HOW TO MAINTAIN PASSION IN THE WORKPLACE WHILE MAINTAINING MAXIMUM PERFORMANCE

Leaders maintain passion in the workplace by always being enthusiastic about their purpose, vision, and mission. Remember, it's the leader who sets the stage for success and maximum performance.

If the leader is not passionate, the team members will not maintain their passion. It takes charismatic leaders to keep the burning passion alive, and they should strive to find things that keep their team moving toward success. The following steps will help to maintain your group's passion and maintain top performance:

Step 1: Have a speedy morning meeting to kick the team into overdrive and set goals for the day. Deliver a quick team-building exercise or ice breaker, and open the floor for questions and honest communication. (Check out Anne's *Ignite Passion—Activate Potential 11-Minute Energizer* video on her website, at www.AnneBruce.com, and get fast, easy-to-use leaders' guidelines that accompany the video.)

Step 2: Spend 10 to 20 percent of your time working directly with your team on the floor; it may be difficult to get away, but it is worth the investment of time.

Step 3: Celebrate failures. This may seem contrary to normal thinking, but great innovative thinkers failed many times before they had a success. If you criticize for failures, your staff will be afraid to take risks that could take the team to the next level.

Step 4: Always greet your employees at the beginning of their shifts, and tell them good night at the end of their shifts. You have probably heard it recommended that married couples start and end each day with positive words; the same applies in the workplace! This helps employees to feel that you are glad they are there today and starts their morning off on a good note.

Step 5: Praise in public and celebrate all successes, big or small. This boosts morale and productivity and is necessary in maintaining peak performance.

Questions for Discussion: Planning to Use the Three Ps

1. Describe how to infuse passion in your work teams.
2. What are some of the ideas from this chapter that you will use in your work teams immediately?
3. What is your team's mission plan?
4. How will you instill in your team a vision to reach your mission?
5. How will you make time to get out of your office and interact with your employees?
6. Look back at Zappos' core values; which ones will you adopt for your teams?

Wrapping It Up

For great leaders, failure is not in their vocabulary! Tying purpose and passion together to increase performance (the three Ps) in teams is the key to success in the workplace. By studying great companies like Zappos, The Ritz-Carlton, and Google, we learn that leaders of superstar companies do things a little differently than the rest of corporate America. By being "a little weird," as Zappos requires its staff to be, and using a "blow up the box" or "step outside the triangle" mentality, you are bound to reach the end of the mission and create many superstars along the way!

CHAPTER 19

Measure What's Important, What's Getting Done, and Forget the Rest

It used to be that performance was measured based on how serious someone took his or her job and how much time was spent "in the grind" of day-to-day tasks. Show up. Do your job. Go home. And whatever you do, don't appear to be having any fun or enjoying what you are doing.

Today, performance has taken on a much more human element (thank goodness), with culture, attitude, and engagement levels becoming normal topics of conversation in leadership circles. Leaders are lightening up!

In fact, many believe that without infusing such traits as attitude into the workplace, leaders cannot achieve optimal levels of performance. Sam Glenn, known as the Authority on Attitude, a speaker, and author of *A Kick in the Attitude*, states, "If you don't take time to charge the attitude batteries of your leaders and employees, your company will be like a cell phone with no energy to make a call. Performance has everything to do with keeping attitude optimal in the workplace. Skills are important, but without the right attitude, your team will struggle to stay engaged."

In past years, most supervisors used one way to assess their employees' performance on the job: They measured how busy everyone stayed. Did people clock in and clock out on time? Were people serious about their work and *not* having any fun? When employees had fun on the job, bosses considered it proof of lack of performance and reduced productivity. It once was believed that no one could have fun at work and still be productive. Fun was just a sign of workers goofing off. Of course, those were the days when managers had an assembly-line mentality and used fear motivation as their primary productivity tool.

These are new times, and here is where your leaders will learn exciting new ways to measure performance and improve productivity, minus the traditional performance review rating system. This chapter reevaluates yesterday's performance evaluation system and offers up a remarkable new way to encourage continuous improvement using effective tools, such as a Performance Builder, a Personal Development Scorecard, and a 90-Day Mailback Worksheet. If your training does not include this element, here is your chance to supplement your leadership development program to emphasize this vital quality.

What You Will Learn in This Chapter:

♦ Characteristics of new and effective performance measurement. Leaders must
 ● ensure continuous learning and improvement
 ● make measurement flexible and easy to revise when necessary
 ● broaden their scope of awareness and sensitivity when it comes to establishing individual performance metrics.
♦ Long-range benefits of performance building. Leaders must
 ● develop their own definition of performance
 ● motivate employees to perform at peak levels
 ● build a bridge between their employees' own interests and talents and the interests and talents of the organization
 ● establish their own easy-to-use BARS measurement tool.

FEAR MOTIVATION: MISS ONE PIECE AND YOU'RE FIRED!

There is probably no better example of the old type of supervision and performance measurement than the 1952 *I Love Lucy* television skit called "Job Switching" (but most widely remembered as "Lucy and Ethel in the Candy Factory"). Get this video on Amazon.com or view on YouTube so you can explain the connection described here to your leaders. Better yet, show it to them.

In the famous skit, Lucy and Ethel get jobs wrapping chocolates in a candy factory. Their supervisor is as tough as nails and shows no compassion for her new hires. Using fear motivation to get as much productivity out of Lucy and Ethel as possible, the supervisor barks the following orders: "All right, girls, if one piece of candy gets past you on this conveyer belt and into the packing room unwrapped, you're fired!" Believe it or not, that quantity-based approach was once one of the most common methods used to measure a worker's performance.

Motivated by fear of losing their jobs, the women panic when the candy conveyer belt starts moving faster than they can wrap. Because they know the number of candies wrapped before reaching the packing room is the measure of their worth, Lucy and Ethel do everything they can to avoid the supervisor's wrath. They stuff unwrapped chocolates into their uniforms and their mouths—it's hilarious classic comedy. What's not so funny is that sheer panic and stressed behavior by employees who are about to undergo traditional performance evaluations still occur in organizations today.

Three Types of Motivation

1. Fear and intimidation
2. Incentives and rewards
3. Personal growth and professional development

Which is most effective for achieving high performance and productivity on the job? Number three.

RE-EVALUATING CURRENT PERFORMANCE MEASUREMENT TOOLS

Is there room for improvement in your performance measurement tools? Will your organization allow leaders to step outside the box, or must they follow the traditional performance review forms and formulas the company has used for years? Either way, the measurement tools and techniques in this chapter will help you open the door for creative and innovative thinking when training your leaders on the value of measurement.

> *In practice, annual ratings are a disease, annihilating long-term planning, demolishing teamwork, nourishing rivalry and politics, leaving people bitter, crushed and bruised, battered, desolate, despondent, unfit for work for weeks after receipt of rating, and unable to comprehend why they are inferior.*
> —W. Edwards Deming

Reframe Evaluations as Coaching, Not Judging

Sixty years ago in the United States, a fascination developed with the concept and application of annual performance evaluations and reviews. The theory was that if managers reviewed an employee on some predetermined criteria every six or 12 months, the employee would use the rating feedback to improve his or her performance. In other words, the review was considered a tool that would make employees better. Although still the belief in many organizations, the theory has not always been supported by practice.

In most organizations, performance reviews are done during the same several-week period each year. Throughout that season, the entire organization may experience extreme trauma. Managers are preparing

> **Key Point:** *Teach your leaders to use judgment, not pass judgment.*

themselves to conduct the painful assessments, and their anticipation of employee responses can be agonizing. In addition, the process leaves most employees feeling demoralized and hiding their hurt feelings or anger. How does an employee explain low job ratings to his or her family? It's humiliating, at the very least.

So what happened to the original idea of using performance evaluations as a method to improve the workforce? Are there exhilarating and beneficial ways to measure an organization's performance through its people? The answer is yes, and it's called leadership!

Real-World Example of a Performance Review's Impact

The following true story was shared by a manager who refused to use the traditional approach when evaluating his employees: "I remember when I was coming up through the ranks in this company. During one of my first evaluations, I only got a satisfactory rating for performance. I think my supervisor graded me a number three on the inane number scale that was used to rate my performance from one to five. I was devastated. Not only did the appraisal squash my confidence, but it took the air out of my sails and slowed my go-get-'em stride. The review haunted me and I eventually left the department because of it."

> **Key Point:** *Use numbers to rank people only if the numbers determine a percentage of growth and learning in a specific skill area such as writing or listening. In that way, the numbers are not representative of the person's ability but of a specific skill area still in development. Even then, the numbers should be self-assigned and not determined by the employee's leader.*

Your leaders' goal in measuring performance is not to prod workers to become the best in the crowd. Rather, the goal should be to encourage all workers to improve themselves continually. The leader who relies on evaluating talent annually via the traditional performance review is missing the point: He or she should be a coach, not a judge.

Leadership means selecting the right people to do the job and then continually educating and training them so that they can master the work. In other words, the measurement and evaluation process is ongoing and is supportive and sustaining rather than judgmental.

The Organization's System Produces Its Behaviors

Using numbers as ratings when measuring an employee's performance points out the person's faults and personalizes the rating instead of focusing on the issues at hand. How can a behavior trait be changed through a scoring process? It can't. It's the organization's system that produces its behaviors. Change the system, and the behaviors will change. This begins with measuring the organization's performance.

According to the old business maxim, "What gets measured is what gets done." That statement is just as relevant as it ever was. No matter how creative and nontraditional their performance, organizations today still have to find ways to measure what's getting done and how much improvement is occurring or needs to be made. You can bet someone is keeping score!

Here are some real-world measurement case studies that you can share with your leaders so that they may begin expanding their thinking when it comes to the many different ways leaders go about measuring an organization's performance. Examples provided include a business school, a high-tech manufacturer, and a start-up airline.

After reviewing the case studies together, ask your leaders to devise their own new and effective ways to measure the performance of their departments or business units. Have them write their own case studies in the case format provided here. Ask this question: What are the measurements that matter most to you, and why? Compile their case studies and distribute them to all of your leaders as a helpful addition to the portfolio of cases presented here.

MEASURING WHAT MATTERS IN THE REAL WORLD: A CASE STUDY PORTFOLIO
London Business School

The Goal: *Have students be transformed by attending this institution of higher learning and be able to look back at the experience as life changing.*

The London Business School was established in 1965 and serves approximately 1,200 graduate students and more than 4,000 executives each year. Outside the United States,

it's ranked as the top business school in the world. According to Dean John A. Quelch, the school isn't in the education business—it's in the *transformation* business. That is a bold and innovative approach to higher-level learning at such a prestigious school.

To measure their success in reaching their goal, the school's leaders developed a tool called a Transformational Benchmarking Questionnaire, which is given to students who have taken programs there. The survey asks such questions as, How much of the program that you took do you recall? Do you stay in touch with faculty? Do you stay in touch with fellow students? How big an impact has the program had on your career and on your quality of life?

How Results Are Measured

Leaders at the school plan to have the survey administered repeatedly as students' careers advance, including one year after they've left the school and then again every five years after that. Survey results provide detailed information about the performance of each student, and leaders will then evaluate that performance against the school's goal of creating a transformational experience for every student.

Before Sun Microsystems Was Acquired by the Oracle Corporation

The Goal: *Sun systems that are up and running at their customers' sites. Sun Microsystems used to call this "system uptime."*

Before Sun Microsystems' merger with Oracle Corporation, it was one of the world's largest computer manufacturers. Sun had offices in 170 countries and provided end-to-end solutions for doing business in the network age. More than a million software developers use its Java programming language.

Behind the technology that put the "dot" in ".com," Sun Microsystems was focused on innovation and high performance in the workplace. Leaders at Sun believed that an organization must closely align its ways of measuring with the ways that its customers measure. In other words, the measures that mattered most to Sun were the measures that mattered most to its customers.

To align its measurement systems appropriately, Sun Microsystems would compile real-time feedback to monitor system uptime and downtime at their customers' sites. That instantaneous feedback was used to determine what the causes of downtime might be. But that's not all that the real-time feedback supplied. Information gathered also was used to train and educate people and to improve existing processes so that Sun's customers could increase their uptime. That, in turn, maximized Sun's ability to serve its customers. This system for measurement was supported by and cascaded down from then-CEO Scott McNealy to Sun's customers and their end users. Today Sun Microsystems is a very successful part of Oracle America.

How Results Are Measured

Before merging with Oracle, Sun used the following two criteria to determine if they were performing to the best of their ability: Are they understanding the real needs of their customers? Are they meeting those needs? Sun believes that the answers to those questions always had the greatest impact on its performance.

JetBlue Airways

The Goal: *Provide the nation with low-fare, hassle-free, high-quality airline service by stressing values and a two-way commitment process between the airline and its people.*

JetBlue, the most heavily capitalized start-up airline in aviation history, is poised to bring to the New York metropolitan area a new brand of travel experience characterized by excellent service, cutting-edge technology, low fares, and great people. Like other carriers, the airline measures closely what is called, in airline lingo, cost per available seat mile. In lay terms, that means how much it costs to make a seat available for sale. That formula brings together every pertinent cost, including fuel, maintenance, and marketing. Unlike some of its competition, however, JetBlue doesn't stop there when it comes to measuring its performance.

One of its measuring tools, which represents two-way employer/employee accountability, is called JetBlue's Two-Way Commitment. It begins during employee orientation with JetBlue's Commitment to You and includes the following five criteria for measuring the airline's accountability to its employees:

- We always will have open, honest, and two-way communication.
- We will provide you with a work environment free from all forms of harassment.
- You will have the opportunity to express your career aspirations and have them acted upon.
- We will return your business-related phone calls within 24 hours.
- We will provide you with the orientation training and proper tools to be successful in your job.

In return, employees are asked to sign a commitment to their employer. The statements somewhat mirror JetBlue's commitment to its people and include the following criteria:

- I will support and use JetBlue-sponsored training and education programs.
- I will treat each customer for who they truly are: They are the very reason we exist!
- I take care of and protect JetBlue assets.
- I am completely honest in my communication with JetBlue employees.
- I take personal responsibility for my decisions, actions, and professional growth.

Other helpful performance metrics include a monthly report to everyone in the company detailing 10 performance issues, such as how the airline is doing in terms of lost baggage, on-time performance, and flight completion.

How Results Are Measured

Twice each year, employees of the airline evaluate the company's leaders and their ability to live up to their commitments, just as employees themselves are appraised by their supervisors. The semiannual review is called the JetBlue Quality of Life Survey (we like that name) and tells the airline's leaders how they're doing. In addition, the airline

ties employee compensation at all levels to the execution of employees' commitments to the organization's values and commitments.

Characteristics of Effective Performance Measurement

Notice that each case study meets the following 10 characteristics of effective leadership and performance measurement:

- relates to and supports the client's goals and objectives
- blends balance among employees, customers, and the bottom line
- focuses on just a few important areas at one time
- indicates where performance can be improved
- indicates if training is needed
- is flexible and easy to revise when necessary
- aligns measurement with the organization's systems
- was established by the people who are performing the jobs
- ensures the well-being of everyone in the organization
- has tools and techniques that translate strategy into action.

Discuss with your leaders how the case studies they have written reflect these characteristics. Are there any gaps that need to be closed? Ask your leaders how they can use that list of characteristics as a way to stay on track when establishing and creating their own performance metrics in the future.

EFFECTIVE MEASUREMENT TOOLS AND TECHNIQUES DEVELOP EMPLOYEE SUCCESS

You must help broaden your leaders' scope of awareness and sensitivity when it comes to measuring their employees' performance. Suggest instead of an annual performance appraisal or review that they consider using, or adding on to their existing format, the following tools.

Enhance Performance Appraisals With a Performance Builder

The Performance Builder is a powerful instrument that your leaders easily can learn to use because it not only helps improve a person's performance but also builds his or her confidence, communications skills, vision, understanding, and accountability.

The great thing about using the Performance Builder is that it actually involves the employee in setting the standards by which he or she will be measured. It incorporates a valuable tool kit with self-scoring tools to help discern where an employee has seen measurable improvement, tools for measuring both personal and professional development, an experiential follow-up assignment for critical feedback from the field, and fast formulas for calculating return-on-investment.

Encourage your leaders to adapt the following format and tools to their unique needs, management style, business sense, and people skills. Remind them that

everything is contextual and they cannot expect every technique and tool to work in every situation.

A leader's objective for learning to use the Performance Builder is to motivate others to perform at peak levels, while building a bridge between employees' own interests and talents and the interests and talents of the organization.

Step 1: Start by defining what performance means to you as a leader. Never assume that your employees will know what you mean by *performance*. It is your responsibility as a leader to define the term clearly in the context of your organization. The word can take on different meanings, depending on whether you manufacture computers, sell software, market travel packages, or design public relations materials.

Define what you mean by *performance* here:

Step 2: Together with your employee, establish clear and specific performance expectations. Invite discussion and encourage your employee to suggest his or her own parameters for measuring performance. By doing this, you'll be getting a good sense of what that employee believes is realistic. As a leader, you must describe the standards of performance that you expect from a particular job. Characterize what you think is outstanding performance and what you consider to be unacceptable performance. Research shows that employees who are involved in their own performance measurement are more likely to accept and meet the challenge of expectations.

So then why don't more managers and leaders take time to have this conversation with their employees? Maybe it's denial, or guilt, or ignorance. Whatever the reason, tell your leaders that it is critical to have a heart-to-heart conversation with every employee about realistic expectations, boundaries, rewards, and consequences. Allow employees to be the architects of how their accountability and performance will be measured moving forward.

Step 3: Stretch your employee and help him or her buy into improving performance. Employees buy into standards worthy of their time, investment, and energy. Getting employee buy-in isn't a matter of creating a manipulative and compelling agenda. Consider performance measurement a joint venture and treat your employees like partners. When leaders do this, employees are more likely to be genuinely motivated to buy into the standards set for them and stretch themselves to reach higher performance levels. Remember, most employees want to take a role in raising their own performance expectations.

Step 4: Be explicit about the scope of responsibility you are giving. Be sure that your employee understands exactly who is responsible for what. When employees understand their responsibilities in relationship to everyone else, the possibility of confusion is quickly eliminated.

Help your employee plan to be spontaneous! This means that an employee's scope of responsibility may change at any time, depending on unforeseen circumstances that may arise. Explain that adapting to unplanned situations is part of the employee's job and that when this happens, it's okay to broaden the scope of responsibility. But again, as the leader, you must be clear about what "broadening the scope of responsibility" means to you.

Step 5: Document what's been agreed on. This is a critical step in the Performance Builder. Create a written list of all the performance standards on which you and your employee have agreed. This, however, will not be enough to guide your employee to achieving success. You must be specific about what it's going to take to reach those expectations and attain those goals. Document those steps and make that your employee's course of action.

Describe the employee's course of action:

Remind your leader to give a copy of this document to the employee and keep one on file. At employee performance reviews, or whenever a project is completed, that document will serve as the platform from which agreed-upon standards of performance can be measured.

Step 6: Follow up. As a leader, it is essential that you make the time to observe and follow up with your employees on how things are going. Don't wait until the next review to check in to see how they're doing. Always observe and give feedback on jobs in progress. With less experienced employees, you may have to check in more often until they feel comfortable with their responsibilities.

Step 7: Offer "speedback" and rewards, and keep your promises. Be clear at the start of the Performance Builder about what can be expected if an employee meets or exceeds the goals set (for example, money, more responsibility, or special recognition such as an award certificate, a day off, a two-hour lunch break, a more flexible work schedule, or a letter from the president). Build in lots of small wins along the way, too. Make recognition a part of the plan and help your employees connect the reward with the behavior. Always remember to keep your promises, and never make a promise without a plan to deliver on that commitment.

The speed with which a leader responds to his or her people also is important. Giving fast feedback not only will validate an employee's contribution but can ultimately determine his or her success. Try these easy-to-use "speedback" tools from your Performance Builder tool kit when measuring and observing from a distance the continuous improvement of your people and their teams.

Figure 19.1 is a checking-in tool that can be emailed, faxed, or even sent by voice mail to the appropriate person or team. When your employee or team answers your questions, send a speedback response (see Figure 19.2 for samples).

FIGURE 19.1 Speedback Questions

Speedback QUESTIONS

Fast! Give me an update! What's happening over there?

What's working?

Any frustrations?

Figure 19.2 Speedback Responses

Sample Responses:

Fast Praise:
"Got your speedback note—great job! Keep up the good work!"

Fast Empathy:
"Sounds frustrating. I can see why you feel the way you do. I'm attaching an article I think may help you."

Fast Corrective Action:
"Hold everything! Before trying that, I think you might want to try this first. I have found it to be very effective. Let me know your thoughts."

Fast Update:
"Have you heard or read the latest on this issue? Thought you might like a quick update for your files. Let's meet and take a proactive approach."

Fast Follow-Up:
"Sounds good. Why don't we meet next week to go over your progress."

Step 8: Provide your employee with the necessary training and resources to be successful. According to management guru Peter Drucker, one of the secrets to IBM's earlier success was that the organization trained and trained and trained. When IBM started to struggle economically, they tightened the training belt, and it had long-term consequences. When it comes to performance-building techniques, training and employee development should be foremost. Focus your training on employee needs. Ask them what they need to learn. Don't arbitrarily decide that for them. And be sure to deliver training "just in time"—that is, get it to people as close as possible to the time they need it.

Give your employees the critical measurement tools that will bolster their confidence and contribute valuable feedback to the organization regarding its investment in training. Measure how effectively training is being used in the field and on the job. Here are three additional measurement tools for your tool kit.

BARS Tools for Monitoring Performance

For jobs that involve performing tasks that can be readily broken down into specific subtasks and steps, our go-to guy on workplace behaviors, speaker and consultant Scott Carbonara, told us that using a BARS tool (behaviorally anchored rating scales) is a great resource for leaders at all levels. (Scott holds master's degrees in psychology and communications and was named "Therapist of the Year" by the state of Michigan.)

"If you can observe a behavior, you can measure it and evaluate it," says Carbonara. BARS is a powerful tool for measuring specific behaviors by individual performers.

As an example, think of the job of a customer service representative. The role involves several steps and substeps, all of which can be measured. Companies measure the ASA (average speed of answer), pleasantness, completeness of the answer, the speed to complete the call, and the verbiage used to complete the call, to name just a few metrics. Each of those steps have long, in-depth processes and procedures defining success. BARS are narrow enough to help leaders measure and evaluate on one small, targeted behavior within the series of behaviors.

So when the XYZ Company trains and coaches its service representatives, the leaders can use BARS to focus on one area, like call completion within 10 minutes. In this hypothetical case, the BARS to evaluate this specific task in this specific job might look like this:

5 — Exceptional performance: Responds to 100 percent of customer inquiries within 10 minutes.

4 — Excellent performance: Responds to 95-99 percent of customer inquiries within 10 minutes.

3 — Fully competent performance: Responds to at least 90-94 percent of customer inquiries within 10 minutes.

2 — Marginal performance: Responds to at least 85-89 percent of customer inquiries within 10 minutes.

1 — Unsatisfactory performance: Responds to fewer than 85 percent of customer inquiries within 10 minutes.

Fast and easy leadership instructions to create your own BARS are to (1) identify a task or subtask that can be observed, and (2) describe and record the ideal, perfect state for successfully performing that task.

What you have described becomes your 5, your perfect rating. For 1–4 ratings, write down performance that is less optimal. These statements can be expressed in percentages of time, quantity, or quality. For example, a 5 might include "Greets each customer with eye contact, a smile, and a welcome within 30 seconds of entering the store 100 percent of the time." That's perfection. You cannot get better than 100 percent. For less optimal ratings, percentages might be scaled down to 95 percent, 90 percent, and so on. Use the following guidelines below in creating your own:

5 — Exceptional performance: Includes all of the ideal, perfect state components you listed. In school, these would be your A + students; in college, *summa cum laude*. These employees are rare, and when you find one, you want to use that employee as an example and mentor to others.

4 — Excellent performance: Includes most of the ideal, perfect state components you listed. Excellent might be missing the highest-level skill described in exceptional performance. These are your straight-A performers, your *magna cum laude.*

3 — Fully competent performance: Includes many of the ideal, perfect state components you listed. Fully competent might be missing the highest-level skills described in exceptional performance. Fully competent is the level where most of your employees will fall. When your employees are performing at this level, they are strong and solid performers. You will accomplish great things with a team of employees performing at this level.

2 — Marginal performance: Includes only a few of the ideal, perfect state components you listed. But a marginal performance rating means these employees are missing key, critical components of the role to be considered successful. In school, these students would be in enrichment classes because they cannot yet perform at a level that keeps up with their peers.

1 — Unsatisfactory performance: Includes almost no ideal, perfect state components you listed. Individuals performing at this level in your BARS observation cannot stay at this level without harming your business, team morale, and customer satisfaction.

Carbonara suggests that there are several benefits to using BARS to measure and evaluate certain job performance.

"BARS are very objective," Carbonara states. "BARS eliminates any potential bias or employee complaints like 'Well, my supervisor doesn't like me. That's why I did

poorly.' When BARS are created correctly, they function like a mirror: they show people a very accurate reflection of how things are, not how people wish them to appear."

Additionally, Carbonara sees other advantages:

- **BARS give leaders credibility.** You have to know a job well to create BARS. So while BARS take some time to create, leaders who take the time to develop them for their employees gain insight and credibility about what it takes to do the job successfully.
- **BARS become coaching "cheat sheets."** Leaders in the coaching role have all of the steps spelled out that are required to perform well. When you want to improve the performance of an employee, the BARS become a starting point for evaluating and conducting coaching.
- **BARS are simple to use and understand.** Employees can study the BARS like they would a training manual. (Hint: Many training manuals are created in BARS-friendly, step-by-step formats for this very reason.) And leaders can listen or watch employees for a brief period of time and still capture relevant, meaningful data to use for coaching and performance management purposes.
- **BARS can be used for self-improvement.** When Carbonara worked to improve the performance of a large call center, he advocated letting customer service reps listen to themselves from recorded calls. Then he suggested that the employee complete the BARS on their own performance! When used in this fashion, employees can use BARS for self-improvement.
- **BARS are customized to the job.** Unlike some performance management tools that include performance criteria that is obsolete or irrelevant to each performer, customized BARS are drilled down to specific jobs. Each person in the same role has the same opportunity to hit the performance standards and be recognized for a job well done.

How to Use the Personal Development Scorecard

Use the Personal Development Scorecard (Figure 19.3) as a template to help employees self-measure their ongoing improvement. Remember, using numbers to score a skill area is acceptable because it is a reflection on the performance skill and not on the person. Furthermore, using numbers works in this example because employees score themselves. A scale of one to 10 makes it easy to assess measurable improvement in percentages. When we offer upper-level management percentages like those, it's easier to assign a dollar value to the significance of the performance improvement and to track return-on-investment.

How to Use the 90-Day Mail-Back Worksheet

After they have completed the 90-Day Mail-Back Worksheet (Figure 19.4), have employees fold it to fit a number 10 envelope and self-address it. Be sure everyone seals his or her worksheet with tape or a sticker. Collect the worksheets and create a tickler file for yourself or note in your calendar to mail back all of the worksheets in 90 days.

FiGURE 19.3 Personal Development Scorecard

This Personal Development Scorecard will help to quickly and easily measure your individual development and improvement in specific areas. The Scorecard is designed as a useful tool to gauge growth and identify areas in which additional improvement and development may be required. The best part is, you are the one doing the grading.

The number 1 is lowest in rating and the number 10 is highest in rating.

SKILL SET	MY PRIOR GRADE	MY GRADE AFTER	% MEASURABLE IMPROVEMENT*
Sample: Creative thinking as a manager	7	10	30%
Creative thinking as a manager			
Brain mapping			
Problem solving			
Stronger decision making			
Turbo charging the work environment			
Becoming an effective catalyst			
Understanding the lightning-in-a bottle concept and thunderbolt thinking			
Getting unstuck from the rut and communicating better			

*Note: It is recognized that there are variations in percentages using tens. The formula is rounded off to the nearest full percentage point for ease of use and flexibility.

Figure 19.3 Continued

The number 1 is lowest in rating and the number 10 is highest in rating.

SKILL SET	MY PRIOR GRADE	MY GRADE AFTER	% MEASURABLE IMPROVEMENT*
Motivating myself and influencing others			
Kicking productivity and performance up a notch			
Building better teams			
Using new tools and techniques as a manager			
Authentic coaching and facilitating other people's success			
Competencies in the workplace			
Empowerment and delegation skills			
Building relationships as a manager			
Conflict-solutions finding			

*Note: It is recognized that there are variations in percentages using tens. The formula is rounded off to the nearest full percentage point for ease of use and flexibility.

FIGURE 19.4 90-Day Mail-Back Worksheet

90-Day Mail-Back Worksheet

Name: _____ Workshop: _____

This worksheet is confidential and for your use only. In the space provided below, record the personal and professional goals you will work toward regarding further development of the skills you have learned in this training program.To help you keep on track and stay focused on your goals and objectives, this worksheet will serve as a helpful reminder of things most important to you that you would like to accomplish and work toward. When you have completed this worksheet, fold, place into the envelope provided, and seal. Address the envelope to yourself. All mail-back worksheets will be collected in class and mailed to you in 90 days.

Skills from this training program that I would like to improve on and develop over the next 90 days include the following:

My personal plan of action to work toward regarding ongoing personal growth and development of these skills will include doing the following:

Note: You will most likely forget about this mail-back tool, and then one day it will appear in your mailbox. The objective is to help keep you on track and moving forward. If you have accomplished your goals, then you will feel a boost of confidence and self-satisfaction. If you do not accomplish all that you hoped for, this will serve as a gentle reminder that it's time to redirect your efforts and get back on course.

The effect this will have on each employee is substantial and becomes an honest way of measuring whether that person stayed on task in pursuit of his or her goals and objectives. If so, employees will gain a sense of self-satisfaction from knowing they followed through. If not, no harm is done because only the employee will have seen the worksheet. It will certainly serve, however, as a hard-hitting reminder of what that employee failed to complete. You'll be surprised at the positive feedback you receive after you mail back those worksheets.

How to Use the Experiential Follow-Up Assignment

Measuring what employees learn in a training classroom and then measuring how effective those lessons are in the real world may offer two different outcomes. The Experiential Follow-Up Assignment (Figure 19.5) tells leaders how employees are using the training techniques and lessons in their jobs. This information will be extremely helpful to management in justifying training time and expense, thereby turning them into valid investments.

Step 9: Help employees calculate return-on-investment. This is a valuable skill when it comes to offering solutions to problems or requesting more money to handle a specific departmental challenge. When employees come closer to thinking like their leaders by first discerning what it's going to take to make something happen and deciding if it's worth the cost, their contribution to the bottom line becomes evident and engenders greater confidence in the team's overall recommendations to management.

How to Use the Fast Formula for Calculating Return-on-Investment

The formula presented in Figure 19.6 is a handy template for quickly calculating the cost of almost any organizational problem. In the example presented there, the tool is used to determine the worth of an organization's customer by calculating the customer's number of transactions per year and the organization's profit on those transactions. Other factors are then taken into the equation—factors we don't often consider on the job. Once the cost of the problem has been determined, it is divided by the cost of fixing the problem in order to get the percentage of return-on-investment. Try calculating other measurable situations for their return-on-investment using this quick and easy format.

Step 10: Expect the best from your employees and don't be surprised if that's what you get. Research shows that a leader's expectations of others directly affect the organization's productivity and profitability. As a leader, you will get better performance from your people if that's what you expect of them. Our expectations of others influence their behavior. When a leader tells his or her employees up front what performance standards are expected of them, those workers achieve higher levels of performance as a result.

FIGURE 19.5 Experiential Follow-Up Assignment

Measuring Tool for Personal Growth and Professional Development on the Job
This on-the-job exercise will measure the effectiveness and results of the new skills you have learned since successfully completing training.

1. What specific skills learned in this training program have you been able to apply on the job?

2. Describe one or more real-world situations that you have been able to handle more effectively as a result of this training. What was your challenge? How did you use your new skills? What were the results?

3. What tools, tips, or techniques learned in your training have you been able to refer to and use?

Your additional comments and feedback:

Deadline: Please complete this follow-up learning assignment and mail no later than_____ to _____

Figure 19.6 Fast Formula for Calculating ROI

Be a hero to your organization by demonstrating return-on-investment. Measure the amount that problems are costing your organization and then invest in solving problems with the greatest payback potential.

Question: How much is this problem costing? Is it worth the investment to correct it?

Example: Customer satisfaction

Step 1: Determine the annual worth of customer patronage.

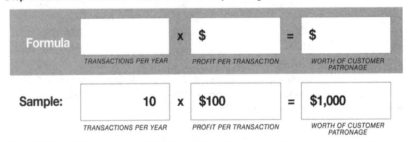

Step 2: Calculate the yearly cost of the problem. (This does not include the cost of negative publicity.)

Step 3: As part of a recommended solution to your organizations problem, include a fast calculation for return-on-investment.

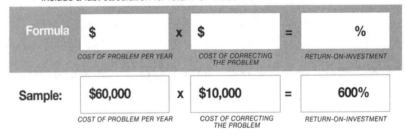

A Successful Measurement System

To be successful, a measurement system usually has to meet four basic criteria:
1. It has to be directly related to the work that is being performed by the employee.
2. It must be simple enough to be understood by everyone using it.
3. There should include performance goals for a specific period of time.
4. It is flexible and changes based on the efforts of the people doing the job.

The reference here to being simple enough to understand is a critical point. Your leaders have access to a myriad of metrics, that is, financials, statistics, ratios, graphs, charts, spreadsheets, and so on.

Refer back to chapter 7, where we discuss how Sutter Health uses dashboard metrics. This limited set of relevant numbers makes measurement fast and easy. Look at the dashboard in your car. At a glance, a few numbers measure, while instruments tell you exactly where you are headed and your current status while driving—compass, fuel, oil, speed, airbags activated, and so on. Dashboard metrics help your leaders to focus on providing services or producing products, not worrying about boring numbers or trying to figure out complicated formulas.

THE ART OF MEASUREMENT

Perhaps what gets measured is what gets done—but what gets measured is also what gets learned, becomes habit, and is reinforced! Use this chapter to guide your leaders in learning and using new and powerful performance measurement techniques that fit their special circumstances. Some tools may work better in certain situations, while others may take special adapting or customization in order to work in your organization. Measuring performance has become something of an art form that is mastered over time and with experience.

The process for measuring performance includes taking the following actions:

- Define what performance means to you as a leader.
- With your employees, establish clear and specific performance expectations.
- Stretch your employees and help them buy into improving performance.
- Be clear about the scope of responsibility you are giving.
- Document what's been agreed on.
- Follow up.
- Offer "speedback" and rewards, and keep your promises.
- Provide your employees with the necessary training and resources to be successful.
- Help employees calculate return-on-investment.
- Expect the best.

Characteristics of effective performance measurement are that it:

- relates to and supports the client's goals and objectives
- blends balance between people, customers, and the bottom line

- focuses on just a few important areas at one time
- indicates where performance can be improved
- indicates if training is needed
- is flexible and easy to revise when necessary
- is aligned with the organization's systems
- was established by the people who are performing the jobs
- ensures the well-being of everyone in the organization
- has tools and techniques that translate strategy into action.

Questions for Discussion: Measuring Performance

1. Can you think of a time when an appraisal of your performance seemed unfair and made you feel incompetent or unappreciated?

2. What is the goal of measuring performance?

3. Why is it valuable for employees to be able to calculate return-on-investment?

4. What are the benefits of a leader using a performance-building method instead of a traditional performance evaluation or in conjunction with an existing review process?

Wrapping It Up

The old, regurgitated measurement devices just won't cut it in today's work environment. Your leaders should be expected to focus on more dynamic, customized, and personal measurement tools that can measure their people's performance quickly and easily, without resorting to practices that have proven ineffective and destructive to employee development.

So where do you go from here? We'll address that question in the conclusion on leadership trends.

Conclusion

LEADERSHIP TRENDS

In all of our domestic and international leadership training workshops, writing, and research, we have found one consistent thread: Successful companies take leadership seriously! So seriously, in fact, that they put hundreds of millions of dollars and countless hours behind making sure it is optimized to the utmost.

A recent BusinessWeek.com/Hay Group survey, "20 Best Companies for Leadership" (O'Connell, 2010), reports that all of the top 20 companies spent millions of dollars annually on leadership. Companies like HP, Goldman Sachs, Cisco, and UPS know that leadership counts not only to the people being led, but also to the bottom line.

Susan Peters, vice president of executive development and chief learning officer of GE (one of the 2010 companies cited in the report) states that what differentiates the top companies from the rest "is not just their emphasis on good leadership, but also how they approach it. They carefully tailor their developing leaders to fit their unique business strategies and organizational cultures."

Southwest Airlines, which values its fun approach to leadership, likens leadership to a game, with all its energy, preparation, and passion. "The future of leadership at Southwest looks like. . . preparing for the Super Bowl," stated Elizabeth Bryant, chief learning officer for Southwest Airlines. "Leaders will embrace the spirit of the game, demonstrate a fierce desire to win, and inspire each team player to be their best."

Leaders see opportunities and promote leadership at all levels and during all economic climates. The survey reports that respondents from the *Best Companies for Leadership* are:

- much more apt to think they will end up in a stronger place after difficult times
- more apt to engage in leadership development
- "twice as likely" to report that each person, despite their level in the business, "has the opportunity to develop and practice capabilities needed to lead others."

Leadership ranks as a higher priority for these companies, and it shows. Companies like Pixar, Google, and Zappos, also cited in this report, find themselves on multiple

lists for best places to work, fastest growing companies, and so on. In fact, Zappos has consistently outperformed even its own profit goals!

Do you see the trend? Success and proactive leadership thrive when they coexist!

YES, LEADERSHIP MATTERS

What does this coexistence mean for you? It means that leadership matters, and that despite whatever tough times you may be facing in the workplace or economy, you have an opportunity to dig deep, apply the skills you have learned in this book, and thrive.

Maybe you think of leadership like preparing for a game—wherein you must condition, train, practice, strategize, and engage your best players. Or maybe you think of it as a family—wherein you care for each individual and help all employees become leaders of their own places in the organization. Whatever story works for you, this book has delivered you with an A-to-Z approach for enhancing your leadership skills and maximizing your workplace performance. Now it's time for you to engage your skills!

Going for the GOLD

Olympic athletes train for years, pack their bags, and head to faraway locations *not* hoping to have a chance at coming in second to last. Why? Because they are driven to lead their own lives and go for the GOLD.

What does this mean in the global marketplace? We like to think of gold in a different context, as it stands for Global Opportunities in Leadership Development. If you, as a leader, have your mind on GOLD, you are apt to inspire your team toward the victory line.

Leading toward GOLD? Try these strategies that can lead you to leadership engagement and success:

Global: Focus on a global approach to leading, problem solving, and business growth. Research how companies are expanding their markets and how the best companies worldwide are leading their people. Step up to the international plate and take a swing!

Opportunities: Find "the gaps" as they might say in football or marathon running, and build a strategy that will get your team through it and to the victory they envision.

Leadership: Follow the principles in this book! Embrace new ideas, one by one.

Development: Fix your mind on the task of training and engaging your leaders.

CREATE YOUR LEADERSHIP LEGACY

Now that you've read this book, you have taken the first step to becoming a best-in-class leader. The next step is to implement what you've read.

The saying goes: *Knowledge is power*. We disagree. The power comes only when you choose to implement the knowledge you've acquired.

What does it take to be one of the best leaders? The 16 statements below mirror several chapters of the book and outline the tactics on developing your leadership strengths. Answer "true" or "false" in terms of where you are today.

1. I am an authentic leader. _____

2. I treat and value my employees as people as well as workers. _____

3. I consciously and intentionally build the knowledge, skills, and _____
 competence of all of my employees.

4. I have an individual development plan for each of my key _____
 employees.

5. I have a strategic plan that is known by all of my employees. _____

6. I spend extra time developing future successors. _____

7. I am proud of the culture that I have created. _____

8. I am known for a high standard of integrity and honesty. _____

9. I am a team builder. _____

10. I take my coaching role seriously. _____

11. I manage performance using effective communications. _____

12. I actively engage my employees. _____

13. I empower others. _____

14. I foster a world-class learning environment. _____

15. I am a visionary. _____

16. I measure performance and instill continuous improvement _____
 methodologies.

These statements and your replies reflect the type of leader you are, and the specific skills you have learned. How did you do? Don't worry. If you didn't answer true to all of the questions, you have the opportunity to continue to learn and grow. Leadership is a process, not a destination! But we will take a guess that you are more confident, equipped, and engaged after reading this book than you were before.

Here is one final true or false question we'd like to add to the list:

When I am out of the office, I know that my people are performing _____
just as well as when I'm there.

The answer to this final question reflects your legacy—what you leave behind. If you can answer true to that final question, it speaks volumes of your legacy. First, it says that you were the kind of leader who taught well—well enough that you can step out of the loop and be confident that your team is leading in your absence. You know how to build and implement a leadership strategy that sticks beyond the initial implementation. You know how to build lasting skills and competence in others.

Second, it says that you *modeled* and *developed* your employees to work autonomously as individuals as well as cohesively as a team, while igniting a desire within your employees to do the right things because they wanted to do them—and not because you were looking over their shoulder. It also says you were quite a motivator, instilling them with energy and passion for what they do.

Finally, it says that you could actually leave the office, attend a workshop, run a meeting, or even go on vacation! And it says that you could do that without feeling guilty—or scared—while you are on that plane to Maui.

Theodore Roosevelt, the twenty-sixth president of the United States (1901–1909) said this: *"The best executive is one who has sense enough to pick good people to do what he wants them to do, and self-restraint enough to keep from meddling with them while they do it."*

All in all, as you engage yourself in the principles in this book and promote leadership in those you reach, you will discover that your legacy is not only one of being a leader—but also of growing leaders around you!

"BUT WAIT! THERE'S MORE!"

When writing a book like this one, a lot of time is spent researching, rewriting, and sharing ideas. The result can be a lot of late nights at the computer, and oftentimes the cheesiest 2 a.m. infomercials become part of the white noise in the background as you write another chapter.

One statement at the end of a few of these wacky late-night infomercials can really stay with you . . . such as: *"But wait! There's more!"* Just when you thought the pitch was over, a voice-over adds one more thing. We got to thinking along the same lines.

You've taken the first step and you bought our book. Thank you! Now you are implementing our leadership development worksheets, exercises, checklists, and discussion stimulators in your own organization. Way to go! But wait! There's more!

At Last! An All-In-One Leadership Solution

We hope you have enjoyed *Leaders Start to Finish: A Road Map for Developing Top Performers* and that you will share it with others who have the same interest and desire to make a real difference.

We understand that it's one thing to grab on to these methods and tools from an intellectual perspective, but it's quite another to actually apply them in the real world and ultimately make them part of your organization.

We want you to know that you are not alone. We have two websites available to guide you in the process of applying this material and then take it to the next higher level of employee development and training.

Two Things You Can Do to Engage With Us for Ongoing Help—24/7

You can write to Stephanie Montanez by visiting her at www.HumanResourcesSources .org and join to get free information and other helpful HR resources, tips, and tools,

giving you privileged access to a world of HR and coaching resources, whitepapers, subject matter experts, podcasts, master trainers, inspiring speakers, and more! This website was created to help you to become a strengths-based developer of top talent. This go-to source for HR solutions offers you:

- announcements of exciting, upcoming keynotes and training events
- substantive and fun videos
- guest authors and columnists
- audio and video programs from Colorado to Cairo
- webinars/teleseminars
- access to assessments
- a leadership blog
- a call-in number to get one-on-one coaching from anywhere in the world
- podcasts, live and archived
- some of the latest research and white papers
- recommended reading and meet the authors behind the books
- opportunities to participate in www.HumanResoucesSources.org's newest projects.

It's free to sign up, and as soon as you do, you'll begin receiving ongoing support and start working toward your leadership goals and special interests. You'll also be joining a community of like-minded people who are fast embracing strengths-based leadership, innate wisdom, and new philosophies.

> *Do not go where the path may lead; go instead where there is no path and leave a trail.*
> —Ralph Waldo Emerson

Next, visit Anne at www.AnneBruce.com for your *all-in-one leadership solutions package* that will guide you beyond this book to maximum impact when it comes to training, coaching, and really engaging your future leaders. Whether it's a conference, meeting energizer, in-person training, high-energy workshops, positively outrageous customer care, or more—Anne can help you tackle the toughest leadership issues, team-building challenges, customized train-the-trainers, or personal growth and development seminars that ignite passion and activate employee potential. You'll be motivating every leader, or aspiring leader, to grow and succeed in ways they never dreamed possible.

WE WANT TO HEAR FROM YOU!

We hope to hear from you. When you join in these initiatives, the end of this book will actually be the start of something greater—something we'd like you to be a part of. We've created the path; now it's your turn to take the next step to greater success as you develop leaders in your organization or among your client base as a consultant.

Pay Close Attention: The Code Is Broken!

The code for leadership has been broken. We're now a global collective consciousness of new and exciting ideas that are changing the way we do business, lead, communicate, build relationships, and provide for our workers and our families.

Pay close attention to what's happening in the global leadership community. There's a strong momentum building, and you can probably sense it right now. This is what happens when a concerted mass of new energy among up-and-coming leaders bubbles to the top. Tomorrow's leaders will be talking about the things that matter most in the world and what we can all do to help sustain new ways of doing business better, more ethically, and with social consciousness.

You're Not Alone. We've Got Your Back!

It's an exciting time to be a leader or a leader in the making. You're not alone. We've got your back. We're in your cheering gallery throughout this entire process, and we look forward to hearing about your successes and accomplishments as you go forward. In fact, we'd love it if you'd email us action photos of you using our book, or these exercises, in your training classes. Anne will get them posted on her photo gallery at her website at www.AnneBruce.com. Just send a description of who is in the photo and what is taking place. Email jpgs to Anne@AnneBruce.com and write Fun Leadership Photo in the subject line.

Now that you're equipped with this book, it is our hope that you will start to free yourself from the overwhelming frustrations you may be facing presently and start transforming your methods and your people into stronger, better leaders who inspire others and will be ready to pass the baton to their successors—all while ditching the drama and any excuses not to be a top performer.

The future of our world will be a reflection of the organizational leaders we nurture, engage, develop, encourage, train, and inspire to touch their greater potential. We hope that this book helps you to touch yours.

Appendix A

Brand Leaders for Talent

After 30-plus years in the HR field, and now a respected talent management expert, Libby Sartain is an active business advisor, board member, and a top HR authority in America. She is the former chief human resource officer (CHRO) of Yahoo! Inc. and the former VP of People at Southwest Airlines, where Libby and Anne first met and worked together. Libby now serves on the Board of Directors of Peet's Coffee & Tea, Inc., and *Human Resources Executive* magazine named her one of the 25 Most Powerful Women in HR. We caught up with Libby and got her ideas on branding for talent.

We highly recommend that you visit **www.BrandforTalent.com**, where you will find all the must-haves for branding leadership talent, including free articles, tips, and non-stop ideas for developing leaders at all levels. It's a great resource you'll visit again and again (also see chapter 4).

With the release of Sartain's latest book (with co-author Mark Schumann), *Brand for Talent: Eight Essentials to Make Your Talent as Famous as Your Brand*, there's been more conversation taking place among company leaders on the topic of branding and its critical importance to developing leadership and company identity. (Sartain's first book on branding, also with Schumann, is titled *Brand From the Inside: Eight Essentials to Emotionally Connect Your Employees to Your Business*.) If you're interested in branding top talent in your organization, this book will be a reliable road map to help you get there.

Visit *www.BrandforTalent.com*

Libby and Mark invite you to join them for hot talent topics on what's new, compelling, confusing, and essential to the world of employer branding. A few of the questions they use to facilitate thought-provoking discussion include:

- What's Working: How to handle sticky situations
- What's Connecting: Experiments using social media to advance employer brands
- Who's Talking: New thoughts from sources
- What Next: New considerations from their crystal ball

MAKING YOUR TALENT AS FAMOUS AS YOUR BRAND

In today's business world, the people in an organization are becoming part of its brand. "Business competes for talent today in a free global marketplace in which traditional definitions of job and employee are increasingly outmoded," says Sartain. "As a direct result, HR leaders and managers must also change traditional ways of working in order to maintain their central role in the organization of the future."

Why the shift? "While many influences are bringing about this change, perhaps the most important is the way in which the worker now approaches and engages with work. Workers today use the sensibilities of consumers to search for overall *work experiences* that not only provide a sense of connection and fulfillment, but also a part of their personal brands," Sartain adds. The result is that employees become engaged in the bigger picture of what is accomplished at work—which also translates to the customers as loyalty and enthusiasm are transferred.

CAREER DEVELOPMENT PLAYS AN ESSENTIAL ROLE IN BRANDING AND EXPANDING TALENT

Career development is an essential part of a worker's experience. Leaders are discovering the important link between talented employees and delivering a brand promise to consumers. So part of that career development is the process a leader uses to connect workers to their roles in delivering the brand promise and in creating an organizational brand for talent that will thrive in the new talent marketplace.

(Sartain also is the co-author of *HR From the Heart: Inspiring Stories and Strategies for Building the People Side of Great Business.* You can reach Libby at her website: www .LibbySartain.com.)

HIGHLIGHTS OF HOW WORLD-CLASS ORGANIZATIONS BRAND TALENT AND STRENGTHS

Throughout this section are some examples of companies that have successfully developed the branding of their employment culture.

Boston Consulting Group: This premiere, global management-consulting group, with more than 60 offices worldwide, has greatly increased the recruitment of minorities, which now make up approximately 25 percent of its staff. This organization possesses the following characteristics:

- It believes no two career paths are the same.
- It offers formal training to support employees.
- There is also informal training to stretch employees.
- It initiates work–life balance with predictable time off.
- The organization takes a "grow further" approach to employee development.

- It believes that a person's potential is only limited by talents and ambitions.
- It provides experience to excel in numerous fields.
- There is 100 percent fertility treatment coverage.

Mayo Clinic: Employees get use of free worldwide Mayo air ambulance service, unlimited lifetime in-network benefits, and free preventive care.

Vanderbilt University: Provides 70 percent tuition subsidy to employees and their dependents.

St. Jude Children's Research Hospital: Workers enjoy organic vegetables from St. Jude's onsite garden and up to $3,600 in tuition reimbursement for growing talent.

Mattell: Workers enjoy half-day Fridays and up to 17 paid holidays, with a week off at the end of the year.

American Express: Women hold more than 30 percent of the leadership positions at AMEX. Everyone has access to onsite healthcare and the use of a "health navigation concierge" to help maximize benefits.

Southern Ohio Medical Center: The company turned National Nurses Week into a community leadership event.

Deloitte: As the largest accounting firm in the United States, Deloitte focuses big on diversity, affinity groups, employee resource groups, cultural competency initiatives, and more. One-third of Deloitte's employees are non-white—the highest percentage of minorities among the Big Four accounting firms. Their commitment to branding a new, diverse workplace is nothing short of brilliant.

Pixar: The Academy Award–winning computer animation studio seeks super fun, tireless talent! Their priority? To combine technology with world-class creative talent. The creators of animated movies such as *Finding Nemo*, *Toy Story*, and *Cars* advertises on its website (using a creative spin on the *Cars* movie) that they are always looking to expand their pit crew of talented employees and that their "creative mechanics" come in all shapes and sizes.

NetApp: This data storage and management company may ask prospective talent to share specific examples of a time when his or her values were challenged. Purpose? To find out whether someone has the integrity required to work there. Some of their attitudes or policies include:

- Collaborative environment—loners need not apply.
- Leave your ego at the door.
- They've ditched a ridiculous travel policy for a commonsense maxim: "We are a frugal company. But don't show up dog-tired to save a few bucks. Use your common sense."

Google: Yes, in tough times it's cut some frills, but not to worry, Googlers still get awesome perks for working there:

- free massages

- onsite car washes and oil changes
- gourmet meals.

Dell Computer: This organization characterizes itself with the following:
- employee commitment to revolutionary innovation
- offers resources you'll need to reach loftiest career goals
- teammates inspiring greatness in each other
- takes energy-smart, green initiatives
- sees bright future for those with integrity, teamwork, and passion for technology.

AFLAC: Onsite daycare includes two centers and more than 500 children and is offered at a modest average cost of $352 a month to the employee. Second-shift workers use the benefit too. Daycare hours extend to 11:30 p.m. Twelve weeks at full pay are given to care for a sick child, parent, or spouse. Also offered are half-day "pampering binges" to lift spirits and motivate employees.

S.C. Johnson & Son: Still family owned, this cleaning products maker has a new building that houses an exhibit gallery, company store, cafeteria, even a bank and concierge desk.

Nordstrom: Celebrating its 111th year in business, this upscale retailer continues to lead by its original doctrine: *Use good judgment in all situations.*

Container Store: This company takes some of the following actions:
- As an alternative to worker layoffs, freeze salaries for everyone.
- Rally troops with motivating sales contests.
- Offer approximately 100 hours of training a year to each employee.

Zappos: Quirky is a "brand attitude" in this culture. The famous e-tailer believes in the "psychic gratification" employees get from helping others. Call center, customer service reps are given tons of freedom; they are allowed to chat as long as they like with customers, write thank you notes, or even send flowers to a customer. Top priority? Make emotional connections! This company hires positive people and then places them where positive thinking is reinforced. CEO Tony Hsieh offers employees a list of branding tips that include:
- Create fun and a little weirdness. (Parties in your PJs, parades, and shaved heads are part of the culture.)
- Pursue growth and learning. (Employees are encouraged to study, read books, and take advanced training courses.)

Bank of Montreal: Talk about an atypical financial institution. This bank's culture is all about innovation and people:
- With tens of thousands of employees worldwide, Bank of Montreal is one of the largest banks in North America.
- Employees are encouraged to develop sense of proprietorship in their work.

- The bank is strongly involved with employees' continuing education.
- Everyone is committed to training and lifelong learning.
- Under its HR umbrella, the Career Center offers employees access to the bank's Possibilities Center (the name alone sums up the organization's unique approach to growing and developing talent to its higher potential).
- The bank's values:
 - We draw our strength from the diversity of our people and our businesses.
 - We insist on respect for everyone and encourage all to have a voice.
 - We share information, learn, and innovate to create consistently superior customer experiences.

Netflix: With more than eight million customers, this movie rental business revolution-izer gives seven great reasons to work for them:
- Netflix delights people.
- Large impact.
- Outstanding people.
- Big pay.
- Rules annoy us.
- Clear values.
- Amazing future.

Levi Strauss and Company:
- Lets employees work on "way-cool" projects at work.
- Managers match their employees' interests to exciting and challenging new projects that ignite passion for the job.
- One leader refers to "the care and feeding of talent" (meaning employees are not attracted to a company by tangibles alone).

J.M. Smucker: Enriches the environment with ongoing job rotations, and keeps employ-ees motivated and interested with ongoing changes in scenery and job responsibilities.

Harley-Davidson: Offers "Easy Own Program" to help employees buy their own Harley:
- Year one employees pay zero—no interest, no payments on new bike.
- Born to be wild and born to be generous.

Intuit: Ultra-green company promotes the following methods to help the environment:
- bottled water banned
- mass-transit subsidies for employees, up to $100 a month
- sets goal to reduce carbon footprint by 15 percent in three years
- replaced its pickup trucks with electric vehicles.

Whole Foods: Enthusiastic, young (28 percent under age 25) workforce whose career paths include:
- mentoring team members through education and on-the-job experience
- encouraging participation and involvement at all levels of the business
- fostering self-responsibility and self-directed teamwork

- rewarding productivity and performance
- offering opportunities that grow with the people
- knowing that best employee ideas are exported to the high-end food seller's stores around the country.

Scottrade: Stock market craziness led to this firm's biggest profits:
- Bonuses were maintained even in turbulent times.
- The company wants to attract talent that can contribute unique talents.
- Internships are offered all year long, not just during the summer.
- 22 percent of branch managers started as interns.
- Hire, on average, 50 percent of graduating interns each semester.
- WOW (Work on Weekends) shift for workers who want to be home during weekdays.

The Walt Disney Company: This long-standing company built on tradition is characterized by:
- D-Think customer training program, branded by the Disney Institute.
- Hiring "cast members" (Disney term for employees).
- All new-hire orientation begins with building pride and morale.
- New hires attend a "Disney Traditions Class" where they are taught Disney's history, philosophy, values, and high-quality guest services.
- "Cast members" train on the job and attend decentralized skill-building classes.
- Learning is done in engaging and powerful ways, where employees are encouraged to keep learning and develop themselves.
- Learning opportunities are designed to build on the competencies and capabilities of the people.
- Disney programs brand and expand talent through:
 - new hire orientation
 - Disney Dimensions, an executive development program
 - Disney Way, designed to showcase the various Disney businesses to managers and above
 - Disney ethics, integrity, and diversity programs
 - professional development
 - management/leadership development
 - computer skills.

In addition, the Walt Disney Company provides educational reimbursement for full-time employees and cast members. And exciting e-learning programs allow employees and cast members around the world to access learning opportunities at their convenience.

Accenture: Every employee is assigned a career counselor, and approximately 78 hours of training are allotted per year, per person. Accenture offers thousands of courses to choose from for employee development.

DreamWorks Animation SKG: Lots of freebies!
- They hold fun wrap parties (completion of movie celebration).
- Offer free gourmet breakfasts and lunches.
- Rural Glendale, California, campus is surrounded by storyboards and movie characters, like Bob from Monsters vs. Aliens.

THE BUCKINGHAM BRAND: FOCUS ON YOUR LEADERS' STRENGTHS!

Marcus Buckingham has been called "arguably the business world's most in-demand management guru" by *BusinessWeek*. Buckingham has taken the corporate world by storm with his Strengths Revolution—a strategy arising from his two decades as a Senior Researcher at the Gallup Organization. The Strengths Revolution is not about fixing weaknesses, but identifying and building upon one's strengths—which is something we recommend and use in developing leaders in our seminars and workshops.

Buckingham proves time and again that companies that focus on cultivating employees' strengths dramatically increase efficiency while allowing for maximum personal growth and success. A tremendous resource for your leaders, Buckingham's work challenges conventional wisdom and shows the link between engaged leaders, employees and productivity, profit, customer satisfaction, and the rate of turnover. Go to Amazon.com and check out all of Buckingham's books for developing your leadership talent, because strengths-based leadership has a direct impact on your organization's ultimate performance and success.

Three Critical Leadership Lessons About Strengths

Buckingham stresses this important lesson for leadership: *We learn faster in the areas we have strengths. Next, our strengths are multipliers. Your leaders are more creative and collaborative in the areas in which they are strong. They are more insightful and innovative too. Finally, a person's strengths are their best reinforcer. If your leaders do suffer a setback or poor performance in an area of strength, they will bounce back much more quickly, because they feel confident and secure in their competencies and talents.*

Recently, Marcus Buckingham came out with his latest book and strengths assessment, called *StandOut* (Thomas Nelson). Following the success of *Now, Follow Your Strengths* (Free Press) and *Strengths-Finder* (Gallup Press), Buckingham was always being asked, "Okay, now what do I do with these strengths?" So his focus with *StandOut* is to help people know exactly what to do to win at their careers.

Appendix B

Road Map to "Top-Performance Coaching" Feedback

Coaching (see chapter 12) is key not only to preventing unwanted behavior, but also to promoting desired actions. Also important is delivering the right feedback at the right time (see chapter 13). Engagement consultant Scott Carbonara (visit www.Leader shipTherapist.com for more tools), provided us with a "Top-Performance Coaching" feedback tool that is useful in determining what type of feedback to provide in various situations, so that you can keep your employees traveling on the road to productive work. We have successfully used this tool in our seminars and workshops—with Scott's permission, of course.

As Carbonara states, "When you see an employee doing something you like, don't ignore it! This is a great coaching opportunity that you need to take advantage of to cement their behavior and develop their engagement and loyalty to you." Deliver *Positive Reinforcing Feedback*.

When employees are new, or working on a task for the first time, they learn best with *Mild Corrective Feedback*. This feedback is so mild that most employees will hear it as a suggestion or a helpful hint.

If an employee has demonstrated success in the past but is currently performing at a subpar level, you might need to use *Moderate Corrective Feedback*. When using this type of feedback, you add more information about the problem and the consequence of the problem as a way to point out pitfalls to avoid.

Finally, if an employee continues to perform poorly, you need to deliver *Strong Corrective Feedback*. As the name suggests, this kind of feedback is delivered when the problem has become serious. In most cases, if you are delivering this type of feedback, this employee is progressing down the road of corrective disciplinary action that could include termination.

WHEN TO DELIVER FEEDBACK

Positive Reinforcing	Mild Corrective	Moderate Corrective	Strong Corrective
When you see an employee engaging in any desired behavior that is part of the job.	When you want to give the performer the benefit of the doubt.	When numerous mild feedback sessions have not been effective.	When numerous mild and moderate sessions have not been effective.
When you have data indicating that employee performance has made even a slight improvement.	When you see an occasional dip in performance below normal levels.	When a negative natural consequence exists for continued poor performance.	When data shows that performance has been poor for an extended period of time.
When someone has implemented your previous feedback and taken steps to correct the undesired behavior.	When you are certain that the performer can't do what is required because of inexperience or lack of knowledge.	When you assume responsibility for new employees and have data indicating that performance is subpar.	When keeping the performer at current performance levels will cause more damage in the long run than letting the performer go.
Use throughout each day to reinforce desired behaviors.	When you want to provide encouraging redirection.	When you think the performer needs extra information in order to perform well.	When you know the performer can do what is expected.

WHAT TO INCLUDE IN FEEDBACK

Steps in Delivering Feedback	Mild	Moderate	Strong
Empathize: Demonstrate empathy with the performer's attempt to perform a certain task that may be difficult.	X		
Give a specific description of the problem situation: Don't assign blame, but specifically outline what you see as the problem.		X	X
Specify the consequence of the problem behavior: State the possible negative consequences of the problem behavior. This points out the natural consequences of the action to the work process, individual or team performance, or even to customer satisfaction.		X	X
Specify the consequence of continued poor performance: This is in line with a threat. The consequence of continued poor performance may influence the employee's position within the organization.			X
Give a specific description of the appropriate action: Outline the specific steps to performing the task correctly.	X	X	X
Give a rationale for the appropriate action: Point out the positive consequences to the worker and team for following the appropriate action.	X	X	X
Create an opportunity for positive practice: Have the performer practice the appropriate action. Review appropriate steps, observe the steps being completed, and provide immediate feedback on what was observed. Ask if there are questions and establish a follow-up plan to observe the performer again. Reinforce the performer anytime you see improvement on the previously discussed performance issue.	X	X	X

STRONG CORRECTIVE FEEDBACK WORKSHEET

Before delivering your feedback during a coaching session, jot down a few notes to serve as a guide in your discussion with your employee.

Specific description of the problem	
Specific consequence of the problem	
Specific consequence of continued poor performance	
Specific description of the appropriate action	
Rationale for the appropriate action	
Create an opportunity to practice; then provide praise	

MODERATE CORRECTIVE FEEDBACK WORKSHEET

Before delivering your feedback during a coaching session, jot down a few notes to serve as a guide in your discussion with your employee.

Specific description of the problem	
Specific consequence of the problem	
Specific description of the appropriate action	
Rationale for the appropriate action	
Create an opportunity to practice; then provide praise	

MILD CORRECTIVE FEEDBACK WORKSHEET

Before delivering your feedback during a coaching session, jot down a few notes to serve as a guide in your discussion with your employee.

Empathize with the challenge	
Specific description of the appropriate action	
Rationale for the appropriate action	
Create an opportunity to practice; then provide praise to reinforce it	

Printed with permission of Scott Carbonara.

Appendix C

The Marathon Margin Success System for Leaders Tool Kit

In chapter 15, "Hope and Trust Start on the Path to Leadership Empowerment," we introduced the Marathon Margin—a proprietary system for leaders wishing to optimize the process and pace by which they achieve their goals—created by Jocelyn Godfrey of Spiritus Communications (for more on coaching or training for your team, go to www .SpiritusCommunications.com), a communications consulting firm in North Carolina. This tool will help you turbo-charge and implement the Marathon Margin Success System for Leaders. Share with your leaders and remember to adapt, delete, modify, and expand whatever works best for you and the people you are training.

The Marathon Margin is based on a concept used in marathon training. Runners start by committing to a race, then measuring their **baseline maximum threshold of achievement**. That is, they determine their fastest pace for a mile, the distance of their longest run in the recent past, and their maximum heart rate. Then runners develop a training program that pushes them hard enough each day to increase their stamina and conditioning, without causing injury or burnout. This often involves increasing their distance by one mile per week.

A runner can't train at his or her maximum threshold each day, while also adding distance, any more than a leader can perform at his or her maximum output, while also learning new skills and achieving new goals. **Instead, a leader must stay within the Marathon Margin—that optimal range wherein his or her skills are being advanced, and the goals become closer—but burnout or overwork to the point of being counterproductive are avoided.** Through implementing the Marathon Margin, leaders optimize their efforts for the highest rate of return on their investment, while protecting themselves against burnout.

This Marathon Margin can also be applied to a team. You may have heard that success is a marathon, not a sprint. Your team can't achieve overnight success, but they can reach success by strengthening themselves to add one mile, and then another. . . on the trail to your goals.

THE EIGHT "MARATHON MARGIN" MILE MARKERS TO OPTIMIZING YOUR LEADERSHIP SUCCESS

Mile Marker 1: Sign up for the race. Set and commit to your goal. Perhaps you want to lead a fully operational sales force within a year. What is your goal? Write it out. Commit to it like a marathon runner commits to a race—signing up for it months or a year in advance.

Mile Marker 2: Determine your current state. Find all of the metrics you can to tell you how you are performing today. Unless you know where you are today, you'll never know when you've made an improvement. Outline all of the processes utilized today. What are the relevant work flows and hand-offs involved in getting work done? On your **best** day, how much can your current team achieve?

Determine your maximum output today, knowing that this is not a result that can be achieved day in and day out. This step will help you temper your expectations and set realistic goals.

Mile Marker 3: Establish your team's marathon margin. Now that you know the maximum your team can achieve, what is realistic to expect from them, on average, if they were to push themselves each day beyond their "coasting" level, but not as high as their maximum output? The goal here is to set a pace for your team that promotes growth and conditioning, without burning them out. For a sales team, if they are currently acquiring 50 new leads per day, perhaps this means that they can add 10 new leads per day. Or perhaps it means pushing for a higher conversion rate. Determine specific skills or mini-goals that will push them toward growth and your organization toward its overall goal. Communicate these goals and expectations. What are they?

Mile Marker 4: Cut out the junk. Just like a marathon runner has to pay attention to what he or she eats, your team also needs to set boundaries to protect its conditioning efforts. Some work processes may have to go if they are not serving your goal. Some work behaviors may have to go, too. For example, you might find a need to replace gossip with effective communication, much in the same way a runner will replace a candy bar with a high-protein energy shake. Put systems in place to cut out influences that keep you from your goal, while establishing new processes and practices that make work more productive. Reward those who stay disciplined in pushing within their margin of optimal growth. What needs to be cut out from your current processes or systems in order for the Marathon Margin to be preserved?

Mile Marker 5: Learn from the best. While you may have a hunch how to train, or achieve your goal, don't operate in a box. Research. Read. Reflect. Find a mentor. Apply any helpful information in leading your team. Who can you study and emulate? What resources do you have to increase your knowledge in the area of your goal?

Utilize best practices from those who have gone before you and have been successful. Not only may they save you from repeating mistakes they made along the way, but they will also serve as encouragement while you gain the confidence that you, too, will be successful.

Mile Marker 6: Measure progress. As your team members achieve a higher level of conditioning, log their improvements while keeping an overall eye on the goal. You may need to periodically reassess your team's maximum output, as it will likely increase as your team is conditioned. As you add more responsibilities or opportunities for growth, keep it within the Marathon Margin—not too much or too little. What can you ask of your team that will help mobilize them toward your goal?

Mile Marker 7: Run the race. On race day, or when you are pushing the final leg toward your goal, show up and run the race. If you have trained, your team should be capable of achieving what you have set out for them. Don't let fear cause you to stop just before the finish line. What will your race look like when it's done?

Mile Marker 8: Rest and reassess. A key part of training is recovery. No one can run a marathon every day. Once your team meets a goal or milestone, allow proper time to recuperate, rejoice, and rest. At this time, evaluate the race, and work on setting new goals. What new long-term goals could you set after your team achieves the goal set in Mile Marker 1?

The Marathon Margin is a powerful and useful tool we have used in our seminars and around the world. We hope you will benefit from it as well.

Printed with permission of Jocelyn Godfrey.

References

Bruce, Anne. (2008). *Be Your Own Mentor*. New York: McGraw-Hill.

Bruce, Anne. (2004). *Discover True North*. New York: McGraw-Hill.

Bruce, Anne. (2010). *Perfect Phrases for Employee Development Plans*. New York: McGraw-Hill.

Bruce, Anne, Brenda Hampel, and Erika Lamont. (2011). *Solving Employee Performance Problems: How to Spot Problems Early, Take Appropriate Action, and Bring Out the Best in Everyone.* New York: McGraw-Hill.

Buckingham, Marcus. (2001). *Now Discover Your Strengths*. New York: The Free Press.

Burson-Marsteller. (2006). The Burson-Marsteller/PRWeek CEO Survey. *PR Week*.

Carbonara, Scott, Sam Glenn, and Doug McKinley. (2012). *Go Positive: Lead to Engage*. Hoboken, NJ: Pfeiffer.

Chism, Marlene. (2011). *Stop Workplace Drama*. Hoboken, NJ: John Wiley & Sons, Inc.

The Civility Initiative at Johns Hopkins. (2003, January). *The Baltimore Workplace Civility Study*. Baltimore: Johns Hopkins

Clemons, David, and Michael Kroth. (2010). *Managing the Mobile Workforce*. New York: McGraw-Hill.

Eriksen, Karen. (2012). *Perfect Phrases for Creativity and Innovation*. New York: McGraw-Hill.

Fast Company. (2005, August). The "Fast Track Leadership Survey" on Business Ethics and Integrity. *Fast Company*. Retrieved from http://images.fastcompany.com/magazine/98/fasttrack-survey.pdf.

Ferrell, O.C. (1999). *Workplace Incivility: The Target's Eye View*. Chapel Hill: Kenan-Flager Business School University of North Carolina.

Ferriss, Timothy. (2009). *The 4-Hour Workweek*. New York: Crown Publishing Group.

Glenn, Sam. (2010). *A Kick in the Attitude*. Hoboken, NJ: Wiley.

Goleman, Daniel. (1995). *Emotional Intelligence*. New York: Bantam Books.

Goleman, Daniel. (1998). *Working With Emotional Intelligence*. New York: Bantam Books.

Hampel, Brenda and Erika Lamont. (2011). *Perfect Phrases for New Employee Orientation and Onboarding*. New York: McGraw-Hill.

Kouzes, James and Barry Posner. (2008). *The Leadership Challenge,* 4th edition. San Francisco: Jossey-Bass.

Lewin, Roger and Birute Regine. (2000). *The Soul at Work*. New York: Simon & Schuster.

Lohr, Steve. (2011, January 20). Apple's Big Hole: Steve Intuition. *Telegraph*. Retrieved from www.telegraphindia.com.

O'Connell, Patricia. (2010, February 16). How Companies Develop Great Leaders. *BusinessWeek*. Retrieved from www.businessweek.com.

Pearson, Christine and Christine Porath. (2009). *The Cost of Bad Behavior: How Incivility Is Damaging Your Business and What to Do About It*. New York: The Penguin Group.

Polsky, Lawrence and Antoine Gerschel. (2011). *Perfect Phrases for Conflict Resolution*. New York: McGraw-Hill.

Post, Peggy. (2009). *Emily Post's Etiquette*. 17th edition. New York: HarperCollins Publishers.

Regine, Birute. (2010). *Iron Butterflies: Women Transforming Themselves and the World*. New York: Prometheus Books.

Sartain, Libby. (2003). *HR From the Heart: Inspiring Stories and Strategies for Building the People Side of Great Business*. New York: AMACOM.

Sartain, Libby and Mark Schumann. (2009). *Brand for Talent: Eight Essentials to Make Your Talent as Famous as Your Brand*. San Francisco: Jossey-Bass.

Sartain, Libby and Mark Schumann. (2006). *Brand From the Inside: Eight Essentials to Emotionally Connect Your Employees to Your Business*. San Francisco: Jossey-Bass.

Seligman, Martin. (2002). *Authentic Happiness: Using the New Positive Psychology to Realize Your Potential for Lasting Fulfillment*. New York: The Free Press.

Sessa, Valerie I., Robert Kaiser, Jodi K. Taylor, and Richard J. Campbell. (1998). *Executive Selection—A Research Report on What Works and What Doesn't*. Greensboro, NC: Center for Creative Leadership.

Smart, Bradford. (2005). *Topgrading: How Leading Companies Win by Hiring, Coaching, and Keeping the Best People,* Revised and Updated. New York: Penguin.

Thaler, Linda Kaplan and Robin Koval. (2006). *The Power of Nice: How to Conquer the Business World With Kindness*. New York: Doubleday.

Wooden, John. (2005). *Wooden on Leadership*. New York: McGraw-Hill.

Ziglar, Zig. (1990). *Zig Ziglar's Little Book of Big Quotes*. Dallas, TX: Zig Ziglar.

Index

About the Authors

G et ready to have **Anne Bruce** energize and transform your organization's teams with her interactive, highly entertaining keynotes and super FUN training programs!

Anne dispenses humor, wit, wisdom, and real-world insights from the speaker's platform and international seminar stage with her popular presentations, including: *America's Got Talent in the Workplace! The Art of Leadership, Motivating and Developing Superstar Talent! Nurturing the Technical Professional, Outrageous Customer Care to Extreme Customer Loyalty!* and her famous meetings' kick-off: *Ignite Passion—Activate Potential!* (Get your free 11-minute energizer video at www.AnneBruce.com.)

Anne is a bestselling, award-winning author of 16 books, which have been translated into 24 languages. Thousands of people around the world have adopted Anne's no-nonsense approach to *Discover True North* and have learned to be the author of their life story. Anne has had the privilege to speak for teams and leaders at the White House, the Pentagon, GEICO, Saks Fifth Avenue, Coca-Cola, IBM, Southwest Airlines and JetBlue Airways, Harvard and Stanford Law Schools, Ben & Jerry's, Baylor Medical University, the American Red Cross, the Conference Board of Europe, and the American Society of Training & Development (ASTD).

For information on training, keynotes, fees, and availability on programs associated with this book and other Anne Bruce bestsellers, go to Anne's website: **www.Anne Bruce.com, call 214-507-8242, or email Anne@AnneBruce.com**.

Stephanie Montanez has been called one of California's HR thought leaders, as well as a subject matter expert in improving employee performance through a wide variety of tried-and-true methods. Her philosophy is to improve performance and avoid employee performance hurdles by using praise in progress and direct and specific feedback methodologies, along with effective formal employee coaching and development plans.

Formerly an HR professional with Imperial Wallcoverings and Qualex, Inc., a wholly owned subsidiary of KODAK, Stephanie now heads up the HR division as director in one of America's most highly regarded and successful medical billing companies, MedAmerica Billing Services, Inc. She also created the organization's employee development and coaching division, with locations throughout California and Arizona.

Currently, Montanez is the executive producer and the voice and face of www .HumanResourcesSources.org and its popular internal media programming channel, where along with the HumanResourcesSources.org website, tips, tools, and cutting-edge HR techniques can be found in interviews, teleseminars, webinars, tool kits, TV programs, MP3 downloads, and podcasts broadcasted continually and at HR conference settings around the world.

For further information or questions associated with this book or the Human ResourcesSources.org website, you can email Stephanie at Steff@HumanResources Sources.org.

TEST 2, WRITING TASK 2

SAMPLE ANSWER

This is an answer written by a candidate who achieved a **Band 7.5** score. Here is the examiner's comment:

> This is a thoughtful and well-argued response to the task. The candidate examines the opposing views of the topic and gives a clear opinion that is well developed and supported. To reach the highest band a more clearly-signalled conclusion would be needed. The argument is well organised and linking is well managed throughout. The development of the answer is not helped, however, by poor control of paragraphing which sometimes confuses the links across different sections. This is a weak feature of the script which limits the overall rating. In contrast, an excellent range of vocabulary is used with a sophisticated level of control and only rare slips. The range of structures is also wide and most sentences are accurate and precise, but there are some errors and omissions. These, however, are only minor and do not affect communication.

Fixing punishments for each type of crime has been a debateable issue. There are many arguments supporting both views, those for and those against fixed punishments.

On the one hand, fixed punishments will have a deterring effect on society. Individuals knowing that they will be subject to a certain punishment if they are convicted with a given crime, will reconsider committing this act in the first place.

This deterring effect also leads to social stability and security, through minimising the number of crimes committed.

If people knew they would be able to convince the court or the jury of a reason for having committed the crime they are accused of, penal decisions would be largely arbitrary. This would result into criminals getting away with their crimes and into a high level of injustice caused by the subjective approach of different courts.

On the other hand, taking the circumstances of a crime and its motivation into consideration is a prerequisite for establishing and ensuring justice and equity.

A person killing in self-defense cannot be compared to a serial killer, moving from one victim to the next. In my opinion an intermediary position between both solutions is the perfect way to establish and ensure justice and equity.

There have to be fixed punishments for all crimes. However, criminal laws have to provide for a minimum and a maximum for the punishment and the laws also have to foresee certain cases of exemptions.

An example for setting minimum and maximum penalties is Competition Law where a person being held liable of a crime under this law will be convicted to pay a fine, according to the harm caused by the violation and the profit gained by the violator through committing the crime.

As for the exemptions, in some countries the law exempts thiefs stealing food during a period of famine taking into consideration the distress and hunger.

Also, a person killing in self-defense will be exempted from punishment.

TEST 3, WRITING TASK 1

SAMPLE ANSWER

This is an answer written by a candidate who achieved a **Band 6.5** score. Here is the examiner's comment:

> This answer clearly presents and illustrates the key points of the information. The writer groups the data effectively and draws clear comparisons, although these could be more appropriately extended in the overview. Information is well organised across the response and a range of linking devices is used.
>
> The opening paragraph, however, is an inadequate paraphrase of language given in the task, and although there are some appropriate collocations in the response, overall the range of vocabulary is rather restricted. Control is good, however, with few examples of error.
>
> A variety of structures is used with some fluency. There are occasional errors in punctuation and there are also some omissions and errors in grammar, but these tend to be minor and do not reduce communication.

The chart gives information about the percentage change in average house prices in five different cities located in five different countries over 12 year period between 1990 and 2002 compared with the average house prices in 1989.

According to the chart, during the period from 1990 to 1995 the average prices of houses in three cities decreased significantly by five percent in New York (U,SA) and about 7.5 percent in both Tokyo (Japan) and London (UK). While the average house prices increased slightly in two cities Madrid (,Spain) and Frankfurt (Germany) by about 1.5 percent and 2 percent respectively.

As far as the next period (1996-2002) is concerned, it is clear that the average house prices decreased only in Tokyo (Japan) by 5 percent. In contrast the average house prices increased in the rest of cities. In New York it increased consideraply by 5 percent, in Madrid it increased slightly by 4 percent, in Frankfurt it increased by 2 percent.

London has the largest increase in the average house price over the 6-year period from 1996 to 2002 as it increased dramatically by 11 percent.

All in all, there are a wide differences in house prices between the five cities which illustrated in this chart. These differences may be a result of the number of population or the number of houses required in a certain city.

TEST 3, WRITING TASK 2

MODEL ANSWER

This model has been prepared by an examiner as an example of a very good answer. However, please note that this is just one example out of many possible approaches.

Nowadays many adults have full-time jobs and the proportion of their lives spent doing such jobs is very high. So feelings about one's job must reflect how an individual feels about his or her life as a whole, and because of this, job satisfaction is indeed very important for the wellbeing of that person.

Employees get job satisfaction in a number of ways. Firstly, a person needs to feel that they are doing valued and valuable work, so positive feedback from superiors is very important in this respect. A sense of fulfilment is also encouraged if a worker feels the job is worth doing because it contributes to the society or the economy as a whole. Secondly, when someone feels they are improving or developing their skills through training opportunities, for example, then there is a sense of progression and purpose that rewards a worker. The sense of belonging to a team or a working community also contributes to job satisfaction because colleagues help each other to enjoy their working lives. Satisfaction is also increased by a sense of responsibility for and loyalty to a team.

Of course not everyone enjoys their work. Hard economic realities mean that many people have little choice in the kind of job they can get. In some cases an employee is working in a job that suits neither their skills nor their personality. Some jobs are repetitive and boring, and labour relations may be poor and lead to resentment and insecurity rather than to job satisfaction.

However, even though it is unlikely that all workers do feel happy in their work, I think it is not unrealistic to promote more job satisfaction in any job. If the factors identified above are implemented, then any job can be improved and more workers can feel greater degrees of job satisfaction.

TEST 4, WRITING TASK 1

MODEL ANSWER

This model has been prepared by an examiner as an example of a very good answer. However, please note that this is just one example out of many possible approaches.

The charts compare the sources of electricity in Australia and France in the years 1980 and 2000. Between these years electricity production almost doubled, rising from 100 units to 170 in Australia, and from 90 to 180 units in France.

In 1980 Australia used coal as the main electricity source (50 units) and the remainder was produced from natural gas, hydro power (each producing 20 units) and oil (which produced only 10 units). By 2000, coal had become the fuel for more than 75% of electricity produced and only hydro continued to be another significant source supplying approximately 20%.

In contrast, France used coal as a source for only 25 units of electricity in 1980, which was matched by natural gas. The remaining 40 units were produced largely from oil and nuclear power, with hydro contributing only 5 units. But by 2000 nuclear power, which was not used at all in Australia, had developed into the main source, producing almost 75% of electricity, at 126 units, while coal and oil together produced only 50 units. Other sources were no longer significant.

Overall, it is clear that by 2000 these two countries relied on different principal fuel sources: Australia relied on coal and France on nuclear power.

TEST 4, WRITING TASK 2

SAMPLE ANSWER

This is an answer written by a candidate who achieved a Band 5 score. Here is the examiner's comment:

> This answer is less than 250 words and it does not address all parts of the question, so it loses marks. Nevertheless, some relevant ideas and a position on the issue are presented. Ideas are organised and the structure of the answer is clearly signalled. Paragraphing is not always logical, however. There is some good use of linkers, but there is also a lot of repetition due to inadequate use of referencing and substitution. The high level of repetition ['knowledge and skills' is repeated nine times] also indicates limitations in the range of vocabulary although, apart from language given in the rubric, there is just sufficient additional vocabulary for the task. The answer includes attempts at complex sentence forms, but these are generally awkwardly phrased and tend to require some re-reading to understand. Nevertheless, there are examples of accurate complex structures.

What knowledge and skills should universities provide has been argued for many years. Some people think that the true function of universities provide knowledge for their own purpose, but nowadays, more and more people point out that universities should provide graduates with the knowledge and skills according to the workplace.

The first reason for universities should provide these knowledge and skill is the students' needs. Obviously, the most of the students go to university purpose of is to get some knowledge

and skills which could make them have the ability to get a job. If a university does not provide these knowledge and skills, the students might not get a job and they would be very disappointed. As a result, the university would lose its students.

Moreover, providing knowledge and skills needed in the workplace maks a university progress. The new skills and information always are initiated in the workplace, so focusing on the needs of the workplace the university could get sound strategies to do research and make it more mordenization.

Lastly, providing these knowledge and skills could benefit our country which usually gives a financial support to universities. Having these knowledge and skills, students are more easy to get a job, and this can make our countries' economy strong.

In conclusion, it can be said that providing the knowledge and skills which the workplace needs is every universities' basic function.

TEST A, WRITING TASK 1 (GENERAL TRAINING)

MODEL ANSWER

This model has been prepared by an examiner as an example of a very good answer. However, please note that this is just one example out of many possible approaches.

Dear Jenny,

I hope this finds you and your family well, and I'm sorry I haven't been in touch recently. I'm writing now to let you know about my new job.

You remember that I was working for that construction company a few miles outside the city? Well, I just got so fed up with it – I was working really long hours and, to be honest, the pay wasn't great. So basically I applied for a job at a new international company that was looking for admin staff for a new branch in the city centre.

I was a bit nervous in the interview, but in the end I got a job as one of the senior administrators. I am so happy! The pay is better, the working conditions are great and I don't have to drive to work anymore.

Anyway, I have to stop now because my sister is staying with me and has brought my baby nephew to meet me. She sends you lots of love and is asking when we can all meet up. Soon, I hope.

With love,

Tina

TEST A, WRITING TASK 2 (GENERAL TRAINING)

SAMPLE ANSWER

This is an answer written by a candidate who achieved a **Band 7** score. Here is the examiner's comment:

The response looks at the advantages of living in apartments and houses then briefly considers some disadvantages before giving the candidate's own opinion. Fuller development of the disadvantages would raise the candidate's score here. The ideas are clearly organised and paragraphing is logical. There is some under-use of cohesive devices and some incorrect referencing, but links between sentences and paragraphs can be clearly followed. The range of vocabulary used is varied and there is some good use of collocation, but there are occasional examples of inappropriate word choice, and better control of spelling would help to raise the candidate's score. The range of complex structures could be wider, but there is sufficient variation in sentence forms and sufficient control of grammar and punctuation to reach this band. Some errors occur, but most are minor and do not reduce communication.

In big business cities there are two options available for the type of accommodation: houses and apartments. Some people prefer to live in apartments and some like to live in houses.

In big business cities, where almost everyone is going out daily for work or study, apartments provide a much more comfortable and safe way of living. The advantages include the fact that there is one key and lock they have to take care of, and also the sense of being a part of a big family. Usually a guard sits at the main gate, so children can play around in the compound with their next door friends. In addition, not much daily cleaning is required in apartments as no staircase has to be clean, which is a difficult task – all house wives know it very well. But a key advantage is that it is safe to go on voccation for a long trip.

On the other hand, houses have their own attraction for its inhabitants. Garden lovers usually prefer houses as they can have their own garden. It is also easy to keep a pet, especially a dog in a house because dog can play around the garden. If someone is interested in maintaing cars himself, it can only be possible in houses where one can have his own garage.

Where people are sometimes much more concerned about their privacy, living in apartments can be a very difficult for them. It may also be the case that someone is not able to deal with other people, for instance next door neighboures, and than house can be a best choice for such people.

However, sometimes houses can be a bad choice for low income people. Maintaing a big house and running it properly can be a problem for such cases.

At the end I must say both options can be good or bad, depending on the personal considerations. But from my point of view, I must say apartments seem a gift of modern way of life which is not common in my home town.

TEST B, WRITING TASK 1 (GENERAL TRAINING)

SAMPLE ANSWER

This is an answer written by a candidate who achieved a **Band 5** score. Here is the examiner's comment:

> This answer does not cover the bullets well because there are no thanks for the holiday and giving the address is not logical in the context. The second bullet is given rather too much focus, so the purpose of the letter is less clear, and the tone is inappropriate at the end of the letter. The information is organised according to the ordering of the task, and although few linkers are used, there is some clear referencing. The range of vocabulary is rather restricted, but generally sufficient for the task, although inappropriacies and some word form errors occur. A mix of structures is attempted but short, simple sentences are frequent. Control of tenses and verb phrases is weak in more complex structures and this impacts on the message at times.

Dear Taufik and Lina,

I'm so glad receiving your photos when we were in Singapore. The photos are so nice and bright. They remind me for my special holiday with you.

I'm sorry because I don't write a letter to you as soon as possible. After I came back to Melbourne, my boss asked me to had two weeks training in Wellington, New Zealand. I don't' have any time to tell you because it happened suddenly.

My company wants to change the system of the computer into the online system. All of the staffs must have training first, before the system running.

I hope you can come and stay with me during next holiday. My address is: 888 Little Collins Street, Melbourne, Victoria, 3000. You can contact me first if you have a plan to visit.

Thanks for your kindness and I'm looking forward for your reply.

Yours sincerely,

Victor

TEST B, WRITING TASK 2 (GENERAL TRAINING)

MODEL ANSWER

This model has been prepared by an examiner as an example of a very good answer. However, please note that this is just one example out of many possible approaches.

I agree with the view that stars in the entertainment business are usually over paid. This is true whether we are considering stars of film, sport or popular music, and it often seems that the amount of money they are able to earn in a short time cannot possibly be justified by the amount of work they do.

However, it is also true that it is only those who reach the very top of their profession who can get these huge salaries. So the size of salary that stars expect is closely linked to the competition they have to overcome in order to reach success. They are, in effect, rare talents.

Furthermore, the majority of stars do not hold their top positions long. Sport stars and pop stars, for example, are soon replaced by the next younger, more energetic, generation, while the good looks of most film stars quickly fade. So this relatively short working life may be some justification for the very high pay.

Unfortunately, professionals from other fields, who make a much greater contribution to human society, are paid so much less that it is hard to disagree with the statement. Teachers, nurses, laboratory researchers etc. are never listed among the best-paid professionals, yet they are more important to our well-being and our future than the stars who earn their fortunes so quickly.

In conclusion, I think there may be some reasons why entertainment stars earn high salaries but overall I agree that they are overpaid. The gaps between their earnings and those of people who work less selfishly for the good of society cannot be justified. Such professionals should be much better appreciated and better paid.

Sample answer sheets

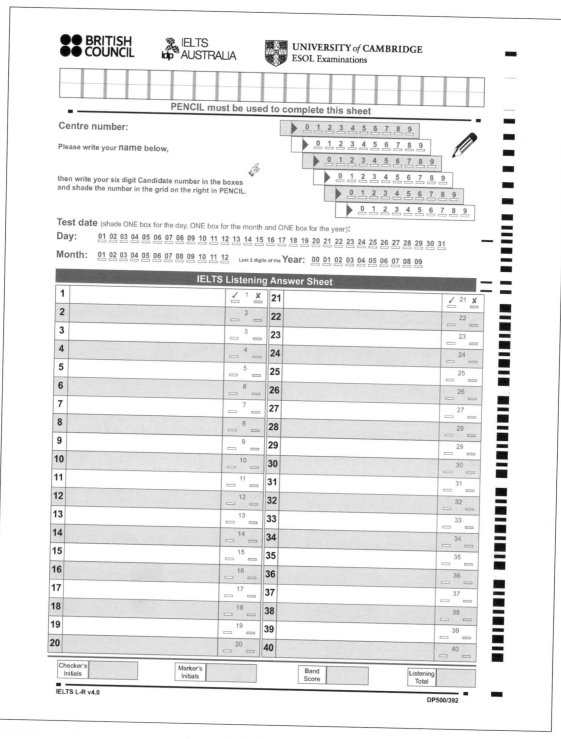

Acknowledgements

The authors and publishers are grateful for permission to reproduce copyright material. While every effort has been made, it has not always been possible to identify the sources of all the material used, or to trace all copyright holders. If any omissions are brought to our notice, we will be happy to include the appropriate acknowledgements on reprinting.

The publishers are grateful to the following for permission to reproduce copyright material:

Brockman, Inc. for the text on pp. 18–19 'Let's Go Bats' from *The Blind Watchmaker* by Richard Dawkins. Reproduced by permission of Brockman, Inc. on behalf of the author; Scientific American, Inc. for the adapted text on pp. 23–24 'Making Every Drop Count' by Peter Gleick, *Scientific American* February 2001. Copyright © 2001 Scientific American, Inc. All rights reserved; Prof Bernie Neville for the text on pp. 26–27 from *Educating Psyche*, published by Collins Dove. Reproduced by permission of Prof Bernie Neville; The Economist for the text on pp. 40–41 'Why Pagodas don't fall down' from 'An Engineering Mystery', *The Economist* 20 December 2007. Copyright © The Economist Newspaper Limited, London, 2007; The Independent for adapted text on pp. 44–45 'The true cost of food' from 'The Way We Eat' by Michael McCarthy, *The Independent* 5 September 2001. Copyright © Independent News & Media Limited; ITDG Publishing for the adapted text on pp. 49–50 'Makete Integrated Transport Project' by T Stransberg from *Appropriate Technology* Vol 20, No 1, June 1993. Reproduced by permission of ITDG Publishing; text on pp. 65–66 'Ant Intelligence' from *Sydney Morning Herald*; Annual Reviews for the text on pp. 70–71 'Population movements and genetics' by Mulligan, Hunley, Cole, Long. *Annual Reviews*, 2004. Reproduced by permission of Annual Reviews; Council of Europe for the text on pp. 74–75 'Europe acts to defend forests' from *Forum Magazine*, February 1991. Copyright © Council of Europe, 1991; New Scientist for the text on pp. 89–90 'Pulling strings to build pyramids from 'Kite Fantastic' New Scientist 27 October 2001, for the text on pp. 112–113 'A very special dog' from 'Pay attention to Rover' written by Amy Davis Mozdy, *New Scientist* 10 May 1997. Copyright © New Scientist Magazine. www.newscientist.com; Kieran Mulvaney for the text on pp. 92–93 'Endless Harvest' from *Living Planet*, Issue 3, March–May 2001. Reproduced by kind permission of Kieran Mulvaney; text on pp. 96–97 'Effects of Noise' from *Environmental Psychology* by E W Hilgard; Crimson Business Ltd for the adapted text on p. 108 'Choosing premises for a new business' from www.startups.co.uk. Reproduced by permission of Crimson Business Ltd.

Photo credits: IELTS 7

The publishers are grateful to the following for permission to include photographs:

Blickwinkel/Alamy p. 18, Raine Vara/Alamy p. 23, Headline Photo Agency/Alamy p. 40, WildPictures/Alamy p. 65, Tim Gartside/Alamy p. 74, Billy Gadbury/Shutterstock p. 112, AA World Travel Library/Alamy p. 125.

Design concept by Peter Ducker MSTD

Cover design by David Lawton

The audio CDs which accompany this book were recorded by Studio AVP, London and dsound, London.

Page make up by Servis Filmsetting Ltd, Stockport, Cheshire.

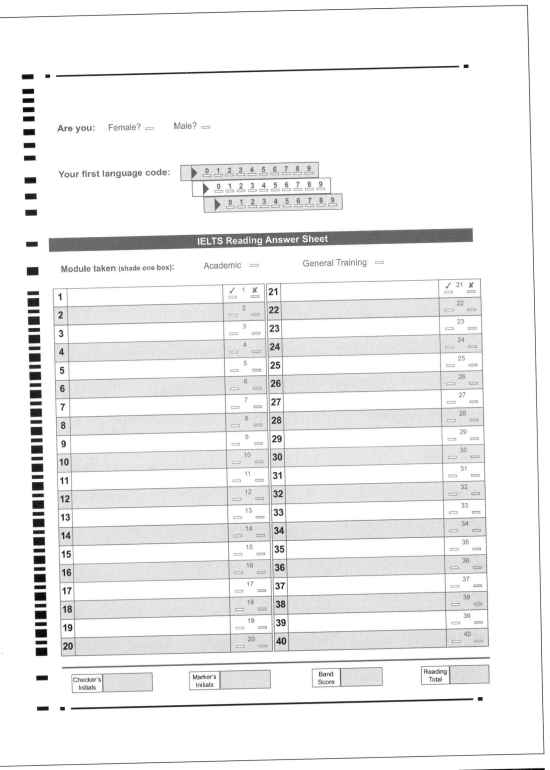

Are you: Female? ⊐ Male? ⊐

Your first language code: ▶ 0 1 2 3 4 5 6 7 8 9
▶ 0 1 2 3 4 5 6 7 8 9
▶ 0 1 2 3 4 5 6 7 8 9

IELTS Reading Answer Sheet

Module taken (shade one box): Academic ⊐ General Training ⊐

		✓ 1 ✗	21		✓ 21 ✗
1			21		
2		2	22		22
3		3	23		23
4		4	24		24
5		5	25		25
6		6	26		26
7		7	27		27
8		8	28		28
9		9	29		29
10		10	30		30
11		11	31		31
12		12	32		32
13		13	33		33
14		14	34		34
15		15	35		35
16		16	36		36
17		17	37		37
18		18	38		38
19		19	39		39
20		20	40		40

Checker's Initials		Marker's Initials		Band Score		Reading Total	